Gay
men & women
who enriched
the world

Gay men & women who enriched the world

THOMAS COWAN

Boston ♦ Alyson Publications, Inc.

Published as a trade paperback by Alyson Publications, Inc.,
40 Plympton Street, Boston, Mass. 02118.
Distributed in England by GMP Publishers,
P.O. Box 247, London N17 9QR England.

First published by William Mulvey, Inc., 1988
First Alyson edition, first printing: February 1992

5 4 3 2 1

ISBN 1-55583-147-8
(previously ISBN 0-934791-16-3)

This book is dedicated to Jack Maguire
who enriches my world.

◇————————————————————————————————————◇

Special thanks go to William Mulvey for his foresight and efficiency in the book publishing world; MacLennan Farrell for his meticulous copy editing and helpful suggestions; Susan Lee Cohen, my agent, for her steadfast interest in this project; and, last but not least, Jack Maguire, whose daily support and encouragement as well as his assistance in research and text development were invaluable.

◇—————————————————————————◇

The illustrations that accompany each chapter in this new edition of Gay Men & Women Who Enriched the World *were drawn by Michael Willhoite.*

Contents

◊———————————————————————————◊

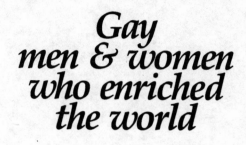

Gay
men & women
who enriched
the world

PURPOSE AND MEANING
IN THE GAY EXPERIENCE

The ability to enrich the world is exceptional by nature. Homosexuality is exceptional by nature. It is not surprising that the two should meet in the lives of some very remarkable men and women.

Courage is also an exceptional trait, possibly because the situations that require it are, for most people, rare. Nevertheless, for many gay men and women, and especially for the 40 individuals whose lives comprise this book, courage is a recurring necessity, if not a daily fact of life. Confronting and accepting the value of one's gay identity, in spite of the efforts of society to deny the worth of gay people, can provide the basis for the strength and self-confidence needed to leave one's personal mark on the world.

To grow up gay or lesbian in modern times means to grow up an outsider. The gay child finds he or she is out of step with the values and standards of a predominantly heterosexual society. The social rituals of falling in love with the opposite sex, dating, marrying, and raising children—the standard gender-determined roles—are counteracted by another equally forceful set of thoughts and desires: falling in love, dating, settling down, building a life together with a member of one's own sex.

Gay teenagers who are even slightly self-aware pass through periods of search, self-reflection, and analysis of the values and lifestyles offered by the dominant culture, wondering to what extent they can accept them, wondering if they can force themselves to fit the molds. Gay youths are faced with a considerable challenge: to evaluate life's options from the standpoint that many of them are unacceptable and to search for alternative opportunities that are acceptable. No gay person can live an unexamined life.

Gay people need to "invent" themselves more self-consciously than their straight counterparts by sifting through the elements offered by society and finding the ones appropriate to their gay identities. Often they have no support or encouragement in doing this. They are left on their own, but they do it. Forging an identity that can adjust and survive in society and not compromise one's own deepest values and personal needs requires exceptional creativity and courage.

Ideally each individual must find a career and lifestyle that supports his or her gay identity. Gertrude Stein, for example, established herself as a unique arbiter of twentieth-century art and literature, extending the traditional female role of salon hostess, and assuming the husband's role in a strong lesbian marriage with her "wife," Alice B. Toklas. Benjamin Britten became a singular force in British music, drawing on his preoccupation with rebellious male heroes, many of them homosexual. His domestic relationship with his lover, Peter Pears, included professional collaboration in the pieces he composed for Pears and in their many concerts together.

Acknowledging oneself as an outsider can be a source of strength. The outsider's perspective offers the freedom to fantasize and imagine a life that may not occur to those who fit more comfortably into the dominant culture. The daydreams of gay youth have a special quality, even as they have a special content in that they challenge the cultural norms. In a sense the gay imagination must stretch far to answer the basic questions of life: Who am I? Where did I come from? What is my purpose?

Studies over the last century have uncovered some rather definite answers to at least the third of these questions: What purpose do gay people serve? A resounding conclusion is that gay people are interpreters for the larger culture. In many nonwestern cultures, for example, gay men and lesbians have been honored with the roles of spiritual leader and healer. In modern western civilization they have tended to be artists and writers. In our own age a large number of gay men and women are attracted to careers in teaching, religion, social work, entertainment, fashion, and design. Because gay people stand "between the worlds," as it were—the worlds of men and women, the worlds of the traditional and nontraditional—they have served historically as bridgers and mediators.

Among the individuals in this book we find T. E. Lawrence mediating between Arab and colonial factions, Horatio Alger interpreting adult American values for young boys, John Maynard Keynes persuading industrialized democracies to accept new economic principles, James Baldwin making peace between white and black Americans, Yukio Mishima preserving traditional Japanese values among postwar youth, Erasmus inspiring church reform, Andy Warhol exciting a whole generation with new perspectives in art, Marguerite Yourcenar translating great works of literature from Japanese, Greek, Latin, English, and German into French.

Living between the worlds requires imagination and a sense of make-believe which has always been a survival strategy for gay people. Having learned how to use make-believe in childhood and adolescence—either pretending an interest in the opposite sex or pretending *not* to be interested in one's own—gay people often retain a strong sense of make-believe in their adult lives. They also often retain the youthful spirit in which that sense of make-believe can flourish.

As wives, husbands, parents, business people, or socially prominent personalities, gay people develop skill and expertise in adapting to straight society. Yet they always retain a certain distance, a slightly offbeat perspective, that can see through the hypocrisies, absurdities, and injustices of conventional society. Such a perspective is often needed for social reform and personal transformation; because unless one can step outside the established patterns and see them for what they are, it is difficult to imagine how they can be changed.

We should not be misled into supposing that the gay traditions of cross-dressing, acting out sexual fantasies, and spoofing life with "camp" humor are only valuable in criticizing sexual mores. The gay perspective is much broader than that, penetrating every aspect of thought and culture: science, politics, business, art, religion, philosophy, and literature. The song lyrics of Noël Coward or Bessie Smith provide shrewd social commentary upon heterosexual relationships viewed as much from the outside as from within. The villains and heroes portrayed by Charles Laughton spring from the weaknesses and sufferings of their outcast creator. Willa Cather's strong pioneers struggling with themselves and the harsh prairie landscape stem from her own struggle to find her place in America and American letters. Herman Melville's alienation from nineteeth-century American values and his lifelong fascination with the "rover" adrift at sea attest to his sense of being a stranger in a strange land.

Creativity studies have shown that among the many factors and circumstances that contribute to the creative individual is androgyny—the ability to recognize and express both the male and female sides of one's personality. The creative self operates closely with the unconscious elements of the psyche, especially those valuable archetypes of gender, the anima and animus. For many gay men and women this "other side" of their personalities is more conscious and instrumental in shaping thoughts and desires. As experiments in creativity indicate, the man or woman who can unite opposites and find room to express both the masculine and feminine elements of human nature stands a better chance of living a more creative and enriching life than individuals bound by an ego-consciousness based on physical gender.

When gay people are fortunate enough to learn early in life to trust the unique sources of creativity within them, they survive and even prevail against the enormous cultural odds arrayed against them. Forced to enrich their own world without many of the social, legal, economic, and spiritual benefits available to those who fit the heterosexual model more completely, they can emerge as strong, self-confident personalities capable of enriching the world at large. Many men and women in this book have done just that. From their own gay perspectives they have offered outstanding contributions in art, literature, philosophy, military strategy, economics, mathematics, music, and entertainment—contributions that are unique because of the gay sensibilities of their creators.

Our gay heritage includes many men and women who deserve to be in this book, but space has allowed for only 40. In selecting the entries for this volume, I followed certain guidelines. First, I wanted to span the centuries with people from the ancient world, as well as our own contemporaries. Admittedly the more recent individuals still need to stand the test of time alongside their heroic forerunners like Michelangelo and Leonardo da Vinci. But recent gay men and women like James Baldwin, Andy Warhol, Marguerite Yourcenar, Michael Bennett, regardless of how society evaluates them a hundred years from now, have enriched our own lives in a more direct and immediate way than, say, Madame de Staël or Frederick the Great.

Second, I wanted to include men and women from non-English-speaking cultures, for to write about enriching the world means precisely that. My selection, however, has focused on those individuals whose impact has been significant in our own English-speaking countries.

Third, it seemed important to include a large proportion of people who were not in the arts. Many gay people gravitate to the art and entertainment fields because those fields allow for greater personal self-expression and are more tolerant in general of minorities and individuals whose lifestyles fall outside the mainstream. The gay sensibility can provide that nonordinary perspective that keeps art and literature fresh and exciting. In order to make room for those who can fill out the rich mosaic of achievement beyond arts and letters, I have omitted many famous gay poets and writers, such as Rimbaud, W. H. Auden, Carson McCullers, Hart Crane, and Truman Capote, as well as such Hollywood actors as Rock Hudson, Tyrone Power, and Montgomery Clift.

Fourth, I have omitted individuals whose sexuality is still to be established by solid historical and biographical evidence. It is very difficult to "prove" sexual experience in historical terms, except in the case of women who bear children. There tend to be no witnesses to sexual activities, gay or straight; and the partners involved are not always trustworthy in their accounts. The prudish deny it; the boastful exaggerate. Ascertaining someone's sexual identity, therefore, is not the same as "proving" that he or she actually had sex. For both homosexuals and heterosexuals the historian must evaluate the circumstances of their lives—marital status, best friends, acquaintances, living arrangements, diaries, letters—and derive reasonable conclusions.

This being the case, I omitted some individuals even though they appear repeatedly in lists of gay people. Take Shakespeare, for example. Joseph Pequiney's fascinating study, *Such Is My Love*, makes a very convincing case that Shakespeare wrote all 154 sonnets to a young man with whom he was romantically involved. But to date there is no historical evidence from Shakespeare's life that he was homosexual. I have decided not to include individuals like Shakespeare for whom we have only their literary works as evidence of their homosexuality.

In a similar vein, Dag Hammarskjöld, secretary general of the United Nations, a lifelong bachelor, was often rumored to be gay, and he always denied it. I have not found any biographical studies that indicate evidence that he was gay. In cases like this I think it is only fair to honor the reputations the individuals themselves chose to present until historical evidence emerges to indicate something to the contrary.

It may come as a surprise to some readers that a good number of the men and women in this book had heterosexual marriages, had children, and/or had lovers of the opposite sex. It is one of the myths of a homophobic society that gay people either do not like members of the opposite sex or cannot fall in love and function sexually with them. This is a rather modern notion. In classical Greece and Rome, in Semitic cultures, as well as in many indigenous cultures around the world, such as traditional Native American communities, homosexuality was viewed as but one form of sexual expression in a rich continuum of sexual experience available to most individuals. In fact, in some cultures being gay was a special calling and conferred a mark of honor.

Not all cultures view gay people in the narrow framework we have come to accept in the western world of the twentieth century. As K. J. Dover has pointed out in *Greek Homosexuality*, the Greek attitude toward homosexuality was unlike our culture's in four important respects. First, it was assumed that an individual could function homosexually on certain occasions and with certain partners, and heterosexually at other times. Second, the Greeks did not perceive this to be a problem either for the individual or for society; and indeed it was not a problem, since Greek society, unlike our own, had legitimate institutions and traditions to accommodate homosexuality. Third, the fact that a person was homosexual was not something that needed to be concealed. And fourth, homosexual relationships were openly discussed and portrayed in art and literature without any sense of shame or embarrassment.

Clearly individuals like Sappho, Plato, Alexander the Great, and the many gay people of the ancient Mediterranean world did not grow up with the same heterosexual constraints as do gay people growing up in our own society. Nevertheless, it appears that homosexuality, no matter how highly it is regarded in a given society, is always a minority position and for that reason calls for additional sources of courage and self-confidence from those who find themselves gay or lesbian.

The spectrum of sexual experience was not always rigidly labeled and categorized. The word *homosexual*, for example, was coined as recently as 1869. As the term sifted into the general culture, it became almost exclusively a psychiatric concept which implied that "something went wrong." The word became mired in concepts of sin and sickness. The positive qualities of the gay spirit that extend beyond sexual desire were seldom discussed. Furthermore, *homosexual* became an exclusive label, implying that a person whose sexual drives were homosexual could not have equally strong heterosexual urges.

The entire concept of bisexuality, so apparent to so many cultures before us, was almost totally lost or relegated to an even more peculiar category of "what went wrong." Regrettably even gay men and lesbians fall into this trap of denying the existence of bisexuality in order to bolster their own positions. We seem to have forgotten that many individuals in the past saw themselves simply as "sexual" and that the object of their sexual interests could and did vary. From all historical and psychological evidence, and certainly from the lives of many individuals in this book, it appears that the object of falling in love and commitment is a person, not a sex.

James Baldwin has pointed out that the word *homosexual* (and of course the word *heterosexual* too) is an adjective, not a noun. In other words it is not a category of people, but an adjective to describe certain thoughts, acts, desires, fantasies, and dreams which most people have at one time or another. But in the popular culture the term *homosexual* has come to mean those individuals who act upon those thoughts, dreams, and desires to the exclusion of all others.

Many individuals who lived before the last century would not have understood all the confusion we have made over our terms for sexuality. Nor would they have drawn such fine lines of distinction to separate people into mutually exclusive categories where, unfortunately, they find it difficult, if not impossible, to even communicate with one another. Nor have human societies always surrounded expressions of homosexuality and lesbianism with the pejorative terms that come so easily to twentieth-century "fag bashers" and "dyke busters."

Throughout much of human history it seems that people— both gay and straight—could live comfortably without a name for the "love that dare not speak its name." In biblical times it was enough for David to simply say that his love for Jonathan "was wonderful, passing the love of women." Our own modern attempts to define *heterosexual, homosexual, bisexual, lesbian,* and *gay* meet with varying degrees of success. Perhaps the most recent and accepted definitions will be outmoded within a few years. I hope they are, so that we can rethink and reevaluate who we are and what we call ourselves in the light of our changing society.

Because of this confusion in terminology and because so many gay people, especially the young, agonize over what words to use to describe themselves, creating a title for this book presented problems. Ideally the title should be historically accurate and politically correct for the various segments in the gay and lesbian communities. I settled on the phrase "Gay Men and Women" as being the most comprehensive, the least objectionable, and, I hope, the least anachronistic. I realize it will not please everyone—certainly it would not have pleased Alexander the Great.

My criterion for selecting the men and women in this book was to choose individuals who, at the right times in their lives and with certain partners, acknowledged the gay dimension of their natures in personal relationships. Regardless of whether the main thrust of their lives was heterosexual or, in a few cases, asexual, each entry in this book expressed a solid gay or lesbian identity at some point in his or her life.

For example Lord Byron, whose fierce sexual escapades with women have dominated his legend, was involved in homosexual relationships from early life to his final days. Similarly, Virginia Woolf, who appears to have been remarkably asexual, had a year-long relationship with Vita Sackville-West which, in the opinion of her biographers, was probably the most meaningful relationship of her life. John Maynard Keynes seems to have balanced his bisexual nature rather smoothly with male lovers in the early part of his life and a satisfying marriage to Lydia Lopokova in the second half.

In other words the 40 men and women in this book display a wide range of sexual and romantic involvements, emanating from a wide range of sexual and romantic needs. Not all of them handled their sexuality with grace and confidence. As the American heiress and salon hostess Nathalie Barney observed of her own lesbian acquaintances around the turn of the last century: "In those days people were still afraid to be involved in scandal." Tennessee Williams and E. M. Forster seem to have been embarrassed at times by their homosexuality. Tchaikovsky was obsessed by what he felt was the need to conceal it. Willa Cather destroyed valuable letters and personal documents near the end of her life to preserve her secrets. Others, like Gertrude Stein, Alan Turing, Jean Cocteau, and Pier Paolo Pasolini, were unashamedly gay or lesbian.

The gay sensibility has both its dark and light sides. Some of the 40 men and women in this volume, had we known them, might have shocked or worried us with their neurotic habits and reckless, even dangerous, lifestyles. Yet even those who struggled most severely with their gay identities and their fear of scandal found the strength and courage to leave their marks on the world. In many cases the struggle itself, the lifelong grappling with the inner self and the outer world, created a personality strong and sensitive enough to enrich the world.

ALEXANDER THE GREAT

356–323 B.C.

To win support among the warrior nobles of the Macedonian highlands, King Philip required that their sons be trained as royal pages in his capital at Pella. As not-so-subtle hostages for their fathers' behavior, the young boys benefited from the experience. They received an excellent military education; they learned Greek; they studied art and poetry; their political horizons were broadened beyond their fathers' petty kingdoms. In short, they became Greek-speaking Macedonian soldiers first, and highland princes second. They also became friends and lovers. In the intensely masculine world of boot camp and gymnasium, male bonding occurred easily and naturally. Some friendships lasted for life.

Studying among Philip's pages was his son Alexander; from the highlands came the young prince Hephaistion. Contemporary accounts describe the ensuing relationship in Homeric terms: Hephaistion was the Patroclus to Alexander's Achilles. And in the tradition of Homeric heroes, it was assumed that the friendship would have a sexual element.

Alexander kept Hephaistion by his side after he ascended the throne at age 20 on Philip's death. When he fulfilled his father's dream of taking over the remaining Greek territories from the Adriatic to the Danube, Hephaistion was with him. As he crossed the Hellespont in 334 B.C. and invaded Persia, and as he marched his troops to India and the "edge of the world" and back, he relied on the help and support of his beloved friend. He appointed Hephaistion to the highest-ranking offices in his army. He honored him with the title of chiliarch, the right-hand man who stood nearest the king and commanded an elite cavalry unit. He arranged political marriages for himself and Hephaistion so that his friend's sons and daughters would be his own nephews and nieces.

When Hephaistion died of a fever while on the return march from India, Alexander's grief was extreme. He refused food and drink for three days; he cut his hair; he hacked the tails and manes off his horses (a Persian custom). Rumors indicated he had ordered Hephaistion's doctors hanged and that the inconsolable warrior lay on the body of his dead friend both day and night. Like Achilles mourning Patroclus, the young conqueror ordered official mourning throughout the eastern empire. He arranged a lavish funeral celebration that would surpass all others. He may have personally driven the funeral chariot.

Alexander's identification with Achilles was a lifelong preoccupation. From his boyhood days of studying with Aristotle and reading the Greek classics, Alexander found a sense of purpose and meaning in the tales of the Greek heroes and their codes of conduct. While on his campaigns he carried a copy of the *Iliad* and viewed himself as a second Achilles. Like the famed hero of the Trojan War, Alexander was headstrong, action-oriented, decisive, and willing to take extraordinary risks. Physically and temperamentally he met the Greek ideal: solidly built, courageous, strong-willed, generous to friends and enemies. A consummate military tactician with an almost clairvoyant insight into strategy, he delighted in battle. He honored the gods, respected the fates, and thought of himself as enjoying divine protection. Throughout his life he nourished a deeply felt relationship with the gods. He was also young, and inspired commitment from men more than twice his age.

By conquering Persia, Alexander fulfilled an ancient Greek goal. For centuries the Persians had threatened the Greek mainland and harassed Greek cities in Asia Minor. After defeating the Persian army, Alexander decided to take the entire Persian empire. In 331 B.C. he took Babylon; the major cities of Susa and Persepolis quickly followed. In a night of drunken excitement, but possibly with a certain amount of forethought, he burned Persepolis. When Darius, the Persian king, was slain by his own men, Alexander became the Great King of Persia.

Although carefully taught by Aristotle that the small, tightly-knit city-state was the only sensible form of government, Alexander dreamed of a confederated Persian empire in league with Greece. Eventually he extended his plans for a confederated political system that could possibly embrace the entire world—or as much of it as would fall under his dominion. Clearly the lands he conquered in his Persian campaigns, which extended from Egypt to present-day Iran, were too big, various, and different from Greece to administer as a Greek colony. The newly acquired territories could not be adequately governed by a garrison system manned by Greek and Macedonian soldiers. Although Alexander encouraged the city-state concept by building new cities from the foundation up (16 of them he named after himself), his political ambitions went beyond the narrow city-state concept of Aristotle.

Alexander also differed with his famed teacher, and most Greeks, by assuming that the Persians and their many ethnic minorities were not "barbarians" inferior to the Greek citizen, slavish by nature and fit only for Greek domination. He tolerated local religions, social customs, and political institutions, rather than impose a Greek model upon them. He saw his influence as one of bringing Hellenic culture to others and in turn learning from their own best traditions.

By treating Persians as equals Alexander caused resentment among some of his officers who thought his policy diluted the old comradeship-in-arms that they enjoyed exclusively. As an even greater insult to some of his men, but as shrewd political drama to solidify his control among the conquered Persians, Alexander adopted native customs. For example, he wore Persian dress. Like Achilles, he married a captive girl, named Roxane, who was the daughter of an Iranian noble; and he acquired a Persian eunuch named Bagoas who, because he was bilingual, could play the traditional role of official spy for his master and who, because of his good looks and irresistible charm, was invited to share his master's bed. Later, on the return from India, Bagoas would be the only non-Greek or Macedonian among the 32 officers honored with the title trierarch. Alexander also drafted Persian cavalry into his own army and required 30,000 Persian boys to be trained in Macedonian combat. In fact, his court marriage to Roxane was partially intended to allay their fathers' fears.

In 327 B.C. Alexander adopted the Persian custom of *proskynesis*, a combination kiss and bow which Persians performed to establish social rank on meeting one another. Depending on the depth of the bow, a man revealed his social status in relation to the other. Social equals kissed each other on the lips. The lowliest inferiors were required to grovel. Catering to Persian custom, Alexander hoped to win over friends and future "partners." His Macedonian officers, however, saw the proverbial writing on the wall and suspected a threat to their own importance by Persian competition. In addition, the Greeks interpreted the custom as implying that the inferior was paying homage to the other as a god.

Alexander arranged a trial for *proskynesis* at a party where each guest would drink a toast and pour a libation to satisfy the Greeks and then offer a kiss and a bow for the Persians' sakes. His guests were all courtiers, so they could satisfy the rule with a slight bow and a kiss on the cheek or the mouth, whichever they preferred. No one would have to grovel. Since Alexander would return a kiss, he clearly intended to dispel the notion that he thought himself divine (gods didn't return kisses). The exchange of kisses would also signify a status of equality among all the men present. It seemed like a good idea.

But when the time came for Callisthenes, a scholar and cousin of Aristotle, to pay homage, he drank the wine but refused the kiss. Because of Callisthenes' protest, Alexander probably did not attempt to force the custom of *proskynesis* on his Macedonian officers.

Later, when an assassination attempt, led by a few discontented royal pages, was discovered, it appeared that Callisthenes, as the boys' teacher, might have prompted them. Although the Persian conspirators had political and social reasons of their own to kill Alexander, it is not unlikely that their disgruntled teacher might have encouraged them in the honored Greek tradition of "death to tyrants." Alexander took no chances and had Callisthenes arrested to stand trial back in Greece. He died in prison before he could be tried. Although not one Greek or Macedonian was implicated with him, there was considerable Greek support for Callisthenes. Many thought Alexander's conquests were too lucrative to be shared with barbarians, especially if the practice deprived loyal Greeks of offices and riches.

After leaving Persia, Alexander reached India and made plans for marching to "Ocean," a mysterious realm believed to border the "edge of the world." His troops refused to go, and in 326 B.C. Alexander agreed to turn around and head for home. Despite growing discontent among his men, Alexander still exhibited his superb talent for leading troops and his personal gift for winning hearts by sharing hardships. When he and his men were lost for 200 miles in the Baluchistan Desert (in what is now southern Iran), food ran short and troops resorted to killing pack animals for food. Alexander sent his own horse to the rear as a replacement and walked on foot. When there was not enough water for everyone, he refused his own ration.

Alexander returned to Babylon in 324 B.C.; his next campaign was to invade Arabia and add it to his growing empire. While solidifying his plans he ventured to the nearby elegant city of Hamadan for an unusual bout of sightseeing. During a week of games and musical contests, sacrifices to the gods, and free wine, his beloved Hephaistion became ill. He rejected doctors' advice to limit his diet and foolishly ate chicken and drank wine. The fever worsened, and on the eighth day the end seemed near. Alexander was notified and rushed to Hephaistion's bedside, but he was too late. Denied the heroic ideal of dying with his friend in combat, Alexander was not even able to be with him at the last.

As the grief-stricken conqueror planned his friend's funeral, a dark cloud hung over the intervening campaigns and military maneuvers. Soldiers noticed their commander's lack of zest. Soothsayers read dire omens that Alexander would soon follow Hephaistion into the next world. The following year Alexander contracted a fever himself, probably malaria. As he lingered on his deathbed, troops rioted, fearing they were not being told the truth about his condition. The day before Alexander died they broke past the bodyguards and entered his chamber. As they filed past his bed, he was too weak to speak but managed to give each of them a nod or a sign with his eyes.

Already Alexander's men were speculating about who would succeed him. Some thought solely in political terms: Who would rule his vast empire, which stretched from present-day Yugoslavia to the Himalayas? Who would carry out his plans for acquiring Arabia? Others wondered more philosophically: Who would match his unique style of heroism, courage, loyalty, passion, and will? According to some accounts, when asked whom he would choose as his successor, the dying warrior answered, "The strongest."

PLATO
427?–347 B.C.

Plato posed the question: Is the love (eros) felt by an older man for a younger man different from that felt by the younger man for the older one? Plato enjoyed this kind of question. His answer was no, the feelings were not different, but the process was.

It was easy for the fourth-century Greeks to account for the love of an older man for a younger man—the younger man had vigor and beauty—but it was more difficult to explain how a younger man could love an older one whose faded physical beauty no longer matched the youth-oriented standards of Athenian society. But Plato had an explanation. The young man is beautiful because he participates in the divine Beauty, which is perceived by the older man and then reflected back to the younger. In this way both the older and younger man serve as conduits through which is channeled the ideal form of Beauty. And in recognizing beauty in any individual, one is really recognizing the ideal Beauty which is changeless and eternal.

In his early life Plato found the ideal Beauty reflected in its lesser form in various young men, Dion, Alexis, and Aster being three names that have survived the centuries. For Aster, Plato wrote some verses, playing on the boy's name, which means star. "Aster is my Aster," Plato wrote. In later life he favored a less erotic, less emotional love which has come to be known by his name: platonic.

In 387 B.C. Plato founded his Academy in a public garden just northwest of Athens to teach students to analyze and think clearly about issues such as beauty, love, justice, and truth. The Academy attracted students from all over the Mediterranean, including his most famous pupil, Aristotle, who studied there for almost 20 years. The school offered instruction in philosophy, science, ethics, mathematics, astronomy, music, logic, and politics. Plato's decision to spend his life teaching and instructing the young came after years of contemplating a political career.

Plato's parents came from distinguished Athenian families. His mother was related to Solon, the famous lawmaker. After his father died, she married a supporter of the statesman Pericles, and Plato was brought up in Pericles' household, where he became interested in politics. But the vicissitudes of the 27-year-long Peloponnesian War between Sparta and Athens and their respective allies disillusioned the young Plato. Eventually the defeated Athens submitted to a pro-Spartan clique of aristocrats, known as the Thirty, who executed the democratic leaders of the city. The infamous Thirty remained in power for only a year before outraged Athenians rose up, threw them out, and reinstated democratic forms of government. Plato was 23 when the Thirty came to power; among them were his mother's brother and cousin. He was asked to join them.

"I thought these men were going to put a stop to the evils that had been happening and govern the city with justice, so I watched their conduct closely to see what they would do. But . . . they very soon showed me that the preceding regime had been a golden age by comparison." When the Thirty met their downfall, Plato considered taking part in the restored democracy, but again the realities of political life disillusioned him. Influential leaders of the democracy accused his old friend and teacher, Socrates, of corrupting the youth of Athens. They put him to death in 399 B.C. The more Plato reflected on the kind of men who were active in politics, the more he realized how difficult it would be to reform public life.

The death of Socrates scarred Plato's spirit. He left Athens and traveled for ten years through Greece, Egypt, and Sicily, where he spent time in Syracuse at the court of the dictator Dionysius I. Here he concluded that "all existing states are badly governed and the condition of their laws practically incurable." The only remedy he could envision to cure "the ills of the human race" was for "sincere and true lovers of wisdom [to] attain political power, or the rulers of our cities [to] learn true philosophy." Having reached this conclusion, Plato soon returned to Athens and founded his Academy to teach wisdom and philosophy, for he, like his mentor, Socrates, believed that virtue was a form of knowledge that could be taught to the young.

Plato spent the rest of his life teaching and writing in Athens, except for two trips back to Syracuse after Dionysius I died. The younger Dionysius, who succeeded his father, seemed amenable to learning and, from all accounts, easily influenced. Plato hoped to make him a test case to see if instruction could turn the young ruler into the wise statesman Plato dreamed of. Plato visited him twice, but the young man tired of study. His suspicious, jealous nature interfered with the ideals of truth and justice that Plato tried to impart. Realizing it was a hopeless cause, Plato returned to Athens.

The 25 dialogues Plato wrote over the course of his life set and defined the terms that would command central importance in European thought and culture for over 2,000 years. Plato's concepts, and the continuing discussion of their relevance, became the basis for the most notable works of speculative thought, applied scientific principles, political theory and practice, and great works of art and literature. The basic questions that Plato asked were: How can the individual discover truth? What is the origin and nature of the world? What is the purpose of life?

For Plato, certain qualities (such as beauty, truth, goodness, justice, whiteness, roundness) are eternal Ideas; that is, permanent realities that impart their essence to the individual objects of the material universe. For example, a young man and an older man each manifest a quality that can be recognized as an expression of the Idea of Beauty. Hence the nature of the universe is double: There is a higher spiritual realm of changeless archetypes, or the world of Being; and there is a lower, physical world of Becoming, where things continually change.

Plato believed that behind the highest Ideal Form is the Supreme Good which is God, who made all the inhabitants of the universe. Originally God intended for human souls to live among the stars, but in time they were drawn by their status as creatures to desire bodies like the material beings of the earth. Birth thus became a process of forgetting the knowledge and wisdom the soul enjoyed among the heavens; and the lessons one learns in life are actually a remembering of that wisdom and knowledge. The soul, according to Plato's famous description, is like a charioteer driving two horses, one a noble steed striving to mount back to the stars, the other an unruly beast pursuing the violent path of physical existence. It is a tough team to control.

Human beings are thus immortal. After death the soul that strove in life to retain its divine nature will be reincarnated in an even wiser individual or rejoin the blessed among the stars. The soul that became enslaved to the material demands of existence will be reborn in a human or animal life of even greater suffering.

A lifelong intellectual obsession of Plato's was the crucial issue of whether or not human society could be reconstructed to be more just and benevolent. His reflections on this question contributed to sociological and political theory for centuries. He viewed society as divided into three classes: the workers, the military, and the rulers, each having its own nature, training, and responsibilities. He believed that women tended to be inferior to men in some areas but superior to men in others, and should therefore be given the same intellectual and physical training as men. Women and men should share equally the duties and offices of public life.

He also proposed a method of eugenics by which the state could breed and educate political leaders from the best human stock. Raised apart from their natural parents, these children would be given rigorous and thorough training in all the disciplines Plato felt would contribute to statecraft, culminating in middle age, when they would be ready to assume the reins of leadership. These individuals, raised by the state, would never handle money or own houses or land, and they would be free of family ties. Such restrictions would prevent them from acquiring the attitudes and values of landlords and tyrants; instead they would become guardians and caretakers.

Plato's famous allegory of the cave describes how he viewed the life of the multitude of human beings. Sitting in the depths of a dark cave with their backs to the entrance, men and women face a wall. Behind them is a fire that throws flickering light around the chamber. Between the fire and the people, artificial objects of living things are passed around, their shadows cast against the wall, distorted by the darting flames. For most of the cave dwellers, these shadows are realities. A few courageous individuals, however, leave the cave and walk out into the bright light of day, where they discover the real natural world. Here they see the truth and realize how they have been duped by the images and their shadows. Their destiny is to return to the cave and try to enlighten those who still sit in darkness, "where men fight with one another over shadows and go mad in struggles for power."

"Until philosophers are kings," Plato said, "or the kings and princes of the world have the spirit and power of philosophy, and political authority and wisdom are united," human communities will never approach Utopia. They will continue to resemble the dark shadows and phantoms of the cave. But what is the wise man or woman, the lover of truth, goodness, and beauty, to do in the meantime? On this point Plato was far from optimistic. These high-minded individuals are like those who "fall among wild beasts." They will not take part in the wickedness, but neither will they single-handedly be able to oppose the fierce natures of the wicked. A man in such a state "holds his peace and goes his own way . . . satisfied if only he can live his own life pure from wrong or unrighteousness and depart in peace and good will with bright hopes."

In such a way did Plato live his own life. At age 80 he died, but his Academy continued to serve as an illustrious center of learning for another 250 years, spawning similar academies throughout Greece and Rome. Some of these, the direct descendants of Plato's original school, survived for almost 900 years until the Christian emperor Justinian abolished them in A.D. 529 and confiscated their property.

SAPPHO
c. 600 B.C.

Plato called her the "tenth Muse." Her image was engraved on coins, her portrait painted on vases, her statue erected in places of honor. Her contemporaries and those who came after her acknowledged her genius. When Solon of Athens heard one of her songs sung at a banquet, he demanded the singer teach it to him at once. Asked why he wished to learn the lyric so quickly, he answered, "So that I may die knowing it."

Her name was Sappho, and little else about her has survived the ages, except that she lived on the island of Lesbos in the Aegean Sea around 600 B.C., had a daughter, was a poet, and loved women.

Sappho's poems are almost exclusively about women: their occupations, their desires and fears, virginity, marriage, their religious mysteries. At a time when women were devalued as both spouses and sexual partners, Sappho celebrated the worth and importance of women's experience. The rise of the city-state and decline of the landholding aristocratic families undermined the need for political and economic marriages and, in the process, undermined the value of women, except as child-bearers. Greek men, of course, still needed sons to carry on their family line and inherit property.

Sexually, men were beginning to regard women with fear, as the tradition of romantic love became increasingly centered on the love of man for man. Statues depicting women were clothed, those depicting men were nude, reflecting the widespread notion that the ideal of physical beauty was the male body, not the female. Furthermore it was a common assumption that women were more sexually potent than men, and that heterosexual activity robbed men of their virility. Male homosexual relations were becoming not only acceptable but desirable. In time the segregation of the sexes became almost total. Required to stay at home, women were allowed only one public function: to officiate at their religious mysteries.

In this society Sappho wrote her lyrical songs, celebrating, almost defiantly, women's experience. In her wedding songs the groom "prays" for the marriage and "dreams" of his lovely bride. Sappho admonishes a young man that, regardless of what he has been taught to the contrary, "no woman was ever lovelier" than the one he is to marry. The homey tasks and duties of women—weaving cloth, gathering flowers, fashioning headbands for their hair—became valued activities full of richness and meaning. Sappho's women are not shrewish and lazy, as depicted in male literature, but industrious and nurturing.

In almost audacious verse Sappho suggests that women can regret losing their virginity, due to the physical trauma itself and in losing what in Greek society was a badge of honor, their chastity. She writes of a bride questioning her virginity: "Virginity, Virginity, have you deserted me, where have you gone?" To whom "Virginity" replies: "I will never return to you again, never return to you again."

In Sappho's poetry, Helen of Troy is a strong, autonomous woman, not the passive creature of the fates and rapacious soldiers, as she is portrayed in Homer. Rather she makes her own decisions. Sappho wrote:

Helen left her husband—
the best of all men—
behind and sailed far away to Troy; she did not spare
a single thought for her child nor for her dear parents
but [the goddess of love] led her . . .

Sappho's Helen is not stolen, but leaves willingly, forsaking the traditional roles of mother and daughter that Greek custom would impose upon her.

Sappho may have conducted a school on Lesbos in which she trained young girls in the religious mysteries of Aphrodite, which would presumably include teaching poetry and song-making for the rituals and celebrations. Some of Sappho's finest lyrics suggest they were written as songs for public worship. To the goddess of love she wrote:

Leave Crete and come to me here, to this holy temple,
where the loveliness of your apple grove
waits for you and your altars smolder
with burning frankincense. . . .

. . . Cyprian goddess, take and pour
gracefully, like wine into golden cups,
a nectar mingled with all the joy
of our celebration.

Women poets posed a problem for Greek men, who consistently denigrated women's talents and genius. Since poets were generally not women in Greek society, those women who were poets often found their poetry discounted as of little value. Many hostile commentators, especially those envious of Sappho's genius, took for granted the deviant lifestyle of a woman who wrote poetry. The scandal surrounding Sappho—that she was a prostitute, that she corrupted young girls, that she committed suicide over an unrequited love for a ferryman—was indicative of many Greek males' inability to come to terms with a woman of literary talent. Stories and rumors abounded, encouraged by those who wished to tarnish her reputation.

Sappho, however, seems to have accepted her role as a poet quite naturally; and on Lesbos, at least, it seems not to have been uncommon for women to compose lyrics. Some of her own verses mention that her female companions or pupils are also poets. She exhorted:

> *I beg you, Gongyla,*
> *take up your lyre [and sing to us;]*
> *for once again an aura of desire*
> *hovers around.*

Ancient commentators asserted that Sappho was the first poet to describe the moon as "silver," an association that today seems commonplace; but like many of Shakespeare's well-known phrases, every cliché has to begin with someone. She also may have been the first to write about finding a kind of immortality in her verses. "I tell you," she wrote, "in time to come, someone will remember us."

Greek men poets wrote of love for women in vague, unexciting terms, reserving romantic intensity for homosexual relationships, frequently expressed in military images of the pursuer and pursued. Sappho, however, writes of her love for women in startlingly clear terms, finding erotic beauty in their clothes, their bodies, their sleep, the garlands they wove to put around each other's necks (a common convention of homosexual courtship). She wrote:

> *. . . your beauty, your dress thrills all those who see you*
> *and the heart in my breast quickens . . .*

> *[Her voice was] far sweeter than any flute . . .*
> *[her hair] more golden than gold . . .*
> *[and her skin] far whiter than an egg . . .*

You've come and you—
            oh, I was longing for you—
have cooled my heart
            which was burning with desire.

In Sappho's poetry submission finds no place in lesbian love. For her, love of woman for woman is love between equals. Women on Lesbos acquired a reputation for being strong, independent sexual partners, whether with other women or in heterosexual marriages. The male poet Anacreon, a contemporary of Sappho who lived on the mainland in Asia Minor, complained that the woman he loved ignored him because "she is from Lesbos and gapes after another woman."

At a time when Greek society was going through severe transitions and the status of women was being undermined, Sappho's poetry created an alternative world of beauty and meaning out of the daily lives and loves of average women, a concern which is unique in ancient literature. Her sensuality and intense celebration of the emotions of lovers became a hallmark for later poets and writers, as did her courage in suggesting that each person's private love is the most beautiful object in the world:

Some an army of horsemen, some an army on foot
and some say a fleet of ships is the loveliest sight
on this dark earth; but I say it is whatever you desire.

LEONARDO
DA VINCI
1452–1519

The government of Renaissance Florence set up special boxes around the city so that citizens could denounce one another in secret. On one occasion a note was left detailing the scurrilous activities of a "boy of ill repute," named Jacopo Saltarelli. He was "17 years of age, or thereabouts," the note read, "[and] behind many misfortunes, and [he] consents to pleasure those persons who wish for this kind of deplorable thing." The anonymous snoop then listed the names of four men who had engaged in the "deplorable" activity. One of them was the 24-year-old artist Leonardo da Vinci.

Arrested, tried, and released because of insufficient evidence, Leonardo returned to more important matters, namely completing his final year under the tutelage of Verrocchio, the renowned artist who greatly influenced Florentine art in the 1470s and whose workshop launched the careers of many and variously talented artists. Whether or not Leonardo needed Verrocchio's instruction was then, and is still now, disputed, for it seems that Verrocchio changed his own style under the influence of his most famous pupil. Although it is not certain when the young

Leonardo began his apprenticeship (possibly around 1470), he was already listed in the Florentine painters' guild as a "master" by 1472, when he was only 20 years old. By the time he was 30, he had received his first two public commissions: *The Virgin of the Rocks* and *The Adoration of the Magi*.

Leonardo was the illegitimate son of Ser Piero da Vinci, a lawyer, and a woman named Caterina about whom little is known except that she came from a "good family." Leonardo grew up in a household bustling with his 11 half-brothers and -sisters, the children of his father's four marriages. In his early years Leonardo was interested in mathematics, music, and drawing. But when his father realized that his son's talent lay in art, he arranged for Leonardo to study with Verrocchio.

A few years after leaving Verrocchio, Leonardo moved to Milan, where he stayed for most of the next 20 years under the patronage of Lodovico Sforza, the usurper who ruled that city until his overthrow in 1499. Sforza was an ideal patron— devoted to the arts and appreciative of the fame that Leonardo's multifaceted wizardry brought to his court. According to the famous résumé letter which Leonardo wrote "to acquaint you [Sforza] with my secrets," the Florentine painter promised to handle almost any military problem that might arise. He could provide portable bridges, scaling ladders, cannon, mortars, new types of projectiles, catapults, technology for offensive and de- fensive naval engagements, mining and tunneling skills, war chariots, and "other engines of wonderful efficacy not in general use." In case peace broke out, he promised Sforza that his architectural skills would be available for both public and private buildings, his knowledge of hydraulics could provide water to any place where it was needed, and he could sculpt in marble, bronze, or clay. He also mentioned that he could paint "as well as any other, whoever he may be."

The years from about age 30 to 50 were happy and prosperous ones. Leonardo designed buildings, painted *The Last Supper*, invented military paraphernalia, sketched out elaborate plans for rebuilding Milan, and constructed canals for Sforza's agricultural reforms. The Sforza court was like a giant playground for his boyish fascination with building and inventing.

In Milan, Leonardo also met Giacomo Caprotti, who became his studio boy at age ten. He first described the boy, nicknamed Salai ("little devil"), in his journal as "thief, liar, obstinate, glutton," and then added a detailed list of the household items the boy had pilfered, along with their costs. In time Salai mellowed and became Leonardo's pupil and lover, staying with him for the rest of his life. He also met Francesco Melzi, a young gentleman of Milan, who became a pupil and lifelong companion. Melzi inherited Leonardo's notebooks and became the executor of his estate.

Returning to Florence in 1500, Leonardo was at the peak of his career as a painter. In a city known for its hard-edged homosexuality (the streets are still studded with statues of naked men), Leonardo found the androgynous youths who became his models and, if they had a modicum of talent, his pupils. Enjoying the company of beautiful young men, Leonardo filled his canvases with their half-tough, half-gentle faces and bodies, complete with the curling, light-tinted hair and the enigmatic smiles that would come to characterize the da Vinci style. For a brief period he accompanied Cesare Borgia on his devastating campaigns through central Italy as his primary military engineer. And he painted the *Mona Lisa*—then and now one of the most celebrated portraits ever painted.

In Florence, Leonardo also began serious anatomical studies at the hospital of Santa Maria Nuova, where he daringly dissected corpses, a practice that would not receive widespread acceptance until the late nineteenth century. He believed that anatomical studies were indispensable for the painter who would accurately depict the human form. He derided those who "seem great draftsmen" but draw their nude figures "looking like wood, devoid of grace; so that you would think you were looking at a sack of walnuts . . . or a bundle of radishes rather than the muscles of [human] figures."

Milan came under French rule in 1506, and Leonardo returned. For the next seven years he cast his brilliant influence over many artists, some of whom studied under him formally and came to be known as the Milanese Leonardesque school of painting. Surprisingly, the two most famous artists influenced by his style were never his pupils. Raphael transformed his own style of painting to emulate Leonardo, and Correggio adapted Leonardo's techniques of counterbalancing different textures and emphasizing the various effects that light has on them.

Leonardo was a masterful teacher, yet he believed that an artist learned more by observing nature directly than from trying to copy the techniques and tricks of the masters. "Since there is such an abundance of things in nature, it is better to go to nature than to the masters who have learned from her," he advised. He perceived the artist as linking God, nature, and human existence. "The mind of the painter is transformed," he wrote, "into a copy of the divine mind" when it wrestles with the natural objects it seeks to paint. Leonardo also recognized the artist's need to identify with his subject in order to render it more exactly and express its divine spirit. The "mind of the painter" must "transform itself into the very mind of nature herself," he wrote, "and to make itself the interpreter between nature and art."

As a teacher, Leonardo expected discipline from his pupils, even as he expected it of himself. The man of genius whose imagination ranged farther than most individuals of his era reminded himself in his journal: "Just as iron rusts without use, and water becomes putrid and with cold freezes, so talent without exercise deteriorates." And yet, most of Leonardo's projects never came to fruition. He spent long periods of time studying and preparing himself before commencing a work; and more often than not he left it unfinished when called to some other project by a demanding patron, or when his own wandering curiosity led him, like a child, to explore something new and strange.

Only when his notebooks were discovered in the last century did the world realize just how truly "Renaissance" this Renaissance man was. Until then, Leonardo's genius rested primarily on his reputation as a painter, but the more than 5,000 notebook pages made it clear that his mind perceptively penetrated the secrets of anatomy, botany, geology, mechanics, and astronomy. In marvelously detailed sketches and commentary, written from right to left with the aid of a mirror (possibly because this direction is more convenient for someone who is left-handed), he sketched out plans for inventions that anticipated the helicopter, the parachute, the submarine, the machine gun, and the automobile. He made meticulous drawings, accurate down to the slightest detail, fascinated by both internal structures and outward form: a horse's foreleg, the individual petals of a flower, the human embryo in its mother's womb, the internal organs of the male and female bodies during sexual intercourse, branching stems, bone structure in the human hand, topographic maps for irrigation systems, the moon approaching total eclipse, the ribbing for a wooden wing (and the hand crank to operate it), and the human eye. On pages crammed with calculations and diagrams, he left plans for inventions that would not be realized for centuries. He imagined scientific and aesthetic truths that only later generations would discover.

With boundless energy and great physical stamina, Leonardo undertook his ravenous investigations and experiments into almost every aspect of life and nature. On one of his works he signed his name simply "Leonardo da Vinci, disciple of experiment." Always he sought to ground his work in reality, to secure even the wildest flights of his imagination in physical laws. In his notebooks he wrote: "First I shall make some experiments before I proceed further, because my intention is to consult experience first and then by means of reasoning show why such experiment is bound to work in such a way." If Leonardo seems to have studied and mastered everything he set his hand to, he was equally convinced of the necessity of understanding one's own nature. "One can have no greater and no lesser mastery," he wrote, "than that which one has over oneself."

From 1513 to 1515 Leonardo stayed in Rome, where he was commissioned for several Vatican paintings and some architectural and engineering projects. While on a trip in Bologna, he met King Francis I, who invited him to France. In the winter of 1516–17, at age 64, accompanied by his faithful friends Melzi and Salai, he made the trek to France, where he lived in the villa of Cloux at Amboise. Here he spent his last years, drawing up plans, sketching out ideas, recording his perceptive impressions of the natural world. He died on May 2, 1519, comforted by his deep faith in the church and, as expressed in his will, a deep affection for all those who had been close to him.

Shortly after his death Francesco Melzi wrote to the artist's half-brothers: "As long as my body holds together, I shall feel perpetual unhappiness, and rightly so, for he showed me daily a very warm and complete love. The loss of such a man is a sorrow to everyone, for nature will not be able to create his equal again."

DESIDERIUS ERASMUS

1466–1536

In 1498 the 32-year-old Augustinian monk Erasmus, on leave from his Dutch monastery to study and teach theology in Paris, accepted two young English pupils with whom he became inordinately enamored (especially for a monk). With one of his students, Thomas Grey, a handsome, athletic 22-year-old, Erasmus had problems: Grey's traveling companion and tutor, a stern Scot, objected to Erasmus' ardor and made trouble for the two. With the other student, William Blount, the 4th Lord Mountjoy, the relationship proceeded more smoothly, and the young Englishman invited Erasmus to England. "Whither would I not follow so humane, so kind, so lovable a young man?" Erasmus wrote. The trip to England was a turning point in the scholar's professional life, for there he met humanists Thomas More and John Colet, who inspired him to work on a new translation of the New Testament, which was to have immeasurable impact on the Reformation and the shaping of modern Christianity.

Erasmus, the illegitimate son of a priest and a physician's daughter, was born near Rotterdam, Holland, in 1466. Both parents died of bubonic plague when he was 17. As a boy, Erasmus spent ten years in schools run by the Brethren of the Common Life, a religious community of men without vows who led a communal life of meditation, study, and simplicity. Their schools were acknowledged as the best in Europe, and their publications included such popular works as *The Imitation of Christ*. With the brethren, Erasmus met Rudolph Agricola, a flamboyant humanist scholar who criticized medieval religious authority and promoted what the Renaissance thinkers called the New Learning, the Greek and Roman classics that were being rediscovered in Italy.

Under strong pressure from three guardians who had squandered his money, Erasmus entered the Augustinian monastery at Steyn when he was 22. Without much enthusiasm he joined the order of monks, even though he knew he had no true calling, and came to detest the monastic life. Erasmus also complained that the monk's life closed the door to real knowledge; and in defiance of his monastery's rules, he continued to read the classics. Of Greek philosophy, he wrote: "A heathen wrote this to a heathen, yet it has justice, sanctity, truth. I can hardly refrain from saying, 'Saint Socrates, pray for me!'"

At Steyn, Erasmus fell in love with a fellow monk, Servatius Roger, who did not reciprocate Erasmus' feelings. Erasmus wrote to him: "My mind is such that I think nothing can rank higher than friendship in this life, nothing should be desired more ardently, nothing should be treasured more jealously." But Servatius did not respond so ardently. Later Erasmus wrote: "Do not be so reserved; I have become yours so completely that nothing of myself is left. You know my weakness: when it has no one to lean upon, it drives me to despair of life." Servatius merely told him to be more guarded about his feelings in the future. Years later, in 1514, Servatius Roger, then prior of the monastery, ordered Erasmus, who had then been living in the "world" for the last 21 years, to return, but Erasmus solicited papal permission to continue his worldly ministry and never set foot in the monastery again.

Although still under monastic vows, Erasmus had received permission in 1493 to serve as secretary to the Bishop of Cambrai, who gave him leave to study at the University of Paris, where he received a bachelor's degree of theology in 1498. After his trip to England with Lord Mountjoy, he returned to Paris and wrote his first collection of the *Adages*, which he dedicated to Mountjoy. The *Adages* were an ongoing compilation of proverbs and wise sayings from classical literature, that eventually totaled over 3,000 entries and introduced the wisdom of the ancients to many Renaissance readers longing for an alternative to the strict medieval orthodoxy.

In 1503 he published his *Handbook of a Christian Knight*, in which he discussed what he called the "philosophy of Christ." The *Handbook* was a serious call to Christians to return to the simplicity and purity of the early church. Eschewing rigid dogmatism, which provoked schism and hatred, Erasmus called for the militant Christian to return to the simple preaching of Jesus, uncorrupted by the layers of church doctrine and theology. There was no need for stiff outward rituals and observances, he argued; what was paramount was the soul's inward journey toward God, a journey that could be made with learning, knowledge, and prayer. He hoped that the church would reduce the number of dogmas to as "few as possible, leaving opinion free on the rest."

In 1511 he wrote *The Praise of Folly* in one week while staying with Thomas More in England. A best-seller for its day (like the *Handbook*), it articulated the failings of the church and society. A product of the intellectual ferment of the Renaissance, Erasmus attacked the church for hypocrisy and churchmen in particular for ignorance and worldliness, and for straying from the path of simplicity laid down by the apostles. He decried the misplaced emphasis on miracles, shrines, indulgences, and pilgrimages, as well as self-indulgent monks, cardinals, and popes who misused the luxuries and riches of their offices. He also criticized secular society for engaging in commercialism, war, and other cruelties.

In Erasmus' work "Folly" announces that she is essential for life. "Without me the world cannot exist for a moment. For is not all that is done . . . among mortals full of folly: is it not performed by fools and for fools?" The antithesis of reason, in Erasmus' view, folly is responsible for war, worldliness, and the evils of life, even as she makes life bearable. "No society, no cohabitation can be pleasant or lasting without folly; so much so that a people could not stand its prince, nor the master his man, nor the maid her mistress, nor the tutor his pupil, nor the friend his friend, nor the wife her husband for a moment longer if they did not now and then err together, now flatter each other; now sensibly conniving at things, now smearing themselves with some honey of folly."

Urbane, scholarly, and an intellectual charmer, Erasmus' greatest achievement was his ground-breaking Latin translation of the New Testament (1516), which he made from early Greek texts of the Gospels and Epistles. Erasmus' translation challenged orthodoxy and rocked the citadels of dogma. It shrewdly pointed up the many mistakes in the Vulgate, the church's official Latin translation. Erasmus' version was praised by humanists both because it made a scholarly contribution to sacred literature and because it provided a solid base from which to attack the orthodox church. William Tyndale used it to translate the New Testament into English, and Tyndale's version became the basis for the later King James Version. Luther used Erasmus' translation in his lectures at Wittenberg and for his own German translation. In short, Erasmus' New Testament laid the groundwork for modern biblical criticism.

Even in his own day, Erasmus was attacked on two sides for his role in the Reformation. He was accused by conservatives of "laying the egg that Luther hatched," for Erasmus' ideas and writings encouraged those who were unhappy with the abuses of the medieval church. In fact, it was Erasmus who sent Luther's theses to a colleague in London in 1517, thus introducing the German reformer and his ideas to the British Isles. But Erasmus detested revolution and thought that Luther and others had carried reform too far. This, in turn, convinced radical reformers that Erasmus had become lukewarm, especially when he refused to support Luther after the Diet of Worms in 1521. Many thought he had deserted the cause, while still others perceived his writings and criticism of the church as having been the cause of all the trouble in the first place.

Erasmus wanted true reform, not revolt. After watching a congregation of Protestants leave a church service, he related: "I have seen them returning from hearing a sermon as if inspired by an evil spirit. The faces of all showed a curious wrath and ferocity." Erasmus may have had a revolutionary mind, but not a revolutionary heart. He felt that revolution was worse than tyranny, and did not want to weaken the faith of the masses. Reform from within the church, he believed, could come from education and learning, a process which, he admitted, would be slow.

In the highly charged theological battles of his era, Erasmus held to a middle-of-the-road position. In fact, he frequently tried to be ambiguous, intellectually caught in a position where he advocated change but feared what would happen when change got out of hand, or out of the right hands. Radical reformers like Luther replied that changing the church and society as Erasmus would do it had proven unworkable. It was too late for slow, steady reform from within. For the rest of his life, Erasmus was on the defensive.

Hoping for a restoration of Christian unity, Erasmus continued his studies and translations, leaving a legacy of classical writers and church fathers for the new era. He edited or translated Aristotle, Cicero, Demosthenes, Lucian, Livy, Suetonius, Ovid, Plautus, Plutarch, Terence, and Seneca; and among the church fathers: Ambrose, Athanasius, Basil, Jerome, John Chrysostom, and Origen. He remained dedicated to primitive Christianity, and continued to believe that education and good literature would bring reform.

Erasmus' main philosophical themes were exemplified in his own life: simplicity, moderation, and a return to the basic message of Christ. Called by one historian the "first journalist"—he had views on everything and expressed his opinions at the drop of a hat—Erasmus wrote in a clear, elegant Latin style. His writings popularized the New Learning, stretched people's minds, made them dream great dreams. A friend called him "the glory of our age." "Truly," Erasmus wrote, "the yoke of Christ would be sweet, and His burden light, if petty human institutions added nothing to what He Himself imposed. He commanded us nothing save love for one another."

MICHELANGELO
1475–1564

When Michelangelo completed his colossal statue of David for the Florentine government, the city's chief executive, Pietro Soderini, complained that the giant-slayer's nose was too big, or so it seemed to him. Michelangelo grabbed his chisel and hammer, along with a handful of marble dust from the ground, climbed the scaffolding, made a few chisel sounds in the vicinity of David's nose, and let the dust concealed in his hand fall back to earth. Then the sculptor asked Soderini how it looked. "I like it better now," he replied. "You have given it life."

At age 28 Michelangelo had learned the fine art of pleasing his patrons and critics, and well that he had, for his life would forever orbit around the whims of others. As an artist who idealized the male body (he even used the male models/assistants who shared his studio and bed for his statues of women), Michelangelo's controversial life and work never prevented his being lionized by both secular and ecclesiastical authorities. He lived in an age of contradictions. Political loyalties, artistic rivalries, conflicting ethical codes, warring ideologies, and warring city-states and principalities provided the backdrop for a life of frustration and disappointment. Yet Michelangelo assembled a successful career out of that maelstrom of conflict and chaos, just as beauty could be drawn from a misshapen block of marble.

Michelangelo's struggle to become an artist began early, with his father, over choice of a career. The elder Buonarroti considered it demeaning to work with the hands and classified sculptors and artists along with stonemasons. Although the boy attended school for a few years, his heart was drawn to art against his father's wishes; and at age 13 he was apprenticed to a Florentine painter who later chose him to study at the informal academy at the Medici palace. At 14 the young artist was swept up into the heady intellectual ferment of Lorenzo's household, where philosophy, art, religion, and the recently rediscovered and reappreciated pagan world of Greece and Rome were discussed with zeal and passion. Here, too, opposing forces vied for the young man's mind and spirit, for the new humanists were not allowed to discuss the virtues of the pagan soul or the value of sensual beauty in peace.

In the streets of Florence, the relentless reformer Savonarola preached the wrath of an angry God who would not easily allow his subjects to stray from the moral code of Christianity. The Dominican's sermons made as much impact on Michelangelo's young mind as did the possibilities of humanism. For Michelangelo there would be no mental peace, just as for Italy itself there would be no political peace. Foreign invasions, threats of foreign invasions, revolutions, assassinations, reforms, and the unpredictable changes in political and ecclesiastical leadership would produce an artist who knew the wisdom of concealing marble dust in his hands.

Michelangelo's first two major commissions reflected the conflict of loyalties. In Rome, at age 21, he found a patron who requested a statue of Bacchus, the Greek god of wine, drunkenness, and spiritual ecstasy. Two years later, a French cardinal commissioned a life-sized statue of the Virgin Mary holding her dead Son across her knees for a chapel of Saint Peter's. The two works expressed the internal conflict within the artist as well as they did the cultural upheaval in which he worked.

Michelangelo's contemporary biographer, Vasari, overawed by the beauty of the green marble Virgin and Christ, wrote: "It is a miracle that a stone without shape should have been reduced to such perfection." Others thought so, too. The *Pietà* established the 23-year-old's reputation, and from then on he was sought after by patrons who included Popes Julius II, Leo X, Clement VII, Paul III, Julius III, Paul IV, and Pius IV; Suleiman, the Ottoman sultan; Francis of Valois, king of France; Emperor Charles V; the Signoria of Venice; and Duke Cosimo de' Medici. All offered him what Vasari called "honorable salaries."

In 1501 he returned to Florence, now under the newly established republican form of government headed by Soderini, and was commissioned to sculpture a statue of David to honor the civic mood of heroic patriotism. The 18-foot-high block of marble had sat untouched for 40 years after another sculptor had tried and failed to sculpt a statue of Hercules. The biblical David's replacing the pagan hero was aptly reflective of the new government's pride in its republican virtue, having ousted the sensuous luxury and vice of the Medici family. Michelangelo, himself torn between the two world views, worked day and night in secret behind a wooden enclosure built around the block of marble. He slept in his clothes and ate on the job. In the end, he had liberated from the rough stone a hero who combined gracefulness and muscularity, a sensuous young man who would slay Goliath as much with muscle power as with the skill used to swing the slingshot flung so nonchalantly over his shoulder.

The success of *David* led Soderini (once the nose was "fixed") to offer Michelangelo another public commission, one that canceled a previous contract to create larger-than-life statues of the 12 apostles for the cathedral of Florence. Soderini's new offer was to paint a fresco in the council room of the Palazzo Vecchio, where Leonardo da Vinci was already painting another wall commemorating the Florentine victory at the Battle of Anghiari. For his painting, Michelangelo chose a peculiar subject: not a victory, but the Pisan army's ambush of the Florentine soldiers while they bathed in a river. He had his reasons. It allowed him to deal with a subject which had, according to one biographer, "already obsessed him: the naked male in many postures." Only the cartoons—the sketches that are glued to a wall to guide the painter—were finished before he was summoned to Rome for another project. But, even unfinished, the daring sketches of the nude soldiers bathing in the river created a greater furor than did the nude *David*.

Nevertheless, the sketches were studied and copied by later artists, and ultimately perished from being handled to death. Surviving studies of the scene show that it is one of the first attempts, according to art scholar Kenneth Clark, to show that the human body of ordinary men could express "nobility, life-giving energy and Godlike perfection." Michelangelo's portrayal of the nude body had profound influence on the human mind and spirit for over 400 years, in direct opposition to the dreary medieval view that the body was the source of sin, guilt, and shame, and must be concealed.

In Rome, Michelangelo began work on the tomb of Pope Julius II, a project he would never personally complete due to interruptions by other projects, shifting political and papal alliances, and canceled contracts. Several sculptures for it remain, however, including the lovely, almost peaceful *Dying Slave*, a 7'4"-high figure which some critics say symbolizes the human soul imprisoned in the flesh, as Platonic thought would have it, while others see it as a young man sensuously reclining in the arms of sleep. Michelangelo himself could have appreciated either interpretation.

The most talented and respected sculptor of his day, Michelangelo shaped forever our images of David, Moses, Adam, God the Father, Christ, the Virgin Mary. He rendered the human figure with awesome grandeur, emphasizing even in many of the female figures the genuinely powerful physique. In them we recognize the magnificence of the human spirit, not just imprisoned but nourished by the body.

And yet Michelangelo's poetry reveals another experience. Repeatedly he writes about suffering, pain, and his own inevitable encounter with death. He himself enjoyed robust health, could get by with little food or sleep, and worked long hours. In his letters to his family, he appears to be suspicious of others, difficult to get along with, ill-tempered at times, and yet generous and concerned for others' welfare.

From youth to old age his devotion to the arts withdrew him from the company of others. Some found this eccentric; others thought it a sign of pride. He never married. "I already have a wife who is too much for me," he explained, "one who keeps me unceasingly struggling on. It is my art, and my works are my children."

In 1532, while in Rome, he met the young nobleman Tommaso Cavalieri. The next year, from Florence, he wrote the young man: "If I had not believed that I had made you sure of the very great, rather, the immeasurable, love I bear you, I would not have thought it strange or wondered at the great suspicion you show . . . that I might forget you . . . but perhaps you do it to tempt me or rekindle a new and greater fire, if a greater can be."

That same year he visited Rome again to visit Cavalieri, and the following year, 1534, he moved permanently to Rome, where he lived the rest of his life.

At the age of 60 he was appointed by Pope Paul III Chief Architect, Sculptor, and Painter of the Apostolic Palace; and so he began his great fresco on the altar wall of the Sistine Chapel: *The Last Judgment*, a companion to the mammoth biblical epic he had painted a quarter of a century earlier that depicted the Genesis story from the Creation to the Flood.

When he first undertook the *Creation* project, he had misgivings. Sculpture, not painting, was his forte, and he had no desire to interrupt his work on the tomb of Julius II. But, like God the Father sending a charge of life and energy through his finger to the heavily muscled body of Adam, Michelangelo breathed his own life and spirit into the Genesis scenes. He worked furiously for the next four years—almost single-handed because, being a perfectionist, he tended to fire his assistants. He completed the task, his misgivings now clearly unfounded, giving the western world a new standard for painting and unforgettable images of the Old Testament.

The newer piece, *The Last Judgment*, attracted the same criticism for nudity that followed Michelangelo throughout his life. The pope's chamberlain sniffed that the work belonged in a brothel, not a chapel. Michelangelo's revenge was to paint the chamberlain among the devils in hell.

From age 60 to 89 he lived quietly, worked as hard as ever, and grew deeper in his spiritual devotions. One night, when Vasari caught him working by candlelight, he dropped the candle so his friend could not see what he was working on and said: "I am so old that death often pulls me by the cloak . . . and one day this body of mine will fall like the lamp, and the light of my life will be spent." After his 70th birthday his days and nights were chiefly concerned with architecture—working on the great dome of Saint Peter's, designing a church, constructing city gates—and poetry.

In a few special people—and in his work—Michelangelo found escape from what, in a sonnet, he called "the evil, foolish and invidious mob." Always he felt pulled by opposing forces of thought, of devotion, of politics, of loyalty, of spirit and flesh. But he always managed to stand in awe of beauty and, with brain and hand, release it from stone or sketch it on parchment or paint it on plastered walls and ceilings.

In a sonnet to Cavalieri, he said that, in beholding mortal beauty, "some other beauty shines into the heart," some divine light "that the soul can sense" shines forth. It was this "other beauty" that he made visible in his heroic masterpieces. "What I sense and I search . . . I'm shown by others," he wrote for Cavalieri, "This happens to me since I saw you . . . /Moved by a yes and no, a sweet and bitter;/I'm sure it must have been those eyes of yours."

In Rome, at age 89, he died as he had lived, working on projects he loved, destined never to be completed by his own hand. Death pulled at his cloak to take him to that "other beauty." Or, as he had written in a sonnet years before:

> . . . *burning love, by which the soul's let loose,*
> *Since it's a magnet to its matching blaze,*
> *Like gold purged in a fire, returns to God.*

FRANCIS BACON

1561–1626

In the winter of 1626 Sir Francis Bacon stopped his carriage to gather some snow, which he packed into the carcass of a dead chicken. His objective? To see whether cold would halt the process of decay. Unfortunately he caught pneumonia and died shortly thereafter. This was the only scientific experiment Bacon is known to have performed.

Fooling around with dead chickens in the snow, however, was not what his mother had worried most about during his life. A rigidly moralistic woman, Lady Bacon wrote frequent letters of advice to both her homosexual sons, warning them of the dangers to body and soul that could result from their reckless lifestyles. Regarding Francis, she wrote to his older brother, Anthony: "I pity your brother yet as long as he pities not himself but keepeth that bloody Percy—yea, as a coach companion and bed companion: a proud, profane costly fellow, whose being about him I verily perceive the Lord God doth mislike, and doth less bless your brother in credit and otherwise in his health."

Lady Bacon had good reason to fret. Her sons were born and raised in an environment rife with money, political favors, sex, privilege, and patronage. Their father was the Lord Keeper of the Great Seal for Queen Elizabeth; their mother, a cousin to Robert Cecil, the chief minister to both Elizabeth and James I. From childhood the royal court was their home; as adults it was their life.

Francis was educated at Cambridge and spent three years in France before studying law at Gray's Inn, a place that worried Lady Bacon because of "practices unmeet," by which she meant both sex with men and boys and the "pernicious and obscene plays and theatres able to poison the very godly!" Both sons lived as they wished, however, ignoring her advice on sexual matters as well as her recommendations to eschew the theater, maintain a strict diet, and get a goodly amount of sleep.

In 1584, at age 23, Bacon, now a barrister, took his seat in Parliament, where he became a shrewd adviser to the Queen on the troubling issues of the day. He advocated toleration on the pernicious religious question that divided the nation. He favored union with Scotland. He warned of the growing rift between Parliament and the Crown, which would escalate into civil war a generation later. In 1593 he lost the Queen's favor by opposing, on principle, royal subsidies to wage the ongoing war with Spain. Around 1592 both Francis and Anthony became political advisers to the Earl of Essex. Ten years later, when Essex had fallen out of favor by the failure of his Ireland policy and his attempt to rouse Londoners to rebellion, Bacon, as the Queen's counsel, found himself in the unenviable position of opposing and convicting his patron. Essex went to the scaffold.

On Elizabeth's death in 1603, James I ascended the throne, and Bacon's hoped-for career began to blossom. He was dubbed a knight in 1603, became solicitor general in 1607, attorney general in 1613, and finally lord chancellor in 1618. A firm believer in the divine right of kings, he sided with the royal prerogative against parliamentary encroachments, often wisely foreseeing the constitutional imbroglios that would erupt in civil war. In 1621 he was accused of taking bribes in conjunction with cases he was representing. In an agile leap of logic, he admitted he had received "gifts" but denied that they influenced his decisions.

The investigation into his professional probity was politically motivated. It was possible that a charge of sodomy would be brought, an issue which King James, a homosexual himself, clearly could not allow to surface as an issue with any real political significance. A hostile contemporary wrote of Bacon in his diary that the lord chancellor "would not relinquish the practice of his most horrible and secret sin, keeping still one Goderick, a very effeminate youth, to be his catamite and bedfellow. Nor did he ever, that I could hear, forbear his old custom of making his servants his bedfellows." In the end, Bacon lost his office because of professional indiscretions, spent a brief time in the Tower, and was banished from court. A full pardon never came.

Unaware that he had only a few remaining years to live, Bacon relished having been ousted from public life. He had admitted as early as 1605 that he was more fit to hold a book than an office. "I have led my life in civil causes, for which I was not very fit by nature, and more unfit by the preoccupation of my mind." In short he was a scholar first, a politician second. On leaving office he remarked: "If I be left to myself I will graze and bear natural philosophy." And he did just that. In his final years he dedicated himself to the literary works that had preoccupied him since he was a young man.

For 28 years he had been writing essays; ten were published in 1597, 58 in 1625. "Dispersed meditations," as he called them, the essays ranged over topics as various as ambition, riches, honor, love, reputation, and friendship. In an essay on deformity he postulated that physically malformed individuals held a secret weapon in their deformity. "It stirreth in them industry, and especially to watch and observe the weakness of others, that they may have somewhat to repay. So that in a great wit, Deformity is an advantage to rising. . . . Whosoever hath anything fixed in his person that doth induce contempt hath also a perpetual spur in himself to rescue and deliver himself from scorn." In general, his essays were cool advice, written straight-forwardly, in an unsentimental style, informing his readers how to rise up in the world. He took his own advice. In his personal notebook are entries reminding himself to flatter so-and-so, study the weakness of someone else, work in his garden, control his breathing, and break his habit of interrupting others in conversation.

In 1609 he published *The Wisdom of the Ancients,* his most popular book next to the *Essays,* which interpreted the wisdom of ancient myths. In 1622 he wrote a *History of the Reign of Henry VII.* In 1614 he began the *New Atlantis,* a utopian tract about an ideal commonwealth on an island named Bensalem in the Pacific. Among its many features were Christianity as a state religion, a strong commitment to family life, and monarchy as a form of government. The Atlanteans also created Solomon's House, a scientific research institute to promote discoveries and inventions for the general welfare. It was always one of Bacon's cardinal beliefs that scientific knowledge should be used to make life better for the average person. "Truth and utility," he wrote, "are here the very same thing." Years later Solomon's House became a model for the Royal Society of London for the Advancement of Science, established by Charles II in 1662.

Bacon's monumental work, *The Great Instauratio,* was intended to be a grand scheme to reform all human knowledge and the methods for acquiring it. The main elements of his masterwork were well established by the time he was 32, and he worked on it off and on over his entire life, without finishing it. Affirming that the true end of knowledge is "the glory of the creator and relief of man's estate," he hoped for a grand synthesis of all knowledge based on his new method. His own life, riddled with political obligations and the machinations of court life, left him little time for the "task which lies beyond my powers and expectations."

In the section called *The Advancement of Learning,* Bacon criticized the contemporary attitudes that impeded learning. To rectify matters he argued that knowledge should be categorized according to what he viewed as the three parts of the human psyche: memory, imagination, and reason. Furthermore, human life and society should be studied inductively. Unproven metaphysical assumptions, he warned, are only useful as part of a materialist approach to understanding natural phenomena. In other words, he severed human knowledge from faith, arguing that knowledge is limited to the sensible, observable, material world.

Claiming that he became disillusioned with Aristotelian logic as early as his Cambridge days, Bacon believed that scholasticism draws artificial distinctions which prevent the human mind from seeing the observable facts about nature. Living in an age when new lands were being discovered and explored, Bacon shared the spirit of the times in his enthusiasm for exploring natural phenomena as well. He argued against the notion that all knowledge had been revealed either by God or by Aristotle. In his day it was a radical position to advocate the study of nature, which, in the cramped, religious world view of the seventeenth century, was depraved and even dangerous.

In the section titled *Novum Organum*, the new method of reasoning, Bacon discussed what he viewed as the major defects in human understanding, or the psychological reasons for human error. Using the metaphor of the Idol, he suggested there were four basic Idols: The Idols of the Tribe create errors that are basic to human nature, such as the tendency to oversimplify. The Idols of the Cave are responsible for errors arising out of human prejudice. Idols of the Market Place produce errors due to the imperfections in human language, such as using words superficially, inaccurately, or deceptively. Idols of the Theater are errors that come from flaws in systems of thought, such as Bacon's personal bête noire, Aristotelian logic. Bacon's remedy for the errors in human understanding was the inductive method for discovering the unique qualities of individual phenomena.

The core of Bacon's legacy to the scientific revolution of the seventeenth century was the notion that science is inductive.

Later philosophers of science, and scientists themselves, would dispute this on the ground that in practice most scientific discoveries are not made by the inductive method. Nevertheless, Bacon's writings had tremendous influence in freeing the scientists and philosophers who came after him from the metaphysical and religious categories in which knowledge had been mired since the Middle Ages. He exhorted his contemporaries to contemplate "things as they are, without superstition or imposture, error or confusion." He inspired scientific inquiry by calling for the need to test scientific evidence and to view science as a handmaid of technological progress that could ameliorate human society.

Bacon had a dry sense of humor, and could meet adversity with patience, intellectual vigor, and strength of character. Although he was known for being coldhearted and subservient to the powerful, these qualities were a kind of armament for survival in the ruthless world of privilege, patronage, and court intrigue. He was accused by his detractors of living like a prince, enjoying a well-set table, music, coaches, and racehorses. Ahead of his time he offered his monarchs advice which was almost always rejected. Nevertheless, he made the most of the opportunities that befell him—and they were considerable—and he enjoyed life.

His insights into science and technology were also ahead of his day. He seems to have foretold the eventual discoveries of hearing aids, microscopes, plastic surgery, and perhaps even the invention of radio from what he called "sound houses." On the fateful day he stopped to pack the chicken with snow, he was investigating the powers of refrigeration. "I have taken all knowledge to be my province," he once boasted. And as he frequently admonished his servant Hunt, "The world was made for man, Hunt, and not man for the world."

CHRISTOPHER MARLOWE
1564–1593

On May 12, 1593, Thomas Kyd was arrested by Her Majesty's government for treasonable activity. Among the papers found in his room was a treatise "denying the deity of Christ." Under torture Kyd claimed the blasphemous paper belonged, not to him, but to the playwright Christopher Marlowe, with whom he had shared a room in 1591. Six days later the Queen's Privy Council issued a warrant for Marlowe's arrest. Unlike Kyd, Marlowe was given surprisingly lenient treatment: He had to appear before their lordships in the Privy Council each day until the matter could be cleared up. On May 30 the matter was cleared up. Marlowe was stabbed to death in a drunken tavern brawl.

Informants and hangers-on who claimed they knew Marlowe came forth with various degrees of evidence or hearsay about his treasonable activities. A purely fictitious account of his death was that he was killed "by a bawdy serving-man, a rival of his in his lewde love." But Marlowe's homosexuality had little to do with his death. He was loose-tongued in his cups and had an impish love of destroying other people's cherished idols. He had a caustic wit and lambasted ignorance and superstition. In spite of being brilliant, well read, and one of the first university-trained English playwrights, he was violent, reckless, and sarcastic, and made enemies easily. Not much is known about his personal life except for when he was in scrapes with the law: quarreling with associates, roaringly drunk, disturbing the peace, or under suspicion of murder.

Marlowe's father was a shoemaker in Canterbury. His mother was the daughter of a clergyman. In 1579 he entered King's School and graduated after only two years, at which time he was accepted at Corpus Christi College, Cambridge. When his university scholarship expired he was able to renew it on condition that he pursue a course of study leading to vows as an Anglican clergyman, a fact that has led some biographers to claim that Marlowe had initially planned upon a career in the church. But life as a rural clergyman was probably too dreadful to contemplate for the restless, self-probing, self-torturing young man who had the soul of a freethinking poet and the daring of an Elizabethan adventurer. In time Marlowe grew cynical about the way religion had become a tool of foreign and domestic political policies.

In 1587 the college was reluctant to grant Marlowe a master's degree, possibly because of excessive absences or, as some think, because Marlowe was winning a reputation for himself as an atheist. There were also rumors that he was planning to study in an English college in France that prepared Catholic missionary priests to win England back to the old faith. A letter from the Privy Council absolved Marlowe for his absences, stating that he had been engaged "on matters touching the benefit of the country." It also denied that he was about to enter the papist college in France—unless, of course, he was going to infiltrate it as a double agent.

Marlowe seems to have been involved in Queen Elizabeth's secret service run by Sir Francis Walsingham, the first English courtier to create a large intelligence network. Walsingham had spies in over 40 towns abroad and spent £2,500 a year on espionage activities (a sum Elizabeth thought excessive). "Knowledge is never too dear" was Walsingham's credo. His agents were active in all aspects of domestic and foreign intrigue: They knew about the Spanish Armada before it sailed; they wrested secrets from political prisoners; they exposed Catholic plots to undermine the Anglican church; and they foiled efforts by Mary Queen of Scots to undermine Elizabeth. Since Walsingham's nephew Thomas was Marlowe's patron, it's possible the young poet smuggled intelligence reports to Francis.

In his six short years as a playwright, Marlowe dominated the London stage, his only serious rival being William Shakespeare, born the same year. Shakespeare acknowledged Marlowe's genius and honored him by incorporating references to Marlowe into over half his plays, sometimes lifting entire lines. Marlowe's line about Helen of Troy, "the face that launched a thousand ships," found its way into Shakespeare's *Troilus and Cressida*, and "Who ever loved that loved not at first sight?" from Marlowe's *Hero and Leander* shows up in *As You Like It*.

Marlowe had a working knowledge of a vast array of subjects, and his insatiable imagination shaped the material into bold and soaring drama. In *Tamburlaine the Great* Marlowe draws on detailed knowledge of foreign locales he knew only from reading and study: Scythia, Egypt, Africa, Babylon, and Damascus. He reveals a basic understanding of Islam and emphasizes that a Moslem can honor Christ. In *The Tragical History of Dr. Faustus*, a morality play with all the conventions of that genre, he deals with a man hungry for all the knowledge of the universe. *The Famous Tragedy of the Rich Jew of Malta* shows Marlowe's sophisticated understanding of Christians, Turks, and Jews. *The Massacre at Paris* deals with events in English and French history. The conflict in *The Troublesome Reign and Lamentable Death of Edward II, King of England* turns on erudite theological issues. Clearly Marlowe was a playwright who could write well on a diversity of subjects. In addition he wrote a humorous account of the *Aeneid* in his play *Dido, Queen of Carthage*. His long poem *Hero and*

Leander was written in competition with Shakespeare for the patronage of the Earl of Southampton.

Ideas excited Marlowe. His innate curiosity led him to dream about the nature of the universe, the meaning of human life, the relationship between God and man. He was not interested in the daily life of Elizabethan England, and his nine plays, unlike Shakespeare's, do not open a window onto sixteenth-century life. Marlowe's imagination roamed to foreign countries and scaled the lofty heights of speculative thought far above the mundane concerns of average men and women. "Tire thy brains to find a deity" was his challenge in *Faustus*. If a man could not become a deity, he argued, he was nothing. And yet such ambition was bound to be thwarted. "Yet art thou still but Faustus and a man!" he wrote, revealing his own sense of disillusionment.

Marlowe rejected the trappings of organized religion and its institutional authorities. He believed that churches govern the souls of men with threats of punishment, rather than challenging them to discover the wonders of God on their own. Although he was continually accused of atheism, his works exhibit a profound belief in a Supreme Being. His own spiritual comfort and inspiration, however, came from the pre-Christian past and the sacred quality of poetic experience.

Among the accusations hurled against him at the time of his death was that he was a member of Sir Walter Raleigh's "study," a gathering of scientists, scholars, and poets who discussed subjects and matters that bordered on heresy. Here Marlowe was supposed to have read "an atheistical lecture" to convert others to his beliefs. The term *atheism* was bandied about very loosely in the sixteenth century, much as *liberal* and *communist* are today. The term could include a variety of freethinkers of varying degrees of belief and unbelief.

Nevertheless, Marlowe's quick tongue and lack of circumspection, especially at table after heavy drinking, led to reckless remarks about religion in an age that equated religious loyalty with national loyalty. He was accused of saying that "the first beginning of religion was only to keep men in awe," a belief based partly on his own opinion of contemporary churchmen who dominated the minds and souls of their parishioners. He argued that Moses purposely kept the Israelites wandering in the desert for 40 years on a trip that could be made in one year, in order for the majority of them to die off so that a new generation could be indoctrinated into the myths and legends that Moses wanted them to believe about the Exodus. Marlowe called Moses a "juggler," a term he used for Saint Paul as well.

Marlowe was one of the first to suggest that Jesus and the "beloved disciple" John were lovers. Thomas Kyd reported that Marlowe believed that "Saint John was our Savior's Alexis. . . . Christ did love him with an extraordinary love." The allusion is to Virgil's poem about Corydon's invitation to Alexis to live with him, the classical male lovers that Marlowe had in mind when he wrote his famous couplet: "Come live with me and be my love, / And we will all the pleasures prove . . . " An informer named Richard Baines reported to the authorities that Marlowe thought "Saint John the Evangelist was bedfellow to Christ and leaned always on his bosom." Baines's testimony also included Marlowe's remark "that all they that love not tobacco and boys were fools." How much of Marlowe's "table talk" had a basis in fact is, as it was then, up to those concerned to decide.

Marlowe spent his last day at a tavern owned by Dame Eleanor Bull in the company of three associates, each of whom had a sleazy connection with the underworld, foreign intrigue, and Walsingham's spy network. The four men spent the greater part of the day drinking, walking in the garden, eating, playing backgammon, and, in Marlowe's case, sleeping off the effects of liquor. Why they argued and over what (the bill for their expenses?) is not known. Ingram Frizer, who stabbed Marlowe in the temple with his dagger, was pardoned on June 28, the verdict being self-defense. The following day he was back in Walsingham's service.

Many questions remain unanswered: about the four men's relationship, the nature of the business that kept them in the tavern all day, the lack of involvement by the other two men in the fatal scuffle. It has been suggested that the Privy Council let Marlowe off from Kyd's accusation of treason precisely to keep him at large where he could be killed. Did members of the Privy Council fear that Marlowe knew too much about their lordships and would talk under torture? Did others among Walsingham's secret service fear the same? The stab wounds were not deep, nor (by today's estimates) fatal, and yet 24 hours elapsed before the body was examined. Was there a deliberate delay?

That the English-speaking world lost one of its greatest playwrights on May 30 is without a doubt. At age 29 Marlowe had already achieved fame and glory. *Tamburlaine* was quoted, parodied, and imitated for years. Shakespeare based *The Merchant of Venice* on Marlowe's *Jew of Malta*. Goethe's own Faust was inspired by Marlowe's forerunner. On his death many of the leading literary figures of the day paid their tributes, even as Puritan churchmen used his brutal slaying as "a manifest sign of God's judgement" on an atheistic rascal.

Judging by the mind behind his greatest works, perhaps Marlowe's passing was in the same spirit of Mortimer, a character in *Edward II* whose death speech implores:

> . . . *weep not for Mortimer*
> *That scorns the world, and, as a traveler,*
> *Goes to discover countries yet unknown.*

FREDERICK
THE GREAT
1712–1786

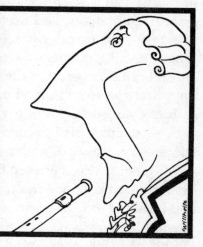

While on a trip with his father in August of 1730, Frederick, the 18-year-old crown prince of Prussia, and his lover, Lieutenant Hans von Katte, plotted their escape to England. The two were caught, imprisoned, and court-martialed for desertion. Because of the two men's high status in the army and their noble backgrounds, the death penalty was not advised. But King Frederick William I took the occasion to teach his son a lesson about what he called the boy's "unmanly, lascivious, female occupations, highly unsuited for a man." In defiance of the court, the king personally ordered that the 26-year-old Katte be executed. In the early morning hours, as the young officer and former royal bodyguard was led to his death, the prince was awakened and forced to go to the place of execution. When he realized what was about to happen, he blew his friend a kiss and said, "My dear Katte, a thousand pardons, please." The lieutenant replied, "My prince, there is nothing to apologize for." Refusing the blindfold, Katte was then beheaded.

The execution of Katte was the ultimate insult in a long string of physical and psychological abuses inflicted on Frederick by a stern, puritanical, and brutish father. Complaining that he could never figure out what secret thoughts inhabited his son's brain, the king frequently whipped or caned Frederick before servants and officers. On one occasion he tried to strangle the boy. Beatings were normal occurrences in the king's attempt to break his son's resolute will. But the boy remained firm. When his father tried to force Frederick to give up his right to succession in favor of a younger brother, he refused.

The clash of wills between father and son extended back into Frederick's childhood, when a French-Swiss tutor encouraged and nurtured the young prince's native intelligence and artistic talents. The king was no match for his exceptionally bright son. On his part, Frederick found his father's military and hunting interests dull and boorish. His own pastimes centered around books and the arts, the "female occupations" which his father thought unmanned him for statecraft.

When it became clear that the 16-year-old prince and a royal page, named Keith, had an ongoing sexual relationship, Frederick William assumed that Prussia itself would suffer should his son inherit the throne. Even after Katte's execution two years later, Frederick insisted on his right to the throne. Finally his father relented; and under a severe surveillance which amounted to house arrest, Frederick was trained for royal duties.

In 1733, three years after the aborted escape attempt, the king arranged a political marriage for Frederick to Princess Elizabeth Christine of Brunswick. Frederick wrote his sister Wilhelmina that he found his fiancée "repugnant." "We have neither friendship nor compatibility," he wrote. And, he added, "She dances like a goose." But the arrangements proceeded. The marriage produced no children, which has led some historians to surmise that it was unconsummated. Never relishing the company of women, Frederick gave his bride her own palace, refused to allow her to live in his other residences, and visited her infrequently, usually a few weeks at Christmas.

The king gave Frederick a residence of his own at Rheinsberg, along with a regiment. The four years at Rheinsberg from 1735 to 1739 were the pinnacle of Frederick's education and military training. Here Frederick saw to his military duties, studied philosophy, read literature, composed music for the flute (over 100 sonatas and concertos in his lifetime), wrote poetry, gave parties, sponsored theatrical presentations, and soaked up the cultural and intellectual trends of the French Enlightenment. He devoured Voltaire, and began a correspondence with the French philosopher that would span 42 years and comprise over 1,000 letters.

The Rheinsberg court was composed of soldiers, philosophers, scientists, writers, and artists. It was an exceedingly masculine environment based on friendship and self-development. Absent were the excessive hunting, drinking, gambling, and womanizing that characterized most eighteenth-century European courts. Frederick held himself to a stringent schedule of waking at four (he needed only five to six hours of sleep a night) and studying or working until noon. Often he read till after midnight. In the process, he became the most knowledgeable and sophisticated prince in Europe.

In 1740, Frederick William died, and the 28-year-old Frederick became King of Prussia. He wrote to Voltaire that he would now reluctantly have to bid farewell to music, poetry, and pleasure. And so it seemed. In October of that year, the 23-year-old Maria Theresa ascended the Austrian throne, and Frederick took the opportunity to strike a lightning raid for the Austrian territory of Silesia, the first in a series of "lightning wars" that became a model for Prussian military strategy. In his first assault, the lightning struck slowly, but when the War of the Austrian Succession finally ended, in 1748, Silesia was under Frederick's rule.

In the course of his long reign, Frederick's military prowess and courage became the envy of all Europe. His unpredictable lightning strikes changed the slow, mechanical style of warfare forever, as he developed and used the offensive maneuver far beyond the customary standards of his day. Also, allies and enemies alike studied and imitated his strategy of attrition, a tactic of inflicting repeated blows against an enemy army until it lost the will to fight. Frederick became the preceptor of modern warfare and made Prussia a respected military power.

Frederick's enlightened despotism lifted Prussia out of the Middle Ages and laid the course for her entry into the family of modern nation-states. He abolished torture and other extreme forms of punishment, and reformed the judicial system, requiring judges to pass government examinations, which in turn made them salaried officials and government servants. In legal matters, Frederick believed that the king should exercise a hands-off policy. "In the courts the law should speak and the ruler must be silent," he wrote. "The law alone must rule." The new system guaranteed property rights and thus laid a more secure foundation for economic development.

Although strong remnants of the feudal system continued to exist, especially in the eastern provinces, Frederick opened the country to capital investment by fostering new industries, such as textiles. He freed the new industries from medieval guild regulations and protected them by tariffs. Frederick's policy was intended to liberate the Prussian economy from a primarily agrarian base. He opened up the Oder River and removed obstacles to shipping, began a uniform customs system, and built canals to serve Berlin.

Frederick also improved agricultural methods by introducing the English system of crop rotation and advocating new crops, such as potatoes. He created incentives to stimulate migration within Prussia, so that sparsely settled areas could become more populated. He created 900 new villages and lured an estimated 300,000 immigrants from neighboring principalities, especially people with technical skills or capital to invest.

In all his efforts, Frederick's primary goal was to strengthen the state, for he believed that without a stable and unshakable government, peace and prosperity would never flourish. In his terms, "the consolidation of the authority of the state and the increase of its power" were paramount. The powers and responsibilities which are commonplace today in the modern state were, before Frederick's time, still philosophical dreams. In the Prussia of Frederick the Great, they became reality.

In spite of his "farewell to pleasure" that he wrote to Voltaire on his ascension to the throne, Frederick managed to maintain a rigorous daily schedule that allowed ample time for his intellectual and artistic pursuits. He drew up architectural plans for the famous palace of Sans Souci at Potsdam, outside Berlin, and turned that court into what Voltaire, a long-term resident there, would characterize as "Sparta in the morning, Athens in the afternoon." In a court devoid of women's influence, Frederick would entertain his "Spartan" comrades at lunch so that he could discuss matters of warfare and diplomacy and indulge his need for horseplay. For dinner, he invited the "Athenians," who engaged in stimulating conversation about art, philosophy, and science.

An unrelenting Francophile (French was his primary language; he spoke German with difficulty), Frederick could not appreciate the reawakening of German culture during his lifetime. Significantly, when he reestablished the Academy of Sciences, he appointed a French president. He found his own countrymen pedantic and backward and considered the German intellectual life of Goethe, Herder, and Lessing far inferior to the products of the French Enlightenment. And yet he himself became a mythic figure, a symbol of Germanic virtues who would be hailed in literature, poetry, and popular song, an inspiration to both the elite and the common folk in his own and succeeding generations.

The fact that German culture had the seed of greatness, however, was not lost on him. He firmly believed that someday enlightened German thought and culture would take their rightful place along with other European traditions, especially after he established secure borders and a strong, centralized government, without which culture could not flower. "These beautiful days have not yet arrived, but they are drawing near," he wrote. "I predict their coming; they will appear, but I shall not see them."

As a man of the Enlightenment, Frederick believed in a rationally ordered universe. He never felt comfortable with his Protestant father's belief in a personal, judgmental God; and as an adult he rejected theological dogma. His frame of reference was completely secular, based on rationalism and human understanding. He promoted religious toleration in the belief that "everyone must seek salvation after his own way of thinking." Of course, in annexing Silesia, half of whose population was Catholic, toleration was also a political necessity. He invited French Jesuits to Silesia to counteract the anti-Prussian influence of Silesian monks, thus giving the Jesuits a needed refuge during the years when the order was suppressed by the Vatican. And yet Frederick would have no part of the antireligious extremism so popular in France. Frederick's sense of the divine order was practical and personal. During a critical period in the Seven Years' War, he wrote, "I save myself by looking at the world as a whole, as though from a distant planet. Then everything appears unbelievably small to me, and I pity my enemies who take so much trouble over such insignificant things."

A life structured around a rigorous sense of duty aged the monarch. He looked old before his time. As his friends died or were killed in war, he grew lonely and more isolated. In his later years, he was afflicted with asthma, dropsy, gout, and abscesses on his ear and leg. And yet, even in his last days, he stuck to his self-imposed schedule: filling military vacancies, ordering new books for his library, studying reports from his ministers, selecting a new ambassador, ordering sheep from Spain.

In 1785, the young Lafayette visited the venerable monarch and military genius in Berlin. The Frenchman wrote to General Washington in America: "I could not help being struck by that dress and appearance of an old, broken, dirty Corporal, covered all over with Spanish snuff, with his head almost leaning on one shoulder, and fingers quite distorted by the gout. But what surprised me much more is the fire and sometimes the softness of the most beautiful eyes I ever saw, which give as charming an expression to his physiognomy as he can take a rough and threatening one at the head of his troops." The following year, unable to breathe, feverish and coughing, Frederick died at the age of 74.

MADAME DE STAËL
1766–1817

A gentleman seated between Madame Germaine de Staël and Madame Juliette Récamier noted graciously: "I sit between mind and beauty." He was not being original in his observation or in his comment, for "mind and beauty" was a touchstone phrase for gossipy Parisians who delighted in inviting the two women to the same functions. Madame de Staël replied facetiously to the gentleman that she had never been called a beauty before, deflecting the compliment about intellect to Récamier, who was acknowledged to be the most beautiful, coquettish, and desirable woman of the day.

In spite of their husbands and many male friends, the two women reserved a special place in their hearts for each other. De Staël said to Récamier: "I clasp you to my heart with more devotion than any lover" and "I love you with a love surpassing that of friendship. I go down on my knees to embrace you with all my heart." For her part Récamier allowed such effusive declarations of love only from de Staël. She demanded that her male suitors be more reserved.

According to Récamier, when they met in 1798 in Paris, de Staël looked at her with "great eyes . . . and paid me compliments upon my figure which might have seemed exaggerated and too direct," but de Staël's comments won her heart. Three years later, de Staël confided to Récamier: "I have loved you for three years. It is sacred, is it not? I shall die thinking of it." Twenty years later, when de Staël died, their love and devotion were as strong as ever.

Madame de Staël made a strong impression on everyone who met her. Gouverneur Morris, American minister to the French court, found her to be "a large leonine woman with few beauties and no grace of gesture . . . [she had a] masculine attitude and powerful conversation." De Staël's strength of character was nurtured in a politically powerful family. Her Swiss father, Jacques Necker, was Louis XVI's Minister of Finance. His bombshell report, *Compte-Rendu*, which sold 80,000 copies, revealed that the government wasted 25 million francs each year on friends of the queen and that tax collectors absconded with one-fifth of the revenues. He was dismissed from office.

De Staël's mother, Suzanne Curchod, was a pastor's daughter who hosted an important political and literary salon in Paris. Here young Germaine met some of the leading intellectuals of the day, among them Denis Diderot, Jean d'Alembert, Edward Gibbon, and the Comte de Buffon. By age 15 she had read Montesquieu's *Spirit of the Laws* (and agreed with it), Goethe's *Sorrows of Young Werther*, and Rousseau's *New Héloise* (both of which taught her moral truths about the plight of the individual in society). At home she learned the art of conversation, developed her natural wit, and perfected a keen sense of political and social realities.

When she was 16 years old, de Staël's parents began arranging her marriage. William Pitt the Younger, of England, was a possibility, but she objected on the grounds that she didn't want to live in England. Finally it was decided that she would marry Baron Erik de Staël-Holstein, the Swedish ambassador in Paris, a man 17 years her senior. The marriage negotiations took three years to arrange and involved the Swedish king and the French court. Clearly it was a marriage to advance her father's career, and it was not destined to last. The couple were soon estranged from each other, and the marriage was formally dissolved in 1797. Among other faults Madame de Staël objected to the baron's gambling and his lack of intellect.

In 1788, at age 22, de Staël published *Letters on the Works and Character of Jean-Jacques Rousseau*, a treatise that made her famous. As the French Revolution commenced the following year, many political observers watched what positions de Staël and her father (called back into service by the bungling Louis XVI) would adopt. Necker wisely advised doubling the Third Estate, which represented the common people, so that it would be equal to the other two estates that represented much smaller elements of French society, the nobility and clergy. Necker's proposal was a revolutionary move but crucial to any viable reform. Three days after the fall of the Bastille, the enlarged Third Estate declared itself to be the National Assembly, and the Revolution was under way. In line with her father's political views, de Staël's position was moderate, favoring a constitutional monarchy modeled on the British system.

During the Reign of Terror (1793–94) de Staël fled to England, where she helped rescue many liberal aristocrats. An obsessive writer (her complete works total 17 volumes), she found time to write *A Treatise on the Influence of the Passions upon the Happiness of Individuals and of Nations*. Published in 1796, it was widely read and became a seminal work in the spread of romanticism. When the Terror subsided, she returned to France and settled on the family estate at Coppet near Lake Geneva, Switzerland.

In time de Staël's salon at Coppet became a hotbed of political unrest. A champion of common sense republicanism, she opposed all the political regimes from the Directory in the 1790s to the restoration of the Bourbons after Napoleon's defeat in 1814. The Directory viewed her as a friend of royalists and banished her from Paris, a strategy succeeding governments would adopt to stifle her influence.

De Staël had met Napoleon in 1796 and noted that "no emotions of the heart could act upon him . . . for him nothing exists but himself; all other creatures are ciphers." In 1800 she launched a fierce opposition to him. "Bonaparte is not a man only,"she warned, "but a system; and if he were right, the human species would no longer be what God has made it." At a time when many in France were tired from years of revolution and political wrangling, de Staël kept the fires of resistance burning against Napoleon's efforts to strip France of the republican liberties which it had fought so hard to win. She saw through Napoleon's "art of dazzling multitudes and corrupting individuals." She swore eternal enmity against him.

"Tell her," Napoleon countered, "she must never stand in my way. If she does, I'll smash her. I'll break her. The only practical thing for her to do is to keep her mouth shut." But she would not. He complained that the most influential political and social dignitaries left her salon less loyal to him. But in spite of Napoleon's bitter press campaign against her, de Staël continued to denounce him for usurping political power and buying allegiance with the glitter and pomp he lavishly bestowed on his newly created nobility. He banished her to a 40-mile radius of Paris.

In 1810 de Staël published *On Germany*, based on her travels through that country in 1803–04, when she met the leading cultural figures Goethe, Schiller, Fichte, and August von Schlegel. Her account was a study of German manners and morals, touching upon art, philosophy, literature, and religion. She praised the German spirit, especially the Sturm und Drang movement that flowered into German romanticism. Napoleon thought the work anti-French.

Written into the censorship law was a clause that allowed even a work that had passed the censors to be confiscated if the Minister of Police deemed it dangerous. At Napoleon's direction *On Germany* was deemed dangerous. The government seized 10,000 copies and hacked them to pieces. The Minister of Police explained to de Staël: "Your last work is not at all French." De Staël was exiled from France. She explained that Napoleon "was vexed that I should be the only writer of reputation in France who had published books during his reign without any mention of his gigantic existence." Napoleon offered to stop persecuting her if she would write a poem about the birth of his son, the future king of Rome. She refused and accepted banishment.

At the same time, Napoleon's police state hounded Récamier for her association with de Staël and her negative remarks about the government. The woman Napoleon had once called "beautiful Juliette" became "dangerous Juliette." The official register reported that she was a "bad influence on society." The act of banishment ordered her "to withdraw 40 leagues from Paris, and to remain there in a state of arrest until revocation by the Emperor."

Since Napoleon's police network stretched to virtually all parts of Europe, de Staël chose to flee to neutral Sweden, by way of Russia. She wrote to Récamier: "You are a heavenly creature; had I lived beside you, I would have been very happy. Fate bears me away. Adieu." Had she asked Récamier to accompany her, her friend would have done so. The years 1812–13 found de Staël fleeing across Europe as allied armies tightened the noose around Napoleon. She reached England, where she was asked about the situation on the continent. "I hope that Bonaparte will win and be killed," she replied, not wanting to see foreign troops occupy her beloved France but not wanting Napoleon to remain in power.

De Staël returned to Paris after Napoleon's downfall but found the attempts to reinstate the old regime of the Bourbons a slap in the face to the revolutionaries who had fought and died for liberty. Her work *Considerations on the Principal Events of the French Revolution* (published in 1818) was a call to return to her father's ideal of a constitutional monarchy. It became the basis for all liberal histories of the era.

De Staël continued to champion new ideas that would one day become political realities. All citizens, she argued, had a right to political liberties and the opportunities to use them. She fought for the emancipation of women. Authoritarianism in government and religion, she warned, was an obstacle to the perfect-ibility of human nature. She shocked political and military leaders by suggesting that politics could be a science.

De Staël believed that the great ideas were by no means a French prerogative, but belonged to all nations. By promoting foreign literary works, she planted the seed for the study of comparative literature. In defense of her life and her work, she said that "men were always capable of being moved by the truth, if it was presented to them with force." In her last years she remained that force.

During the Restoration de Staël's salon was as influential as ever, even though the Bourbon government suspected her of disloyalty and many of the returning émigrés shunned her. Soon thereafter a stroke left her partially paralyzed. Récamier visited her at Coppet shortly before her death. Her final words to her friend were: "I embrace you with all that remains to me." She died on July 14, 1817, Bastille Day.

LORD BYRON
1788–1824

On setting out for Constantinople in 1810, Lord Byron wrote a poem about Theresa Macri, the 12-year-old girl whose family he had stayed with in Athens and who had become the object of his affections. "Maid of Athens," he wrote, "ere we part, / Give, oh give me back my heart." On returning to Athens later that year, his heart now recovered, Byron fell in love with Nicolo Giraud, a 15-year-old Neapolitan youth whose devoted, puppylike affection captivated the poet's attentions. When Byron had to leave the boy and sail for England the following summer, he wrote gloomily in his notebook: "At 23 the best of life is over and its bitters double. . . . I am sick at heart." Then he quoted Horace's ode "To Venus": "Nor maid nor youth delights me now." Fortunately for Byron, and for his legend, life was not over. Both youth and maid would continue to delight him, for it was part of the romantic tradition to which he gave his name to bounce back. He had done it before and would do it again.

Judging by letters written on his journeys, his sexual escapades were of the high caliber he had achieved three years earlier in London when he boasted that he was worn out "from *debility*, and literally *too much Love*." To a friend he wrote: "I am buried in an abyss of Sensuality." Finally his physician convinced him that his dissipations were leading to serious health complications. "The *Game* is up," he announced at one point. "For the last five days I have been confined to my room, Laudanum is my sole support." Nevertheless he continued to keep two "nymphs," as he described them, in his lodgings. One, disguised as a boy, he passed off as a brother or cousin. The "game" was really up, however, when, as Byron later explained it, "the young gentleman miscarried in a certain family hotel in Bond Street, to the inexpressible horror of the chambermaids."

The summer months between Theresa Macri and Nicolo Giraud were adventurous. He visited the site of Troy. He had an audience with Sultan Mahmoud II of Constantinople, who seems to have become nervously excited by the lord's handsome countenance. And he swam the Hellespont "with little difficulty" (the second time—the first attempt was foiled by strong currents). Although the swim was not as challenging as his earlier feat of swimming the Tagus River at Lisbon, Portugal, Byron took lifelong pride in his accomplishment because of the Hellespont's romantic associations with Greek myth: Leander swam across it every night to meet his lover, Hero, a priestess of Aphrodite.

While traveling through the Mediterranean, Byron began *Childe Harold's Pilgrimage*, a picturesque travelogue of his journeys in which the hero, Byron himself, repeatedly confronts the disparity between the ideal and reality. Conjured from a brain he described as "a whirling gulf of fantasy and flame," Childe Harold's adventures brought Byron immediate fame when the first two cantos were published in England in 1812. The theme of the lonely soul's disillusionment and world-weariness touched the hearts of readers in the Napoleonic era who were eager to hear that the glory of the world is fleeting and the ideal is always beyond human grasp.

Byron's early life also had a Childe Harold quality. His father was the notoriously irresponsible Captain John ("Mad Jack") Byron, who died in 1791, less than three years after his son's birth. His mother, Catherine Gordon, was descended from a colorful strain of British aristocracy. Raised in Aberdeen, Scotland, until he was ten, the boy Byron became the 6th Lord Byron on the death of a great-uncle. The young lord and his mother then moved to the family property at Newstead Abbey near Nottingham, a gift to the Byrons from Henry VIII. Byron loved growing up in the Gothic ruins of the old monastery that fired his imagination with old, lost times and the lingering presence of spirits and ghosts.

Byron's right foot, crippled from birth, became an object of schoolboy teasing. Although extremely sensitive about his disability, he did not let it interfere with developing romantic attachments among his schoolmates. At Trinity College, Cambridge, in 1805 he met a 17-year-old choirboy, John Edleston, who became the paragon that would haunt his homoerotic fantasies for the rest of his life. Byron later confided that "his *voice* first attracted my attention, his *countenance* fixed it, and his *manners* attached me to him for ever. . . . I certainly love him more than any human being, and neither time nor distance have had the least effect on my (in general) changeable disposition." Edleston's temporary absence would leave Byron wallowing in "a chaos of hope and sorrow." After Byron turned 21 and assumed his seat in the House of Lords, Edleston asked to live with him in London. But Byron had by then decided to travel through the Mediterranean, and Edleston died prematurely before Byron returned.

In addition to Edleston there were other homoerotic infatuations of which Byron would later write: "My school friendships were with me passions." None of them, however, prevented amorous involvements with young girls; and later in life his love for handsome pages and servants never precluded his affairs with women closer to his own age, including his own half-sister, Augusta, five years his senior.

In 1807 Byron's first book of poems, *Hours of Idleness*, appeared, followed two years later by *English Bards, and Scotch Reviewers*, a satire attacking virtually all his contemporary writers as "little wits" and "knaves or fools." Almost immediately after the second book was published, he set sail for the sunny south. Thus, at age 21 in 1809, as he departed for the Mediterranean, he left behind him a dual reputation that would follow and haunt him during his life and become the glorious Byronic legend after his death: a poet of caustic wit and a lover of insatiable appetite.

On his return to London in 1811, he immediately fell into complicated liaisons with various aristocratic ladies, had continual financial problems, and finally entered an ill-fated marriage with Annabella Milbanke, who he soon realized was too "encumbered with virtue" to understand his volatile moods or accept his rakish sexual life. After one year and one daughter, she left him, possibly because she had learned of his homosexual activities or his incestuous relationship with Augusta.

With his social and sexual imbroglios surfacing and his political standing falling apart around him (the discredited Whig party was being vilified by the Tory press), the most talked-about poet in England realized he was becoming an outcast. In 1816 Byron chose self-exile and left for the Continent.

At Lake Geneva in Switzerland, Byron spent time with Percy Bysshe Shelley and Shelley's future wife, Mary Godwin. Traveling with them was the importunate Claire Clairmont, whom Byron had known briefly in England, eager to pursue him across Europe now that she was carrying his child. The foursome spent a stimulating and creative summer together. Shelley eloquently doused Byron with Wordsworthian pantheism; Mary Godwin conceived the story of *Frankenstein* (at Byron's suggestion that they each write a horror story); Byron composed one of his most popular poems, *The Prisoner of Chillon*, and penned new stanzas for *Childe Harold*; while Claire Clairmont produced a daughter to be named Allegra, born the following January.

In 1817 Byron wrote his Faustian poem *Manfred*, in which he delineated the hero's revolt against the hapless conditions of life. For Byron the romantic dilemma was that human existence was "half dust, half deity, alike unfit to sink or soar." Nevertheless the frustrations of "dust" and "deity" tugging at his soul did not deter him from continuing to pursue life to its fullest.

In 1817 he moved to Venice, where he engaged in more bedroom intrigues, first falling in love with a draper's wife and then a baker's wife. Eventually he settled down as *cavalier servente*, an official gentleman-in-waiting, to the Countess Teresa Guiccioli, a 20-year-old beauty unhappily married to a man three times her age. The domestic "arrangement" alternately excited and depressed Byron, the count enigmatically accepting the poet in his household at times and at others threatening violence.

These years in Italy were some of the happiest of Byron's life. He began working on his last great poem, *Don Juan*, a picaresque epic filled with typical Byronic digressions, satirical comments on the abuses of society, and cosmic mood swings. Through the countess's father and brother, he was introduced to the Carbonari, a revolutionary underground dedicated to overthrowing Austrian rule in northern Italy. The Carbonari's spirit for freedom touched something in Byron's own soul. He took part in their plots and revolutionary activities and found himself under surveillance by Austrian and Vatican spies.

In 1821 Byron and the countess moved to Pisa, where he found a congenial expatriate community that included the Shelleys and other friends from England and where yachting was a favorite pastime. On one outing Shelley's boat mysteriously disappeared. Five days later his body washed ashore. Shelley's death stunned Byron, who later called the dead poet "without exception, the *best* and least selfish man I ever knew." Then, in a typical pessimistic insight (perhaps thinking also of what might befall his own reputation), he said: "There is thus another man gone, about whom the world was ill-naturedly, and ignorantly, and brutally mistaken. It will, perhaps, do him justice *now*, when he can be no better for it."

In 1822 Byron felt the need for change. His daughter Allegra died. He had a falling out with his publisher in London. His involvement with the countess was growing stale, and he was bored with the ineffectual Italian revolutionaries. When the London Greek Committee approached him in 1823 to act as their agent in Greece's struggle to oust its Turkish rulers, he readily accepted. It would be a good reason for leaving Italy. Perhaps it would reinstate him with his countrymen back home. Perhaps he could recapture the happiness he knew on his earlier Greek adventures when he was young.

Byron sailed for Greece with English money and supplies, and threw himself wholeheartedly into the struggle for Greek independence. He committed £4,000 of his own money for the Greek fleet and personally paid Greek soldiers, encouraged discipline among their ranks, and took part in forming a military corps for laying siege to the town of Lepanto.

In the midst of military preparations, he fell in love with the dark-eyed page boy Loukas Chalandritsanos, who failed to respond to Byron's courting with either affection or gratitude. Byron wrote: "Yet, though I cannot be beloved, / Still let me love!" When Loukas was soaked from a three-hour ride through the rain and fell ill, Byron gave him his own bed. "I am a fool for passion," he wrote about his unrequited love for the boy, which was the subject of the last poem he ever wrote.

> . . . and yet thou love'st me not,
> And never wilt! Love dwells not in our will.
> Nor can I blame thee, though it be my lot
> To strongly, wrongly, vainly love thee still.

Byron too fell ill in the foul weather. After days of lingering in a weakened condition, feverish and bled by leeches, he rolled over and said: "I want to sleep now." Those were his last words. In a locket which he still carried with him was a strand of hair from John Edleston, the choirboy, who, more than any of the boys or women who captured Byron's affections, had represented the ideal of perfect love.

HERMAN
MELVILLE
1819–1891

Herman Melville and his ship-
mate Richard Tobias Greene jumped ship in 1842 in the Mar-
quesas Islands in the South Pacific and lived for a month with a
gentle, hospitable people who, as described in *Typee*, Melville's
fictional account of the escapade, were "lovers of human flesh."
Although cannibalism is a major theme of the novel, "lovers of
human flesh" was one of Melville's many sexual puns.

The island of Typee was a sexual paradise where intimate
relations between men and women, and men and men, were
open, honest, and loving. Here Melville discovered "tayo," a
prototype of male friendship that was to haunt him for the rest
of his life. A tayo was an intimate friend for whom one "is
bound to do everything," and "make the greatest sacrifices."
On Typee, Melville realized what would become a lifelong fantasy for him: a society in which male bonding was legitimate
and respectable and offered an alternative to the unrelenting
heterosexual demands of Victorian family life.

Of course there is always trouble in paradise. Every tayo was
not devoted and loyal. One faithless tayo jilted his friend be-

cause he "had fallen in love at first sight with a smart sailor who had just stepped ashore quite flush from a lucky whaling-cruise." And so it goes.

Melville's first three novels, and the most popular in his lifetime, were travel adventures. An accepted form of genteel pornography for the nineteenth century, travel accounts legitimized the discussion of alternate sexual practices, much as *National Geographic* a century later would be allowed to flaunt photographs of nude bodies, provided they were "primitives" living in "exotic" cultures. In fact, for nineteenth-century urban homosexuals, the notion of a gay island paradise or an all-male lifestyle out in the American West were the only wishful options for realizing their dreams. The phenomenon of a gay subculture coexisting with the dominant culture in the major cities of the nation was over 100 years away. So Melville placed his male lovers on board ship or on remote islands, with the notable exception of Ishmael and Queequeg in *Moby Dick,* whose symbolic marriage ceremony takes place in New Bedford before they embark on the whaler *Pequod.*

When he was a boy, Melville's emotional life centered on his male cousins and older brother, especially after his family moved from New York City to Albany in 1830, when he was 11. As a teenager he worked in the male-dominated worlds of his uncle's farm and his older brother's fur store. It wasn't until 1841, however, when he sailed from Fairhaven, Massachusetts, aboard the whaler *Acushnet* headed for the South Seas, that he discovered how much male company meant to him. On board ship, Melville's spirit resonated with the all-male society and the freedom from outside restrictions on male friendships.

In a series of sea novels that includes *Typee, Omoo, Mardi, Redburn, White-Jacket, Moby Dick,* and *Billy Budd,* Melville explored the opportunities for man-to-man love. He repeatedly drew on his own experiences, especially the free-and-easy sexual behavior he had seen among men who were not bound by western customs and morality. Often he created a dark-skinned "stranger" in his tales, usually a native of a more natural society, as a foil to a lighter-skinned hero. The two inevitably fall in love, but the tragedy of Melville's vision is that he could not imagine such male attachment surviving beyond the shipboard romance, much less being transplanted to American society. In most cases, the stranger is a "rover," ("omoo" means "rover" in Polynesian; Queequeg was called a rover). In nineteenth-century slang, a rover was a sexual outlaw. Men who went "a-roving"—i.e., most sailors—were at complete odds with heterosexual marriage and domesticity.

Melville was enamored of these men and, lacking an identifiably gay vocabulary, he wrote about his fascination in heterosexual terms. For example, he described Harry Bolton in *Redburn* as "one of those small but perfectly formed beings, with curling hair and silken muscles. His complexion was a mantling brunette, feminine as a girl's; his feet were small, his hands were white; and his eyes were large, black, and womanly." In *Typee*, when Tom is smitten by the young Marnoo who slights him, he says: "Had the belle of the season, in the pride of her beauty and power, been cut in a place of public resort by some supercilious exquisite, she could not have felt greater indignation than I did at this unexpected slight." Billy Budd, Melville's archetypal homosexual icon and victim, is also described in feminine or androgynous terms. Captain Vere, fantasizing about Billy as a heterosexual man would a woman, muses that "in the nude [Billy] might have posed for a statue of young Adam before the Fall."

Throughout his sea novels Melville struggled with the evils of society and the imagined happiness of a culture where men formed intense affectionate bonds and played, rather than fought, with each other. In his brighter moods, Melville imagined a society where men loved one another and worked and played together, free from war. In the famous "sperm-squeezing" scene from *Moby Dick*, Melville grew rapturous over the notion:

"Squeeze! squeeze! squeeze! all the morning long; I squeezed that sperm [from the whale] until I myself almost melted into it;

I squeezed that sperm until a strange sort of insanity came over me; and I found myself unwittingly squeezing my co-laborers' hands in it, mistaking their hands for the gentle globules. Such an abounding, affectionate, friendly, loving feeling did this avocation beget, that at last I was continually squeezing their hands, and looking up into their eyes sentimentally; as much as to say,—Oh! my dear fellow beings, why should we longer cherish any social acerbities, or know the slightest ill-humor or envy! Come; let us squeeze hands all round; nay, let us squeeze ourselves into each other; let us squeeze ourselves universally into the very milk and sperm of kindness."

Although Melville married Elizabeth Shaw in 1847, and had three children, family life does not seem to have played an important role for him. As a young married man he was withdrawn and silent, and overworked to the point of ruining his health, a fact repeatedly called to his attention by family members. In short, he seems to have been a workaholic when it came to his writing, a habit now commonly known to indicate a need to avoid family relationships and intimacy. Frequently irritable with each other, the Melvilles almost separated in 1867, Elizabeth going so far as to consult her minister about the appropriateness of a separation. Only the mysterious, self-inflicted death of their son Malcolm kept them together.

Melville's real concerns were increasingly metaphysical: the question of good and evil as seen in the burning social issues of the day. He wrote about slavery, the exploitation of the land, the injustices of capitalism, and mistreatment of American Indians. He was often depressed that his more speculative novels never sold as well as his potboiler sea adventures.

In 1850 Melville moved his family from New York City to the Berkshire Mountains in western Massachusetts, hoping that farming would supplement the meager income from his novels, and that he would be able to write in the peaceful country setting. The area had already attracted such writers as Oliver Wendell Holmes, Fanny Kemble, and Nathaniel Hawthorne.

Meeting Hawthorne was a turning point in Melville's career. To what extent he fell in love with the older, handsome writer (Hawthorne was 46, Melville was 31), and to what extent he expressed it clearly and certainly, is not known. What is known is that Hawthorne rejected him, possibly because Melville expected an intimacy and affection that went beyond the bonds of friendship acceptable to the strait-laced, puritan-bred Hawthorne. Melville was crushed and used his later writings to deal with the setback. His very next novel, *Pierre*, was a trite romantic novel about rejected love.

On Hawthorne's death Melville wrote:

> *To have known him, to have loved him*
> *After loneliness long—*
> *And then to be estranged in life,*
> *And neither in the wrong:*
> *And now for death to set his seal—*
> *Ease me, a little ease, my song!*

Later, in his long homoerotic poem *Clarel*, Melville implied that physical rejection was also spiritual rejection.

> *But for thy fonder dream of love*
> *In man toward man—the soul's caress—*
> *The negatives of flesh should prove*
> *Analogies of non-cordialness*
> *In spirit.*

In *The Blithedale Romance*, Hawthorne dealt with Melville's overtures in a satirical way. Hollingsworth (Melville) beseeches Coverdale (Hawthorne), "Be my friend of friends for ever" and, "There is not the man in this wide world whom I can love as I could you." But Coverdale offers only an unequivocal "no."

But while pursuing Hawthorne during those halcyon days in the Berkshires, Melville was in his glory. He was working on his masterpiece *Moby Dick*; he was at the height of his creative powers; he was caught up in a mental and emotional ecstasy. He was never so happy again.

When *Moby Dick* was published the following year, it met with mixed reviews. It was criticized for being too speculative and metaphysical, for not fitting the accepted genres of the day, and for leaving the major questions of the story unanswered. Some critics, however, raved. Hawthorne understood the work, and this pleased Melville.

The 1850s were a bleak period for Melville. He became increasingly withdrawn, bitter, obsessed with the darker side of American society and human nature, as the nation headed toward civil war. He tried unsuccessfully to get a government appointment. He worked the lecture circuit, but he was not very good at it. He wrote for magazines. He farmed. Although never reduced to poverty, he had major financial problems. He overdrew on his royalties until he was in serious debt. He had to rely on his wife's legacy to keep them solvent.

The last half of his life took a more conventional tone. In 1863 he returned to New York City; and three years later, at age 47, he found his first permanent salaried job. He was offered a position in the U.S. Customs House. He kept it for 19 years, finding time to write poetry on the side and working on the unpublished manuscript of *Billy Budd*. He continued to become ever more absorbed in the metaphysical questions of the universe, and in his old age he enjoyed his garden and his grandchildren.

When he died in 1891, the obituaries stated that Melville was an author whose popularity had long since waned and whose best work was *Typee*, an adventure story set in the South Seas. He was all but forgotten. Not until a generation later would his work surface, assuring his reputation as one of America's greatest writers and confirming what Hawthorne had written in his notebook about his onetime suitor: "If he were a religious man, he would be one of the most truly religious and reverential; he has a very high and noble nature, and better worth immortality than most of us."

WALT
WHITMAN

1819–1892

On a stormy night in Washington, D.C., in 1865, an 18-year-old streetcar conductor named Peter Doyle had one last passenger. "We felt to each other at once," he recalled. "It was a lonely night, so I thought I would go and talk with him. Something in me made me do it and something in him drew me that way. He used to say there was something in me had the same effect on him. Anyway . . . we were familiar at once—I put my hand on his knee—we understood. He did not get out at the end of the trip—in fact went all the way back with me." And in such ordinary circumstances Walt Whitman met his heart's companion, the dream friend and comrade of his imagination whom he had written about in the lusty, lyrical poems that appeared in two editions of his controversial book *Leaves of Grass*, first published ten years earlier.

Whitman's relationship with Doyle blossomed at once. The 46-year-old poet sent his ex-Confederate friend bouquets and love notes. They took long walks around Washington and Alexandria, Virginia, talking incessantly, reciting poems, picking

flowers. The poet would "hum arias or shout in the woods. . . .
He never seemed to tire," Doyle wrote.

Whitman had come to Washington in 1863 on learning that his
brother George, serving in the Union army, had been listed on a
report of casualties. On seeing the thousands of young men,
from both Union and Confederate armies, lying wounded and
dying in army hospitals, Whitman volunteered as a Delegate of
the Christian Commission, a wartime agency of the YMCA, to
visit soldiers in hospitals. An army nurse who knew Whitman
by reputation (but may not actually have read his poems) wrote
in a letter to her husband: "There comes that odious Walt Whitman to talk evil and unbelief to my boys."

But her "boys" loved him. He spent hours with them, even
entire nights, two or three at a stretch, listening to them if they
could talk, talking to them if they could not, writing letters home
for them, consoling them, holding their hands, sometimes kiss-
ing. It was his "personal presence," he said, "emanating ordinary cheer and magnetism," that boosted the men's spirits more
than medicine, gifts, or money. "I believe no men ever loved
each other as I & some of these poor wounded, sick & dying
men love each other," he recalled.

To support himself in the nation's capital, Whitman worked
as a clerk in the Office of Indian Affairs, from which he was
dismissed when his supervisor, the Secretary of the Interior,
discovered a copy of *Leaves of Grass* in his desk. "I will not have
the author of that book in this Department," he vowed, and
Whitman lost his job. Shortly thereafter he found another position in the Treasury Department, where he worked until 1874,
when, incapacitated by a stroke, he was forced to resign.

Fifty-five years earlier, Walt Whitman had been born on his
grandparents' farm near Huntington, New York. In 1823 the
Whitmans moved to Brooklyn. At age 11 he began working in a
printing office. For the next 24 years, until he published the first
edition of *Leaves of Grass*, Whitman held jobs in printing, typeset-
ting, publishing, journalism, and, for a short period, teaching.
He became involved in Democratic politics, discussing issues of

culture, nationalism, slavery, expansionism, and democracy. He also published short stories, and articles on music, theater, books, and education.

Whitman worked on various newspapers in Manhattan from 1841 to 1845, when he returned to Brooklyn as editor of the *Daily Eagle*, Brooklyn's leading paper and an important voice in Democratic politics. When the Mexican War broke out in 1846, he joined the militants who were eager to wrest territory from what they perceived as the barbarous, decadent nation below the Rio Grande, but he drew the line on opening the new regions to slavery. A free-soiler in 1848, but not an abolitionist (Whitman thought abolitionists were just as dangerous to democratic principles as slave-owners), he broke with northern Democrats who were willing to compromise their free-soil ideals to appease the southern wing of the party.

But Whitman was also discouraged with the limitations of party politics. He had more to say, something that could not be contained in the party rhetoric of the day. In 1842 he attended a lecture by Ralph Waldo Emerson, New England's voice of conscience and culture, who called for a new poetry and a new poet. "He worships in this land," the philosopher from Concord lectured, ". . . he sits on the mosses of the mountain. . . . He visits without fear the factory, the railroad, and the wharf. When he lifts his great voice, men gather to him." Later Whitman said that he had been simmering before hearing Emerson's lecture, and that Emerson brought him to a boil.

In 1848 Whitman got a chance to see the great nation he would sing about in his poems. He and his brother Jeff went to New Orleans, where Whitman had been offered the editorship of a new newspaper. After two months his intransigence on the issue of extending slavery into the western territories became an embarrassment for the southern paper, and he left to return to New York. In the process, however, he traveled the Mississippi River, the Great Lakes, and the Midwest, and saw firsthand how average men and women made their living around the nation. He traveled over 5,000 miles, learning the "song of the open road."

In 1855, at age 36, Whitman personally published 795 copies of the 32 poems he called *Leaves of Grass*. In 1860 a second edition containing 124 new poems swelled the slim volume to 456 pages. For the rest of his life, he would continue to revise, shuffle, rearrange, delete, and add to his *Leaves*. The "death-bed" edition of 1892 was the last he saw to press.

From the very first edition Whitman's poems were controversial. Some readers were puzzled at the long, rambling, boastful, egotistical, sensual poems that did not rhyme or seem to end. Others found them obscene. But to many they were the breath of fresh air that Victorian literature was gasping for. In terms of both literary style and their provocative content, Whitman's poems heralded a new era in poetry. Emerson recognized the book as "the most extraordinary piece of wit & wisdom that America has yet contributed." He wrote Whitman: "I find incomparable things said incomparably well. . . . I greet you at the beginning of a great career." Without Emerson's permission Whitman unashamedly published the letter in the preface of his 1860 edition.

Whitman's poems were pure Whitman and pure America, written from the poet's personal involvement with the nation— opera, theater, literature, the metaphysical movement, the personal-health crusade, the scientific developments he witnessed in the Crystal Palace exhibit at America's first world's fair in 1853, the great political issues of the day, and the rough workmen who piloted New York's ferryboats, drove stages and fire engines, and performed the manual tasks that were building a great nation.

Whitman's courageous delight and celebration of the body and sex in a staunchly prudish era rose directly from his own sexuality, his obsession with health, and the intense but often unfulfilled infatuations he had for the boys and workmen he knew so well. The "Calamus" section of poems offers a manifesto for a new honesty in male sexuality. Edward Carpenter, an English spokesman for progressive causes, who lived openly with his male lover, visited Whitman and honored his role in permitting "men not to be ashamed of the noblest instinct of their nature." "Women are beautiful," Carpenter said, "but to some there is that which passes the love of women." Whitman's sexually explicit poems unwittingly made him the center of a cult to liberate the cramped sexual mores of the Victorian éra. Men and women, heterosexual and homosexual, read in Whitman the celebration of the body and the powers and joys of sexuality that were never spoken about openly and unashamedly.

And yet for all their sensuous and physical imagery, Whitman's poems inspired a spiritual movement among freethinkers who sought a cosmic consciousness not nurtured in the Christian churches of the day. Whitman's poems are as much a dialogue between the poet and his soul as they are about the poet and his body. "I believe in you my soul, the other I am must not abase itself to you, / And you must not be abased to the other." Countless readers recognized Whitman's distinction between "the Me myself" and the "what I am" as opposed to the "pulling and hauling" of daily life. They realized the truth in asserting that "every atom belonging to me as good belongs to you." Whitman had become a sexual and spiritual liberator for a generation that had been "simmering." A hundred years later, he still brings people to "boiling."

The "test of a poem," he suggested, was "how far it can elevate, enlarge, purify, deepen and make happy the attributes of body and soul." The soul was his poem; the road before him was his poem; even the sex organ became a poem. "This poem drooping shy and unseen that I always carry, and that all men carry, / (Know once for all, avow'd on purpose, wherever are men like me, are our lusty lurking masculine poems)."

In 1871 Whitman wrote a series of three essays, published as *Democratic Vistas*, in which he seemed to have lost faith in the great mission of America. Disillusioned with postwar corruption in politics and the ruthless excesses of the Gilded Age, he catalogued the diseases of modern society. But the old "yea-sayer" was not totally disheartened. America, he asserted, could still produce the great moral and spiritual civilization he had hoped for in the heady 1840s. In a notebook entry he stated the basic idea behind his trust: "That the divine efforts of heroes, and their ideas, faithfully lived up to will finally prevail, and be accomplished however long deferred."

During the ten years after the war, when a series of strokes left him unable to hold a permanent job, Whitman's relationship with Peter Doyle sustained him as his health failed and prospects for the nation looked bleak. "I don't know what I should do if I hadn't you to think of and look forward to," he told Doyle. In 1873 Doyle took a job as a brakeman on the Baltimore and Potomac Railroad, and their relationship waned. But the aging poet found other companions. He met Harry Stafford, an 18-year-old errand boy in a print shop in Camden, New Jersey, where Whitman was staying with his brother George's family. Stafford invited Whitman to live with him on his parents' farm. There his health returned, and he began writing his autobiographical sketches, *Specimen Days*. A 25-year-old farmhand in the area, Edward Cattell, became another companion with whom Whitman (according to his diary) had meetings by the pond on moonlit nights.

When he moved back to Camden, where he spent his last years, a close circle of friends and admirers cared for him. Supporters in England sent money. His unofficial "disciples" watched over him. On March 26, 1892, he died of what was diagnosed as "the indirect effects" of paralysis.

Even after his death Whitman's clear, bold verse, his call for sexual honesty and enjoyment, his love of America, and his celebration of comrades were hailed by new generations of readers who found his message relevant for their own times. In the preface to his 1855 edition of *Leaves of Grass*, he had written: "The messages of great poets to each man and woman are, Come to us on equal terms, Only then can you understand us, We are no better than you, . . . What we enjoy you may enjoy. . . . The proof of a poet is that his country absorbs him as affectionately as he has absorbed it."

HORATIO ALGER, JR.

1832–1899

In the late winter of 1866, after 15 months in his first ministry, the Reverend Horatio Alger, Jr., had established what seemed to be an exemplary reputation with all segments of his Cape Cod parish. A friendly, likable man, Alger served the Unitarian parish well; and, unlike other ministers, he always found time to organize activities and entertainments for the young boys of the rural community: outings, ball games, hikes, songfests. His second novel for boys, *Paul Prescott's Charge*, had been published shortly after he arrived, and the parish basked in the honor.

Then the rumors began: The reverend's concern for boys extended beyond their spiritual and intellectual development. The social activities in the woods were not innocent. A parish committee met to investigate the charges and, based on the testimony of two boys, reported that "We learn . . . that Horatio Alger, Jr., has been practicing on them at different times deeds that are too revolting to relate." The shocked community was not appeased by Alger's admission that he had been merely "imprudent." He dissolved his connection with the parish and

90

left town that same night. The committee then wrote to the American Unitarian Association, justifying its actions in the light of "the abominable and revolting crime of unnatural familiarity with *boys*, which is too revolting to think of in the most brutal of our race."

So Horatio Alger had preached his last sermon, but only from the pulpit. He set off for New York in the spring of 1866 to become a famous writer, a goal which had inspired him from his childhood. As for his days in the ministry, Alger viewed them as so much water under a bridge which he was in no way reluctant to burn behind him.

Alger's heart had never really been set on the ministry. A scrawny, asthmatic child with a slight stutter, growing up in the environs of Boston, he was an easy target for the tougher youths and retreated into his own world of reading and studying. His minister father supported his interests, assigning him extra studies to prepare him for the ministry. To give his son a taste for his future work, the senior Alger forced the boy to accompany him on house calls around the parish. Young Horatio never rebelled and seemed to accept the fact that he was destined to follow in his father's footsteps. But his compliance hid other ambitions.

He excelled at Harvard, where he published poetry and prose pieces in the *Pictorial National Library* at age 17. He was graduated Phi Beta Kappa and composed the class's commencement ode. When he was home on vacations, his social conscience was stirred by the temperance and abolition movements, which in most communities went hand in hand. On one home visit, he heard William Lloyd Garrison speak from his father's pulpit on the evils of slavery.

On graduating Alger hoped to make a living as a writer, but estimated that he would have to publish 250 poems and stories a year to make ends meet. So, after a spate of rejection slips from magazines, he ceased resisting his father's advice and entered Harvard Divinity School. During his course of studies, he also taught in a boys' school and worked for a short time as an editor at the Boston *Daily Advertiser*, where he learned that his love for writing was not easily transposed to the nitpicking work of editing. In July 1858 he received his divinity degree. The following year he published 27 stories.

Before settling down to parish work, Alger took a trip abroad to round out his education, wrote some travel pieces, and returned to America in April 1861 to learn that, the preceding week, the state of South Carolina had fired on a federal fort in Charleston Harbor. When President Lincoln called out Northern militias to quell what he called the "rebellion in the Southern states," poor health disqualified Horatio from joining up. As an adult he weighed only 130 pounds and stood five foot two inches. He continued writing for magazines and, as a personal war effort, began *Frank's Campaign,* a novel about a young man in the army. In 1863 the prestigious *North American Review* and *Harper's Weekly* published a prose piece and a short story, respectively.

He then renewed his friendship with William Taylor Adams, also known by his pen name, Oliver Optic. A former teacher, Adams now wrote and edited boys' stories for a publication called *Student and Schoolmate,* which became Alger's chief outlet for stories and poems. Adams also introduced Alger to A. K. Loring, a Boston book publisher, who was interested in publishing *Frank's Campaign.* In the preface to his second book on the Civil War, Alger explained his basic theory of writing for boys: ". . . every boy's life is a campaign, more or less difficult, in which success depends upon integrity and a steadfast adherence to duty." Over the next 30 years, Alger would rework this basic moral in over 100 novels.

In 1867, the year following his ignominious retirement from the ministry, the 35-year-old Alger published *Ragged Dick, or Street Life in New York* as a 12-part serial in *Student and Schoolmate.* The story about the young hero's rise from squalor and thievery to respectability and financial success by luck and pluck caught the pulse of the nation. Mail began to pour in. Reformers and social workers approved of the highly readable account that publicized a cause they had long championed: the miserable plight of the growing number of street waifs—the orphaned or abandoned children of immigrants and the rootless ex-drummer boys and soldiers who moved to the big cities after the war.

Ragged Dick graphically depicted New York's low life, the exploitation of young men by thugs, evil employers, and unscrupulous entrepreneurs, and the unrelenting poverty of the tenements. Editor Adams knew he had a success and negotiated for the exclusive rights to the Alger name, promised his readers further stories from the author, and promoted the magazine by giving commissions to boys' clubs that sold subscriptions.

For his part Horatio Alger made the subject matter of his novel a personal crusade. He met Charles Loring Brace, a New York philanthropist, who in 1854 had established the Newsboys' Lodging House to provide bed, baths, and meals to the city's large number of homeless newsboys. By the 1860s the house could accommodate 250 boys a night, and by 1869 an estimated 8,835 boys had passed through its doors. Brace gave Alger a bed of his own and a desk for writing, and the author moved in on a semipermanent basis. In time he had the run of the place to do research, meet potential heroes for his novels, engage the boys in talk, and listen to their sad and, at times, ennobling tales. Although Horatio Alger novels were as packed with stereotypes, stick figures, stock situations, and miraculous escapes and coincidences as the television soap operas and adventure series of a later era (and just as popular), his stories were always based on the lives of real boys he came to know in his work.

In 1872 Alger wrote a tale about the padrone system of child slavery. *Phil the Fiddler* relates in squalid detail the social evil of the beggar rings composed of young boys lured to America from Sicily and Italy with the promise of the good life, only to discover that they must thieve for their Faginesque patrons. The Society for the Prevention of Cruelty to Children got involved; Alger served on a city commission on child labor and abuse; and in 1874 the New York legislature passed a law protecting children. Four years later the padrone system was abolished.

As he continued to write prolifically, Alger also tutored college students or prepared boys for Columbia College. He was also hired as a resident tutor for the sons of Joseph Seligman, a wealthy banker and businessman, a position that gave Alger the opportunity to observe the lifestyles of the entrepreneurs and captains of industry to which his "well-knit and manly" heroes always aspired. Although he never delved too deeply into the ethical practices of this class that would be known, in time, as the robber barons, the tenor of the age reinforced the possibility that a young boy could, with integrity, hard work, trustworthiness, and a little luck, go either from rags to riches or, more likely, from rags to respectability. In the end Alger always believed that the struggle counted far more than the reward.

In addition to writing and tutoring, Alger took a personal interest in the welfare of many teenage boys over the years. He gave away most of his royalties and customarily used his own money to sponsor individual boys he met, buy them food or clothes, find them lodging, get them into schools, set them up in business, or simply give them a loan. A busy man-about-town, Alger led an active social life that included belonging to clubs and organizations, attending the theater, and volunteering for social programs such as the Fresh Air Fund, an organization to sponsor summer vacations for poor urban boys which Alger was instrumental in founding. He read all the juvenile magazines and newspapers and knew virtually all the editors and publishers personally. He always traveled about town in the company of one or two boys who were his favorites at the time, or older boys he had helped in earlier years who had remained his friends. Having learned how to be discreet, Alger never again raised a hint of scandal.

In 1881, after President Garfield was assassinated, Alger was asked to write a biography of the slain president. Typically, he entitled it *From Canal Boy to President*, and the breathless exploits, invented dialogue, and luck-ridden adventures of young Garfield rose to crescendos befitting a fast-paced magazine serial. It sold well, and persuaded the publishers to commission Alger to write a "great men" series. But his next work, on Lincoln, flopped.

So Alger continued to stick with what he knew best: the nether regions of New York and other big cities (which were merely New York writ small). He did attempt stories set out west (he had visited his brother in California in 1876) and other more rural locales, but the local color was pale, and the farmboy heroes—as "well-knit and manly" as their urban counterparts— always journeyed to New York for at least one chapter. Readers expected it from the author whom the *New York Times* called the city's Prose Laureate.

In his sixties Alger was as vigorous as ever, continuing to crank out three, four, sometimes six books a year. He wrote Irving Blake, a former "Alger boy" with writing talent whom Horatio succeeded in getting hired as a journalist for the New York *Tribune*, that he felt young "particularly because I have so many friends of your age with whom I sympathize." In 1895 he invited Frank Cushman, a 16-year-old distant cousin, to accompany him on a trip through the Catskill Mountains. He wrote Blake: "We are both descended from Reverend Robert Cushman of *Mayflower* memory. [Alger was always proud of his Puritan ancestry.] He is as tall as you, and is a robust boy, weighing 150 pounds. He is quite able to pull me up the mountains, I may need such help."

Alger was always proud of his relations with boys and young men. That same year his popularity forced him to change residences in order to achieve some rest and anonymity. "I gave up my room on 34th Street," he wrote, "because I had too many young callers who were unwelcome." The indefatigable writer and mentor hoped his friends would keep his new address on East 10th Street a secret, but in the end, of course, he was found out. Eventually he moved back to live near his sister and her family in Massachusetts.

He informally adopted two brothers, Tommy and John Down. As his own health began to fail, he worried about what would happen to them. He wrote: "I think of giving Tommy a vacation from work and sending him to a commercial college soon. He will be 18 in March. He has been under my charge a little more than 3½ years. I sent John Down to the same institution at 18. I may not be able to leave Tommy much but I mean to leave him a better education at any rate."

Shortly before he died he wrote Blake: "I wonder, Irving, how it would seem to be as young and full of life and enthusiasm as you are. I shouldn't dare to go back to 19 again, lest my share of success prove to be less than it has been." In 1899, plagued by asthma and bronchitis, he died at the home of his sister and brother-in-law.

But Horatio Alger's career was not over. Edward Stratemeyer, better known as the author of the *Rover Boys* and *Tom Swift*, completed 11 of Alger's unfinished manuscripts for his publisher. Alger stayed in vogue till 1910; and although fewer editions were published by the 1920s, boys continued to read him through the Depression years. Businessmen, ministers, educators, and parents all approved, for Alger's basic story had become part of the American Dream.

OSCAR WILDE
1854–1900

On January 2, 1882, Oscar Wilde arrived in New York City to begin his year-long lecture tour of North America. A customs inspector asked him if he had anything to declare. "Nothing but my genius," he replied. Who was this 28-year-old Irishman from London who lectured in 70 American cities on the arts and literature, as an advance publicity agent for the Gilbert and Sullivan touring company of *Patience*, an operetta that spoofed aesthetes like himself?

He spoke to Mormons in Salt Lake City, silver miners in Colorado, West Coast literati in San Francisco, farmers in Kansas and Iowa. He swung through Quebec and Ontario, down to New Orleans, and stayed with Jefferson Davis at his plantation on the Gulf of Mexico. He visited Walt Whitman for two hours in Camden, New Jersey ("A splendid boy," the old poet reported. "We had a very happy time together"), and ended back in New York. His performances were so popular that he complained, tongue in cheek, that it took three secretaries to manage his act: one to sign fake autographs for him, a second to receive the bouquets of flowers, and a third, with brown hair like his own, to cut locks for the throngs of female admirers. The third secretary, Wilde recounted, nearly went bald.

Wilde grew up in an intellectually bustling Irish household. His mother, a poet with a considerable following who wrote under the pen name Speranza, held literary salons that lasted sometimes from dinner to dawn and included poets, artists, wits, intellectuals; his father, a renowned physician, was interested in myths and folklore. Oscar went to Trinity College, Dublin, where he was known as much for being a pugilist as a poet. At Oxford, where he won a coveted poetry award, he came under the influence of the critics John Ruskin and Walter Pater and the late-nineteenth-century aesthetic movement and found notions such as "art for art's sake" and dedicating one's life to art congenial to his temperament and talents. Furthermore they fed his desire to make himself famous. After leaving Oxford he went to London and did just that.

From 1878 to 1881 Oscar Wilde became well known for being well known. Without any substantial achievements to build on, he insinuated himself into that class of individuals whom he labeled "the beautiful people," wore outrageous clothes, passed himself off as an art critic and aesthete, and built up his reputation for saying shocking things and doing amusing ones. As he put it: "If one tells the truth, one is sure sooner or later to be found out." His natural wit and good humor endeared him to the art and theater world. Through Frank Miles, an upcoming artist and Wilde's lover and roommate, he found easy entry into the cliques that frequented London's theater circuit and drawing rooms. He lionized the popular actresses of the day—Lily Langtry, Sarah Bernhardt, Helena Modjeska, and Ellen Terry—for whom he wrote sonnets and effusive letters of admiration. In short he became a "groupie," a celebrity hound, and soon became a much-desired, all-purpose party guest.

In time, cartoons in *Punch* began to satirize Wilde as the character "Jellaby Postlethwaite," a precious, languid young man who uttered witticisms in a supercilious manner. Wilde, who believed that it was worse not to be talked about than to be talked about, enjoyed the publicity. His velvet coat, knee breeches, silk stockings, pale green tie, cane, shoulder-length hair, loose silk shirts, as well as the lily he occasionally carried through London's Picadilly Circus, made him an easy mark. With his flamboyant reputation as the Great Aesthete, the Gilbert and Sullivan promoters could hardly have chosen a better advance man for the new operetta. And since Wilde was offered all expenses and one-third of the box-office receipts, he could hardly turn the proposition down. After all he was being paid to be himself.

On his return from America he continued to lecture and write, but eventually tired of being the Great Aesthete and speaking to audiences that came primarily to see his funny clothes. He returned to conventional but fashionable dress, toured, wrote two unsuccessful plays and a well-received collection of children's fairy tales, married, fathered two sons, and took a position as editor of *Woman's World*, a monthly magazine for which he wrote literary criticism. Although he was not a professional editor, his previous networking among the notable literary and theater figures in England, America, and Europe provided him with a stable of fascinating writers whom he persuaded to contribute to the magazine. Within two years he tired of journalism—and journalists, whose company lacked the glitter he had come to enjoy and expect in his life. He resigned, and devoted extra time to sparkling at parties and receptions with an unending flood of wit and paradox. As he wrote Arthur Conan Doyle, the creator of Sherlock Holmes: "Between me and life there is a mist of words always. I throw probability out of the window for the sake of a phrase, and the chance of an epigram makes me desert truth." He neglected his family and spent much of his time with friends and lovers, often stepping beyond the bounds of what was considered morally and socially proper.

From 1890 to 1895 Wilde reached the peak of his career, both as poet-playwright and social gadfly. His one novel, *The Picture of Dorian Gray*, raised a storm of indignation with its "purple patches" and thinly veiled allusions to the protagonist's homosexual lifestyle. Walter Pater and a few others saw its true merit as an indictment of bourgeois hypocrisy and favorably compared its macabre quality to that of Edgar Allan Poe. When Wilde came out with a second volume of delightful children's stories, *The House of Pomegranates*, in the same year, readers could not believe the two works were from the same author, a fact that confirmed for Wilde much of what was wrong with society.

Over the next four years a succession of enormously successful plays reintroduced the comedy of manners to the English stage: *Lady Windermere's Fan*, *A Woman of No Importance*, and *The Importance of Being Earnest*, the last being hailed as the first modern comedy in English. Collectively these plays forced Victorian society to reexamine its hypocrisies and delineated, with wit and humor, the arbitrariness of many moral and social taboos which, to the unreflective Victorian eye, appeared to be eternal. Wilde's plays served as midwife in birthing the modern era. In his own person he elevated the role of social critic to an art form and demonstrated that the critique itself could make marvelous theater. He quickly became the leading comic dramatist of his time.

In 1894 his play *Salomé*, which he wrote in French, was translated into English and illustrated by Aubrey Beardsley. Later to be the inspiration for an opera, Wilde's play was not performed in England for 13 years, because a seventeenth-century law forbade the representation of biblical characters on a public stage. It was this kind of hypocrisy and censorship against which much of Wilde's work and life was directed. On hearing that the Lord Chamberlain had banned *Salomé*, Wilde threatened to renounce his British citizenship and become a French citizen. Writing with hindsight years later, Wilde's son Vyvyan, then an adult, remarked how fortunate that ploy would have been.

In 1895 the eighth Marquess of Queensberry, considered quite mad even by members of his immediate family, culminated his persistent public harassment of Wilde for his on-again-off-again sexual relationship with his son, Lord Alfred Douglas, by leaving a card for Wilde at his club accusing him of being a "somdomite" [sic]—a pervert in Queensberry's eyes, no matter how the abominable word was spelled. Wilde, greatly influenced by Douglas, who (along with other members of his family) hoped to see his father put to shame, initiated a libel suit against Queensberry. The solicitor general, representing Wilde's case, asked the playwright if there was any truth in the matter. Wilde said no; and the case proceeded, bringing to light Wilde's homosexual affairs, which were never too well camouflaged to begin with. Queensberry was acquitted, whereupon Wilde was arrested, and, after two trials, found guilty and sentenced to two years of hard labor. Friends urged him to leave England and take up residence on the Continent, where more tolerant sexual standards prevailed, but he refused, partly because Douglas didn't want him to, and, more important, because Wilde believed in accepting with dignity the consequences of his actions. As he would write to Douglas from prison, "The supreme vice is shallowness."

While in prison he composed a 30,000-word letter to Douglas (published after Wilde's death with the title De Profundis), in which he explained—he once quipped that he never justified himself; he explained himself—his tragic downfall. He expounded on the topics that were dear to him: art and life, love and hate, happiness and suffering, the power of the imagination. In an extended passage on the personality of Christ, he wrote: "And while reading the Gospels . . . I see this continual assertion of the imagination as the basis of all spiritual and material life." He presented Christ as the "most supreme of Individualists," and "the true precursor of the romantic movement." He rhapsodized about the Man of Sorrows, saying: "He saw that love was that lost secret of the world for which the wise men had been looking." In spite of his occasionally irritating love-hate attacks upon Douglas, the work is possibly his most important and mature statement on life and art in general and his own life and art in particular. In the concluding lines he tells Douglas: "You came to me to learn the Pleasure of Life and the Pleasure of Art. Perhaps I am chosen to teach you something much more wonderful, the meaning of Sorrow, and its beauty."

After his release Wilde left England to wander around Europe for the last three years of his life, followed by young gay men who were enamored of his legend and of whom he, in turn, was enamored. A broken man, he sank deeper into a reckless life of sex and absinthe from which neither he nor his true, long-term friends, like Robbie Ross, could extricate him.

His one noteworthy piece from this period is *The Ballad of Reading Gaol*, a gripping account of prison brutality based on his own harrowing experiences and a plea for prison reform. Its haunting refrain, "Each man kills the thing he loves," has become part of our folk wisdom.

Reduced to poverty and poor health, he endured his final days living on borrowed money and the kindness of sympathetic friends and hotel managers. In a perfectly Wildean paradox he complained to a friend, "I am dying beyond my means." In 1900, in the Hôtel d'Alsace in Paris, he died of cerebral meningitis, perhaps complicated by the syphilis he had contracted in his college days.

In 1895 he had asked the Frenchman of letters André Gide: "Would you like to know the great drama of my life? It's that I've put my genius into my life; I've put only my talent into my works." But perhaps he best perceived his ultimate legacy two years later when he wrote in *De Profundis*: "I made art a philosophy, and philosophy an art: I altered the minds of men and the colours of things: there was nothing I said or did that did not make people wonder. . . . I treated Art as the supreme reality, and life as a mere mode of fiction: I awoke the imagination of my century so that it created myth and legend around me: I summed up all system in a phrase, and all existence in an epigram."

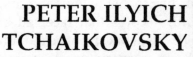

PETER ILYICH TCHAIKOVSKY

1840–1893

In 1875 Peter Ilyich Tchaikovsky accepted a commission from the Imperial Theaters for a ballet entitled *Swan Lake*. He was offered 800 rubles. He accepted it, claiming that the money was the primary attraction, even though, as he admitted to the composer Rimsky-Korsakov, "I have long had a wish to try my hand at this kind of music." Throughout his life he was drawn to writing what he thought of as the great operas. Ironically, these were not his best works. Today his compositions for the classical ballets outdistance his other pieces. At one point he seemed to have suspected this. "Despite all the seductions of opera," he mused, "I write a symphony, sonata, or quartet with infinitely greater pleasure."

Over the next year he finished *Swan Lake*, and in 1877 the Bolshoi prepared for its premiere. At rehearsals dancers complained that parts of the music were "undanceable," so the company administrators substituted other ballet music for the more difficult parts. Production values were shabby; the sets and costumes were of poor quality; the choreographer was second-rate; the conductor was an amateur. On March 4 the curtain rose and fell on a failure. The Bolshoi gave the ballet a few more chances, and then dropped it from its repertoire. Not until years later, after its composer's death, would it be revived.

Tchaikovsky's reputation, both during his lifetime and after his death, suffered many twists of fate. Although he was a musical genius, the manic-depressive composer took critics too seriously and made changes according to their whims and some-times deliberately destroyed entire scores that received bad reviews. Frequently unhappy over his work, he once admitted that he was "very dissatisfied because everything that comes into my head is so commonplace." He often wondered, espe-cially when he was in his forties, "Am I really played out, as they say?" Even when audiences were ecstatic, a cool critical reception would send him into despair. Tsar Alexander III attended the premiere of *The Sleeping Beauty* in 1890 and said it was "very nice." Crestfallen, Tchaikovsky confided in his diary: "His Majesty treated me in a most offhand manner, God be with him." On the other hand, when audiences went wild with enthusiasm, he suspected it was to honor him personally, not his latest work.

As a young boy growing up in an affluent, middle-class household run by his father, a mine manager, and a talented mother who spoke French and German and played the piano and sang, the young Peter Ilyich already displayed his overly sensitive personality. His French governess claimed, "A trifle wounded him deeply. He was as brittle as porcelain." His piano teacher found "nothing remarkable, nothing phenomenal" in Peter's talent and advised his father not to encourage music lessons. But when the young Tchaikovsky heard Mozart's *Don Giovanni*, "It awoke a spiritual ecstasy which was afterwards to bear fruit. With its help I penetrated into that world of artistic beauty where only great genius abides."

After graduating from the strict discipline of the School of Jurisprudence in 1859, Tchaikovsky worked as a clerk for the Ministry of Justice in Saint Petersburg and began music lessons with the Russian Musical Society. When the Russian Conservatory was established, he enrolled there and studied under Anton Rubinstein. Years later the renowned teacher remembered that on one occasion he assigned contrapuntal variations on a given theme, for which, he assumed, Tchaikovsky would write perhaps a dozen. "Not at all," Rubinstein declared. "At the next class he gave me over two hundred."

Unhappy with his clerkship at the Ministry of Justice, Tchaikovsky decided that if he did not receive a promotion, he would resign and study music full time. "Whether I become a celebrated composer or merely a struggling music teacher—it's all the same. In either event my conscience will be clear, and I shall no longer have the right to grumble at my lot." He did not receive the promotion.

But grumbling seems to have been a lifelong motif. He moved to Moscow and began teaching in the conservatory's sister institution in 1866. After a successful performance of his first symphony, *Winter Daydreams,* he made his ill-fated debut as a conductor. He gave all the wrong leads, and the orchestra, it seems, managed to get through the pieces only because they knew the music so well. Afterwards he told a friend that he felt that his head would fall off his shoulders unless he held it tightly in position. His fear of the podium kept him from conducting publicly for the next ten years.

He was equally unhappy over his assumed need to construct elaborate cover-ups for his homosexuality. In 1871, when he wanted to travel through southern France and Italy with his favorite pupil and close friend Vladimir Shilovsky, a boy of 19, he asked his brother Modest to say that he was visiting his sister and her family in the country. Throughout his professional life he worried about gossip and rumors, and his inability to come to terms with his homosexuality became a source of self-inflicted misery.

In 1876 he decided to marry. "I shall make a serious effort to marry, legally, anybody," he wrote his brother. "I am aware that my inclinations are the greatest obstacle to happiness; I must fight my nature with all my strength." So he resolved that, given the opportunity, he would escape into holy wedlock. "In a word, I should like to marry, or by some known liaison with a woman, shut the mouths of all despicable gossips, for whose opinion I do not care a bit, but who can hurt people close to me." And yet, judging by the composer's supersensitive nature, it would seem that he did care more than "a bit." He continually worried over what he called "succumb[ing] to my natural inclinations."

In 1877 Antonina Milyukova, a pupil at the conservatory, began a series of passionate love letters to Tchaikovsky, and in time he yielded to them. He admitted he was not in love with her; but one of her letters hinted at suicide should he reject her, and this drastic appeal made up his mind for him. They were married in July 1877. Within days, while still on his honeymoon, Tchaikovsky realized his mistake. He wrote Modest that he found his new wife "physically repulsive."

Shortly after their return to Moscow, Tchaikovsky was on the verge of a mental and physical breakdown. He escaped for the month of August and went to the Caucasus alone. Back in Moscow for his winter courses at the conservatory, he was miserable. In October he attempted suicide by wandering into the icy waters of the Moskva River, hoping to catch pneumonia. Recovering, he invented a subterfuge that he had to go to Saint Petersburg. In the capital he collapsed and was unconscious for two days. Finally his doctor advised "a complete change of life and scene," whereupon he began formal separation proceedings. His health began to improve immediately. In time, however, Antonina renounced her agreement to the divorce and for years wrote threatening letters to Tchaikovsky and members of his family. In 1896, after a string of many lovers and a large number of children, she was admitted to an asylum and certified insane.

A more fortunate relationship for Tchaikovsky was with his patroness, Nadezhda Filaretovna von Meck, a wealthy widow who bestowed on the composer 6,000 rubles a year, allowing him to resign his teaching position at the conservatory. Over the course of 13 years they wrote 1,100 letters, many quite intimate and passionate. Von Meck allowed Tchaikovsky the use of her villas, and the only stipulation was that the two of them never meet. On occasions when they were both at the same residence, they synchronized their schedules so they would never see each other on afternoon walks. In 1890, for no apparent reason, von Meck ended her generous patronage. Fortunately, the same year witnessed the premiere of *The Queen of Spades*, Tchaikovsky's most successful opera, whose royalties adequately compensated for his loss of von Meck's patronage.

In 1887 Tchaikovsky felt confident enough to embark on his first European tour as a conductor. Audiences were enthusiastic, but critics were more guarded in their reviews. In London, however, the old doubts returned, and he wondered, "Is it worthwhile? . . . I come to the conclusion that it is far better to live quietly, without fame."

In 1892 an American tour included concerts at Philadelphia, Baltimore, and New York, where Tchaikovsky's four performances were part of the inaugural celebration for the new Carnegie Hall. "I am a much more important person here than in Russia," he wrote. "Is it not curious?" When he returned, *The Nutcracker* premiered to great acclaim, and Tchaikovsky was hailed as Russia's foremost composer, but he continued his restless habit of escaping to Europe. "Every place is better than the one which we are in," he once said. He was still worried about the rumors of his homosexuality.

Even though unhappy with the reception critics gave his work, continually agitated over the gossip about his personal life, and driven to move from place to place, Tchaikovsky found moments of happiness; and his music composed during those times attests to them. The piano pieces he wrote while on tour with his friend Vladimir Shilovsky, and which he dedicated to the young man, reveal a joy and contentment with life. While staying with Shilovsky at the boy's estate at Ussovo, he was euphoric as he composed parts of *Swan Lake*. In an outpouring of heightened creativity, he wrote music for *The Tempest* in ten days.

Tchaikovsky also drew strength from his long-term relationship with his "pal" or servant Aleksei Sofronov. The boy came into Tchaikovsky's service when he was 14. Later, when he reached military age, Aleksei had to spend four years in the army. Tchaikovsky was miserable. He wrote his brother that there was not a second in the day he did not think of his young friend, nor was there a night that he didn't dream of him. In his will the composer left Aleksei a share in his estate and royalties and all his household furniture and effects.

Throughout his life Tchaikovsky visited his sister and her family in the Caucasus. He loved the merriment of family life and took a great interest in the children. His nephew Bob found a special place in the composer's heart. Together they played piano duets, and as the boy grew older, he accompanied his uncle on trips to Europe. Whenever Tchaikovsky had to travel alone, he faithfully wrote to Bob. "I idolize you," he told the young boy.

After returning to Russia from his American tour, Tchaikovsky, in a typical slough of despair, felt that his career and life were over. He began his next (and last) symphony assuming that he had no future. He predicted the work would be a failure. In 1893 he conducted its premiere, and, true to form, it received lukewarm reviews. His brother suggested calling it *Pathétique*. Twelve days later Tchaikovsky died in the presence of his faithful brother Modest, his pal Aleksei, and his nephew Bob.

The rumors that Tchaikovsky feared all his life were rife even in death. Mystery still hovers over his final days. Some contemporaries said he died of cholera contracted from inadvertently drinking unboiled water. Others claimed he drank it deliberately, depressed over the failure of his last symphony. Recent scholarship indicates that he may have poisoned himself to avoid a scandal that was about to erupt concerning a sexual relationship with a male member of the imperial family.

The man who claimed that he was "working like a cobbler day in, day out, and often to order" was productive in every field of music: opera, ballet, symphony, piano pieces, music for string quartets, and church music. His neurotic, self-torturing ego is clearly evident in his best work, but so is his exuberant sense of life's promise. Ironically, the man who, while alive, thought Russia did not appreciate him, today is highly esteemed in the Soviet Union.

MARCEL PROUST

1871–1922

A publisher who read the first installment of Marcel Proust's masterpiece, *Remembrance of Things Past*, was confused by the stream-of-consciousness technique. He turned the manuscript down. André Gide, editor of the prestigious *Nouvelle Revue Française*, also rejected the manuscript, practically unread, because he considered Proust a social butterfly and an amateur writer. Still another publisher refused the manuscript, objecting that he couldn't understand why Proust took 30 pages to describe rolling over in bed at night before going to sleep. Discouraged, Proust offered to finance the publication himself and found a willing publisher who accepted the manuscript unread. In November 1913 the work appeared as *Swann's Way*, and went almost unnoticed.

When *Swann's Way* was published Proust had virtually completed the massive work which would eventually tally over 1.25 million words and equal in bulk 13 average-size novels. But World War I halted further publication. In 1919, however, Proust found a publisher for the second part, *Within a Budding Grove*, which drew rave reviews from a member of the Goncourt

Academy; and Proust received the coveted Goncourt Prize, an honor that would assure him a wide readership. Overnight he became famous. In 1920 he was awarded the Legion of Honor, the distinguished-service award instituted by Napoleon.

What was this strangely beautiful, massively detailed, poetic work called *Remembrance of Things Past*? As fictionalized autobiography *Remembrance* draws on Proust's experiences from childhood to middle age, and adroitly chronicles the fading lifestyles of the French aristocracy. But apart from content it inaugurated a new style of writing that would come to dominate twentieth-century fiction.

Proust was born in 1871 in Paris, and his childhood coincided with France's post-Commune era, the rebuilding of Paris into a modern city with new boulevards and modern buildings, the introduction of automobiles and airplanes, the building of the Eiffel Tower, and the construction of the Statue of Liberty, soon to be shipped to America. It was an era of ferment, social change, and new ideas.

Proust grew up in a wealthy family. His father was a doctor of medicine; his mother was the daughter of an affluent Jewish stockbroker. He spent happy days in his family's town home, enjoying the country gardens of friends and relatives, and studying at first-rate schools. "Your school days are the happiest of your life," he later recalled, voicing a sentiment not shared by many gay people since. When he was 18 he joined the infantry for one year, and, strange as it may seem for a sickly, introspective young man, found that experience also enjoyable. The military restrictions, he later explained, contributed to a happy time "in which pleasure is the more constantly with us because we have no time to run about looking for it and so miss it altogether."

In spite of the privileges and opportunities that came with affluence, Proust learned early in life that he was an outsider, a stance he would use to great literary effect. As a Jew, a homosexual, and an asthmatic semi-invalid, Proust adopted a voyeur approach to the social customs he saw around him, a condition that ultimately gave him shrewd insight into individuals he would fictionalize in such credible and revealing detail. As an outsider he was able to view the aristocratic enclaves of Parisian society from a fresh perspective.

From his 18th year, when he was introduced to the world of the salon, he rapidly and determinedly pursued the art of social climbing. In the lively, stimulating drawing rooms of wealthy, socially prominent women, Proust participated in the gatherings of intellectuals, artists, thinkers, writers, and the hangers-on who hoped to become important by brushing shoulders and wits with celebrities. Here the properly coiffed and elegantly clothed guests met to discuss art, music, and science, and to enliven the afternoon or evening with opinions and pronouncements on the social and political issues of the day. Clever, witty, and with a keen eye for social nuances and stupidities, Proust was right at home, watching, absorbing, "telescoping" (a favorite word) the manners and habits of the men and women he met. In the world of the salons he discovered the aristocratic figures who would supply the parts of his grand literary mosaic.

In 1896, when the Dreyfus Affair rocked every corner of high society and splintered even the best-run salons, Proust sided with the Dreyfusards and collected names to force a reopening of the case of the Jewish officer, found guilty of passing military secrets to the Germans and exiled to Devil's Island. Proust risked ostracism in the very social circles he had worked so assiduously to enter. Like any *cause célèbre*, the Dreyfus case quickly mushroomed into a free-for-all in which everyone, liberal and conservative alike, found room to battle for his or her pet social or political concerns. Caught up in the controversy that would not be settled until 1906, when the maligned Dreyfus was reinstated, Proust became disenchanted with the military and social heroes he had formerly lionized. Disenchantment nurtured a more critical eye with which to view the society he was to immortalize in *Remembrance of Things Past.*

Around 1900 Proust's health failed. Never robust, he had suffered from asthma since childhood and was frequently sick in bed or convalescing. In the early years of the new century, he became ever more reclusive, and organized his life around his habit of sleeping during the day and working and socializing at night. When he challenged a journalist to a duel over a homosexual slur, his major worry seemed to be whether it would take place at dawn during his accustomed hour to retire for the day. (It didn't, and neither Proust nor his opponent was hurt.) He spent his days and nights in the great country houses of aristocratic friends and the grand hotels. When he felt vigorous enough he frequented cafés and restaurants, and nurtured platonic friendships with young nobles and military officers with whom he shared literary and artistic interests.

Proust's first known lover was Reynaldo Hahn, a Jewish composer and singer from Venezuela whom Proust met when he was 22 and continued to see for two years. Hahn, handsome and exotic, captivated the attention of high society and performed for the most fashionable clientele, which played nicely into Proust's own desire to see and be seen in the most exclusive company. There were other lovers and amorous entanglements after Hahn, but in later life Proust's sexual attachments focused primarily on a series of gay servants who always shared his residences.

The chauffeur Alfred Agostinelli, whom Proust met in 1907 in Cabourg and with whom he later fell in love, moved in with Proust in 1913 (along with his wife—a situation that did not make for domestic bliss) and became Proust's secretary. He died in an airplane crash the following year. The story of Albertine in *Remembrance*—a tale of love, captivity, jealousy, escape, and death—was based on Proust's experiences and relationship with Agostinelli.

Proust's earliest attempts at transforming his life's experience into fiction left him very unsatisfied. In 1896 he wrote *Jean Santeuil*, a semiautobiographical novel based on many of the same incidents, characters, and themes that would appear in his later work, but he found his writing sterile. The precise relationship between the past and memory, which he tried and failed to capture, would continue to obsess and elude him.

Thirteen years later, in 1909, Proust was given a cup of tea and a madeleine (a small, rich tea cake)—a normal event not unlike many similar incidents. But on this particular day, when he dipped the madeleine into the tea, the secret of time and memory was revealed to him in a flash of understanding. Childhood experiences flooded his memory, showing him the mystery and relationship of past events. His past life came back to him, every important incident falling into place, the minor supporting details appearing as he needed them. He called this "involuntary memory," triggered by spontaneous sense impressions, rather than by mental exercises. By reexperiencing the past through the senses, Proust's memories appeared clear and free from the mental habits and reflexes that colored his present modes of thinking. In effect he had discovered that time does not really fade and pass from consciousness. Everything is preserved in memory.

Proust's discovery and the great work it produced had tremendous influence on subsequent writers who pioneered in applying Freudian theories to literature, drawing on autobiographical material and trying to unlock the deepest memories that seem cut off from recall. As Proust became required reading in literary circles, his open and unambiguous accounts of the homosexual experience were read by a new generation of writers, who learned through him how to delineate the subtleties of homosexual life and character. *Remembrance of Things Past* did much to put to rest the century-old taboo in western European literature of not referring to homosexuality openly and honestly. Proust became so closely associated with the homosexual theme in literature that "Proustian" became a euphemism for homosexual.

In October 1922 Proust went to an evening gathering in poor health, weakened by recent bouts of asthma. He returned home with a cold that developed into bronchitis and pneumonia. A

22222

2222222222

month later he died, having worked on into the middle of the night on his writings, as was his custom.

As his work became available in translation, his reputation grew internationally, as a writer whose fine-tuned sensibilities penetrated and illustrated a fading society along with its varieties of human nature. By refracting his literary perceptions through the prism of time, he discovered that all "characters will later reveal themselves as different from what they were in the present, different from what one believes them to be, a circumstance which, indeed, occurs frequently enough in life." Having witnessed the entire spectrum of human passion, from the decent to the despicable, Proust portrayed "the life which, in a sense, dwells at every instant in all men, and not the artist alone."

WILLA CATHER

1873–1947

In 1908, while working as managing editor at *McClure's Magazine* in New York City, Willa Cather received a letter that was to change her professional and personal life. It was a long letter of advice from her Greenwich Village literary friend and almost-neighbor Sarah Orne Jewett. "You must find a quiet place," she wrote. "You must find your own quiet center of life and write from that." The notion of "a quiet place," one's "own quiet center," stirred something deep inside. At age 35 Willa Cather had indeed moved far beyond the flat, monotonous prairie society of Nebraska which she remembered as suffocating to a writer's soul. It had led her to the excitement of writing for the leading muckraking magazine in New York's publishing world. But as Jewett pointed out to her, she had not found her real voice, her real subject, her real self.

Over the next few years Cather resolved to ease herself out of publishing, and she began working on a novel about the prairies. In 1912 she resigned from *McClure's* and traveled to Winslow, Arizona, to visit her brother Douglass, a lifelong bachelor and outdoorsman who made his life among the railroad men who were then developing the Far West. With Douglass, Cather went backpacking, camping, and horseback riding through the nation's newest state, sometimes staying out on the trail for a week at a time. Her keen eye observed the majestic vistas, the deserts and mountains, the Indians, the cliff dwellers' encampments, the remnants of the Spanish settlers, and all the exotic local customs.

The following year her prairie novel *O Pioneers!* was published. Willa Cather had found her "quiet center"—it was the pioneer spirit that had inspired her as a child but which she felt compelled to escape in order to develop her own creative spirit. In *O Pioneers!*, Cather affirms that a woman with a large, expansive personality, like the heroine, Alexandra, can rise above the petty intolerance of prairie society. She can learn that the world is "wider than my cornfields," that there is "something besides this." But it is the cornfields and the sunsets and endless horizons that produce an Alexandra. *O Pioneers!* was Cather's first novel about the strong Scandinavian women and men who could struggle with their environment and win. Clearly the work shows that Cather could enjoy writing about the prairie and its people. It was a major step in her reconciliation with Nebraska and all that it stood for.

Cather had spent the first 35 years of her life trying to escape her "center." From her childhood days in and around Red Cloud, Nebraska, Willa Cather was known as an unconventional girl. She could not abide the commonplaceness of prairie life. She sought out the eccentrics in the community, the older men and women from whom she hoped to learn less conventional ways of thinking and acting. As she matured, the local town folk regarded her with increasing wonder and concern. She was most criticized for her hobby of dissecting animals, which she hoped would prepare her for becoming a doctor. She wore her hair shorter than most boys, preferred starched shirts and men's ties and hats, and asked to be called William or Willie. She had radical opinions on religion, science, and the imagination;

and in her high-school commencement address she shocked her staid audience with unconventional statements about investigating God's universe. "The dice of God are always loaded," she announced, "and there are two sides which never fall upward, the alpha and omega. Perhaps when we make our final cast with dark old death we may shape them better."

At the University of Nebraska in Lincoln, Cather fell in love with Louise Pound, an older student who did not respond to her attentions as wholeheartedly as Cather would have wished. In her letters to Pound, Cather regrets the fact that society considers intimate friendship between women to be unnatural. But despite the unrequited love of her college days, Willa Cather thrived in Lincoln. As in Red Cloud she was drawn to the company of her elders. She frequently visited the families in Lincoln that she found stimulating. She became editor of the undergraduate literary journal. Eventually she met the novelist Dorothy Canfield, who inspired her with the beauty and power of art and encouraged her aesthetic sensibilities.

While at the university she published her first short story, "Peter," in a Boston journal, a tale that would later be reworked as the suicide of Mr. Shimerda in *My Antonia*. In 1893 she was invited to be a regular contributor to the *State Journal*, for which she was paid one dollar a column. She graduated in 1895, and on a return visit to Lincoln met the founder of a Pittsburgh magazine, the *Home Monthly*, who invited her to join his staff. In 1896 she left Nebraska for Pennsylvania, thrilled with the notion that she was finally putting the dull, small-minded prairies behind her.

The ten years Willa Cather spent in Pittsburgh were equally divided between publishing and teaching. After only one year at the *Home Monthly*, she resigned and joined the *Leader*, Pennsylvania's largest evening newspaper, where she edited and rewrote telegraphic news, a job which she found cramping and limiting. In 1901 Cather began teaching high-school Latin. But more important, she met Isabelle McClung, the daughter of a conservative Pittsburgh judge. The two became best friends;

and on McClung's invitation, Cather left her boardinghouse and lived with her new friend and her family in their ample home. Together they read European novels and discussed art and literature. The following year the two young women traveled together to Europe, where they met up with Dorothy Canfield and visited the poet A. E. Housman in England. With Isabelle McClung, Cather found the strong affectionate bonding with another woman that she had been seeking since girlhood.

From 1902 to 1905, while living in the McClung residence, Cather published her first book of poems, *April Twilights*, and placed prose pieces in *Lippincott's, New England Magazine, Scribner's, Everybody's,* and *McClure's*. In 1905 her first book of short stories, *The Troll Garden,* was published by McClure, Phillips and Company. She had not yet discovered her "quiet place" from which to write; these stories are indictments of prairie life and its people. Typical of turn-of-the-century literature that revolted against the small town and countryside for being mean-spirited, narrow-minded, and inimical to the life of the spirit, *The Troll Garden* was Cather's version of the common literary theme "You can't go home again." She was still resentful of the West and, at the end of a decade in Pittsburgh, disillusioned with the world of business, which she portrayed as equally hostile to the creative spirit.

In 1906 she accepted S. S. McClure's offer to come to New York and join the staff of *McClure's*, a popular magazine that pricked the nation's conscience with factual human-interest stories about corruption in politics, business, and the industrial cities. Eventually Cather became managing editor of *McClure's*, and under her successful stewardship circulation increased. She enjoyed working with socially conscious and innovative writers, but she never liked the factual, scientific reporting the magazine required.

Cather continued to visit Isabelle McClung in Pittsburgh, and in 1908 they traveled to Europe again. Cather invited her friend to live with her in New York, but the move was not in McClung's plans. In 1916 she married, but Cather stayed on good terms with her and her husband and continued to visit and travel with them. Until her death of kidney failure in 1938, McClung remained the primary object of Cather's affection.

But if a relationship with Isabelle McClung did not become the nucleus for a community of women that could satisfy Cather's emotional and artistic needs, her friendship with Edith Lewis did. Cather met Lewis on a visit to Lincoln in 1903. Impressed with Cather's works, Lewis had arranged to meet the author from her native state. Cather, in turn, was equally impressed with the young Lincoln girl's desire to go to New York, even without a job, to try to make a career in publishing. Cather visited Lewis in New York several times, and eventually the two became neighbors living in Washington Square. Willa got Edith a job as proofreader at *McClure's;* and in 1908, after her last trip to Europe with Isabelle, Cather and Lewis took an apartment together. Their relationship lasted for 40 years. And in that same year, 1908, Sarah Orne Jewett told Cather to find her "quiet center."

After publication of *O Pioneers!* and *The Song of the Lark* the following year, Willa Cather and Edith Lewis spent the summers of 1915 and 1916 traveling in the Southwest, where Cather discovered more of the mysteries and beauties of the desert land and its rich assortment of cultures. She became fascinated by its history, by what she called "the previous, the incommunicable past." Two years later *My Antonia* was published, another prairie novel whose protagonist-narrator learns to appreciate the strength and vitality of the Plains women. He eventually realizes, as did Cather, that Nebraska can be more than a place to run away from; it can be a home. For someone with the heroic strength of Antonia, the Plains can draw out the highest nobility of spirit.

The brutalities of World War I disillusioned Willa Cather, as it did many writers and artists. In 1922 she and her parents joined the Episcopal church in Red Cloud, and religion assumed a prominent place in her writings. The writer, whose sensibilities had formerly centered around the aesthetic, now found inspiration and meaning in the religious. Explaining this development, she wrote: "Art and religion (they are the same thing, in the end, of course) have given man the only happiness he has ever had." In *The Professor's House, My Mortal Enemy,* and *Death Comes for the Archbishop,* all published in the 1920s, Cather dealt with the power of religion to illuminate life and provide a coherent base for weathering the storms of fate and destiny. With increasing brilliance she delineated the importance that place and spirit have in forming the human personality. People like the archbishop, who are "sensitive to the shapes of things," can be enriched by the land, the atmosphere, the bits and pieces of daily life that can release "the prisoned spirit of man into the wind, into the blue and gold, into the morning, into the morning!"

Cather's father died in 1928, and her mother followed two years later after a lingering illness. According to Edith Lewis, nursing Cather's mother "was one of those experiences that make a lasting change in the climate of one's mind." Cather never quite recovered. In 1938 both her brother Douglass and her dear Isabelle died. The world that Willa Cather had known and grown to appreciate was slipping away from her. She continued to write about people who embodied "the passionate struggle of a tenacious will," even as she saw the pioneer spirit dying all around her. The New Deal convinced her that America no longer valued independence and freedom of spirit. The great industrialists and pioneers who settled the West were replaced by clerks and civil servants who were not hardy, daring, or creative. She deplored higher education's emphasis on contemporary art and literature, rather than the riches of the past. Education in general, she felt, exalted technology at the expense of humanism, and prepared people for nothing but making money.

When World War II broke out, she wrote: "There seems to be no future at all for people of my generation." Her health and vigor began to fade (among other things, she suffered from gallbladder problems), but she continued to take daily walks, dictate letters, entertain a few friends, and tend to the daily chores of life. According to Edith Lewis, "Her interest in things, her talk, were full of life and spirit. It was only her bodily strength that failed." On April 24, 1947, she died of a massive cerebral hemorrhage.

As Willa Cather's literary executor, Edith Lewis continued to live alone in their Park Avenue apartment for the next 25 years, attending to her dear friend's growing literary reputation as one of America's major writers. When Lewis died in 1972, she was buried next to Cather in Jaffrey, New Hampshire. The Nebraska writer's tombstone looms over both their graves; on it is engraved a line from *My Antonia:* ". . . this is happiness; to be dissolved in something complete and great."

COLETTE
1873–1954

Henri Gauthier-Villars, once described as "one of the most putrid wrecks of the *belle époque*," pressured his 22-year-old wife in 1895 to "write something," claiming as he usually did that there "isn't a sou in the house." Known by his pen name, Willy, Gauthier-Villars was the head of a publishing company that relied on a chain gang of ghostwriters to crank out the risqué novels, histories, memoirs, gossip, and hack journalism that was the pornography of its day. A committed bohemian who gloried in the cheap glitter of café society and the demimonde of struggling writers, artists, and entertainers, the repulsive, prematurely old Willy kept his wife dependent upon him for the small pittance he would bestow as her allowance. Yet his publishing firm, known as the "factory," was a lucrative enterprise.

On that particular day, now a watershed in the literary history of France, he badgered his young wife to write something lurid about her school days. Obediently she created a semiautobiographical heroine named Claudine, and wrote about Claudine's libertine adventures at school. Not finding it particularly suitable, Willy stuffed the manuscript in a drawer. A couple of years later he found it and realized what a fool he had been to dismiss his wife's first literary efforts so high-handedly. Two years later it was published as *Claudine at School* under his own name, Willy. And his wife, Sidonie-Gabrielle Colette, became a writer for the "factory."

During the 13 years of marriage to Willy, Colette pretended to be happy. Without friends her own age (Willy was 14 years her senior), lonely, isolated, and confused, Colette learned to be a writer. Later she would describe her marriage to Willy in terms of self-disgust: It was "a morbid thing, akin to the neuroses of puberty, the habit of eating chalk and coal, of drinking mouthwash, of reading dirty books and sticking pins into the palm of your hand."

The four Claudine novels were runaway successes; the first sold 40,000 copies in two months. The spin-offs of the "Claudine industry" included Claudine lotions, ice cream, perfumes, collars and hats, cigarettes, and postcards with Colette posing in button boots and a little schoolgirl dress. Soon the novels were dramatized, and Willy forced Colette to cut her hair like the actress who portrayed Claudine so they would look like twins. He even spread the gossip that his wife and the actress enacted the passions described in the books. Leaving no promotional stone unturned, no matter how seedy, Willy made Colette the talk of Paris.

In 1902 Colette persuaded Willy to rent a house in the country with a dozen acres where she could find some temporary respite from the cheap world of commercialism. Willy agreed, and here, alone, Colette returned in memory to her happy childhood in Burgundy where her wise, gentle mother taught her to love animals, food, gardens, the changing seasons, the days, the nights. She recalled her father, the wounded officer who served as a tax inspector for the region. She again touched the peasant roots of simplicity, decency, and innocence that would continue to undergird her life and her writings. Here Colette wrote *Dialogues de bêtes* (published in English as *Barks and Purrs*) which proved to a different kind of reader that Colette had more to describe than libertine sexual escapades. Over the next three years she rediscovered her almost animistic love of plants, the weather, landscapes, and the animals, of which she said: "Our perfect companions never have fewer than four feet."

When Colette and Willy separated in 1905, Colette began an eight-year period as a music-hall performer. Until 1913 the primary relationships in her life were women, especially Missy, the Marquise de Morny, a descendant of the Napoleonic aristocracy. Colette and Missy became lovers for six years, living together off and on, Missy sometimes accompanying Colette when she toured.

As a "tumbler," a dancer, a mime, a transvestite, and a singer, Colette found another kind of apprenticeship for her literary talent in the ambisexual world of cabaret. Her years in the lesbian communities of Paris deepened her understanding of her own femininity. She grew to value the essential "feeling of kinship" that she believed characterizes the love for one's own sex. Basing her fictional characters on the people she met and worked with, she created the myth of her own personality: the strong, independent woman very much in charge of her own emotional life.

Colette admired her lesbian friends and acquaintances, seeing them as latter-day revolutionaries, using their controversial lifestyles to demand for Frenchwomen the rights won in 1789 for Frenchmen. At the turn of the twentieth century, women were still governed by the Napoleonic Code, which made them completely subservient to husbands and fathers. They were denied career opportunities based on talent and interest. As wives they could be imprisoned for adultery, a penalty that did not apply to philandering husbands. In the androgynous drawings of the English illustrator Aubrey Beardsley, Colette discovered "what is hidden in me": the blend of masculine and feminine qualities that would be central to so many of both her male and female characters and which she would admire in the gallant lesbians she had come to know and love. It would be 25 years, however, before she would write about her lesbian relationships during this period of her life.

Her music-hall career did not interfere with her writing. In the early 1910s she published *Music-hall Sidelights* and *The Vagabond*, the latter considered for the Goncourt Prize and acclaimed as one of the 12 best French novels of the century.

In 1911 she began an affair with Henri de Jouvenel, a descendant of a baronial family dating back to the fourteenth century, and editor of the prestigious *Le Matin*. The following year they married, and once again Colette embarked upon a writing career for a husband; but this time she wrote a respectable column which eventually branched into genuine journalism. She wrote special reports on a variety of diverse topics, such as criminal trials, dirigibles and balloons, general elections, drama criticism, and cowboy films. During World War I she reported from the fields of battle, and after the war she became the newspaper's literary editor. Despite Colette's growing literary reputation, her appointment to the staff of *Le Matin* raised eyebrows. De Jouvenel's son by a previous mistress recalled: "Everyone was well aware . . . that she had been one of those half-naked dancing-girls whose naughty photographs are still preserved in certain albums."

Colette's only daughter, Bel-Gazou, was born in 1913, when Colette was 40. In two years she had gone from a music-hall dancer to a mother, from a single woman and mistress to the titled Baronne de Jouvenel des Ursins, from a woman who could move freely through the demimonde of Parisian nightlife to the wife of a man whose political career would in time make him a member of the Geneva Disarmament Commission, a senator, a delegate to the League of Nations, and Minister for Public Education.

In 1920 Colette's novel *Chéri* was published to great success; and the character of Léa, the older mistress of the young Chéri, loomed across the pages of the book and across Colette's life as an omen. "Everything one writes comes to pass," Colette said; and soon she began portraying the role of Léa in the stage version of her novel. Scandal rocked the baron's world, and, convinced that Colette was a liability to his rising political career, he walked out on her in 1923.

At age 50 Colette was once again on her own. As one of the best-known writers in France, she had offers to write for *Le Figaro, L'Eclair, Le Quotidien,* and *Le Journal.* She chose *Le Journal.* In 1929 she became drama critic for *La Revue de Paris.* Her career in journalism kept her busy until after World War II, when she became crippled with arthritis.

In 1925 she began an affair with Maurice Goudeket, a pearl dealer 16 years younger than she; they were married in 1935 in order to avoid scandal on their upcoming trip to the United States. She was 63 and happy with a man who loved her deeply.

The following year she was promoted to commander in the Legion of Honor, having been a member since 1928, the year she wrote the most lyrical of her works, *Break of Day.* Part novel, part autobiography, part meditation, it captures the beauties of the natural world in the deeply sensuous images of color, taste, sound, and smell, and the rich textural descriptions that characterize Colette's best work. Here Colette was at her best and solidly established her reputation as an introspective writer who avoided tortured self-analysis for the simple self-discoveries that can be found in rocks, bird song, clouds, and the dawn of day.

While Paris was occupied in World War II, Goudeket, who was a Jew, was imprisoned by the Gestapo. On his release he went into hiding for 18 months. Beset with worry, aging, growing increasingly arthritic, anxious about the safety of her husband, Colette continued to write. Her stories, memoirs, and essays were, as always, her life's blood. During these years of pain and disruption, she wrote one of her best-loved masterpieces, *Gigi,* a charming novel about youth, happiness, and love. In 1951 *Gigi* was adapted for Broadway; while it was still in the casting stage, Colette and Goudeket, on a spring vacation in Monte Carlo, found a delicate English actress with no stage experience filming a movie in the foyer of their hotel. Colette turned to her husband and said they needn't look any further. "This is our Gigi in America," Colette exclaimed. The young actress was Audrey Hepburn.

Colette's mature work continued to win her awards. In 1936 she was elected to the Royal Academy of Language and Literature of Belgium. In 1945 she was the first woman elected to the Goncourt Academy. Four years later she became president of that institution (meetings were held in her room because she was often confined to bed with arthritis). She became a grand officer in the Legion of Honor. The National Institute of Arts and Letters in the United States honored her with its diploma.

Years earlier, observing the opium-addicted entertainers with whom she worked, she had said: "I am hostile to those who let life burn them out." Colette was not one of them. She survived, endured, and became a national institution because she had learned how to grow and thrive even in the soil of adversity. She had learned to step back from her life to observe it and then transform her observations into great literature. In 1954 she died peacefully. Her final word to her husband was "Look!"

AMY LOWELL

1874–1925

Once when Amy Lowell was lecturing, she adjusted the reading lamp on the lectern and casually asked a woman seated in the front row if the light was in her eyes. "No," she replied, "I see another light." To many poets and writers of her generation and the succeeding ones—such as Marianne Moore, Wallace Stevens, e.e. cummings, William Carlos Williams—Amy Lowell was a bright guiding light, illuminating a trail, even as she blazed it, that would be followed by many others. As one contemporary critic put it: "She added new beauty to English poetry."

Who would have thought this shy Lowell heiress, afflicted by illness most of her life, and greatly overweight due to a glandular problem that began when she was eight, would become a "national institution," one of America's foremost poets, a celebrated and controversial figure on the American literary scene? Who would have predicted from her first book of unremarkable poems that she would repudiate the Victorian style of poetry that most critics agree had gone stale by the turn of the century, and champion a new movement called Imagism?

If it had not been for three transforming events in her life, the reluctant debutante might have remained the "empress of Brookline," well ensconced in the baronial estate of Sevenels, outside of Boston, never to become a firebrand for a new poetic sensibility.

The first event was her 1902 encounter with the famous Italian actress Eleanora Duse, whom she first saw at the Tremont Theater in Boston when she was 28 years old. Stunned by the actress's commanding performance, Lowell left the theater overwhelmed by the power of art to carve open life and reveal its mysteries and complexities. She returned for other performances and decided to dedicate her life to poetry that she hoped would have the same penetrating impact as a performance by Duse. She began to study literature and poetry seriously at the Boston Athenaeum, a private library; wrote uninspiring verse, which was published in 1912 to lackluster reviews; and joined a little-theater group for which she acted in, directed, and translated French plays. But her efforts were amorphous, her ambitions undefined. She was groping in the dark, looking for her literary niche and personal identity.

The second event occurred in 1913 when she read a strange little poem signed "H.D., Imagist." Not knowing who the mysterious H.D. was, or what the word *Imagist* meant, Lowell intuitively resonated with the new poetic form and the term *Imagist*. As she laid the poem down, she thought: *Imagist. I am too.*

Lowell studied the new poetry in Boston and, in 1913 and 1914, made two trips to England, where, because of her wealth and family reputation, she easily met the members of the new movement, *The Imagists*. The literary rebellion that was soon to transform the world of arts and letters consisted of struggling poets who met weekly in cafés and teahouses in the Soho section of London to discuss their poetry, French Impressionism, Zen Buddhism, and the rigidly stylized Japanese *haiku* verse form, as well as the need for new directions in the literary world. Regulars included Hilda Doolittle, the American poet who signed her work "H.D."; Ezra Pound, another American and one of the initiators of the movement; Richard Aldington; and John Gould Fletcher. In time Lowell took over the movement's leadership.

In 1915 the Imagists published their manifesto, which called for poetry written in the common language and utilizing what they called the *exact* word; new rhythms and free verse; absolute freedom in the choice of subject matter; the need to present and create an *image*, rather than moralize or preach; poetry that was hard and clear, never blurred or indefinite; and concentration of thought and form as the essence of poetry. Greatly influenced by Zen and Japanese *haiku* (Lowell would later translate and publish a respectable volume of Chinese poetry), the new movement would eventually become a major aesthetic and intellectual stream in art and philosophy throughout the twentieth century.

The third turning point in Lowell's life was meeting the actress Ada Dwyer Russell at a social function in 1912. As she would later write: "Between us lept a gold and scarlet flame/ . . . How it came / We guessed not, nor what thing could be its name." The poet suggested that Russell move in with her, but the actress declined because she had an acting engagement for the coming season. Still, Lowell hoped that her new friend would become a more permanent feature in her life. In her diary she wrote of Russell: "a very intimate friend, a friend whom I should love better than any other girl in the world, and who would feel so toward me. To whom I could tell all that is in my heart, and who would do so to me. We would love to be alone together, both of us."

The two women saw each other off and on over the next two years, and in 1914 Russell gave up her stage career and moved into Sevenels. They lived together until Lowell's death 11 years later.

Inspired by her love for Russell, Lowell's poetry took on new intensity: the images became sharper, her statements more honest; her work took on a new vigor. All her friends and acquaintances credited Russell for having given Lowell "a heart." Russell centered the poet, giving her someone to live for and write for. Lowell called her "Peter" or "Pete," because she thought of her as "my rock." Their relationship became a pivotal topic in Lowell's poetry. Indeed her next volume of poetry, coming out the same year the two women began living together, shows the influences of both the Imagist movement and Ada Russell. *Sword Blades and Poppy Seed* was widely read, inspiring other poets and writers to experiment freely in their own works. It was critically acclaimed and marked the beginning of Lowell's career as a serious poet. Her statements on Impressionism, radical sexual morality, a new social ethic, lesbian themes and perspectives, a more tolerant religious code, and free verse rocked the literary world.

With such a welcome reception, Lowell threw her weight (and it was considerable: she weighed 248 pounds at age 34) behind the movement. Between 1912 and 1921 she produced 12 volumes of poetry and prose and 72 essays and articles on art, poetry, creativity, and foreign influences, often in the most prestigious literary magazines. Almost single-handed she reawakened America's poetic sensibilities. She read and lectured widely. A good friend said she was like a circus barker as she lectured, wrote, or talked informally at Sevenels, shouting: "Poetry! Poetry! This way to Poetry!"

During World War I, Lowell brought out three anthologies of Imagist verse that included work of her own, as well as Aldington, Fletcher, H.D., and D. H. Lawrence. These works fueled the artistic rebellion that was changing the literary landscape in America as surely as the war was changing the political landscape of Europe. To many, the new movement implied a dangerous rebellion against social mores. The poet Robert Frost, for one, would have nothing to do with what he called "Amy's radical Bohemianism." On one occasion Lowell tried to persuade him that he was really an Imagist at heart—or should be, since it was the only legitimate way to write in the new century, but he declined the designation. Nevertheless, Frost and his wife, Elinor, remained on good terms with Lowell and Russell, and the two poets' relationship was one of mutual respect and professional kidding. Lowell was the first to review Frost's *North of Boston* in America, giving it a favorable critique in the *New Republic*.

In 1917 Lowell wrote *Tendencies in Modern American Poetry*, reviewing Frost, Edwin Arlington Robinson, Edgar Lee Masters, and Carl Sandburg, a volume that called for a new sensibility that would reject the puritan, Victorian style of poetry that was written primarily to uplift and moralize over a rigid social code. Didacticism was out. The pure poetic image and honesty of expression and sentiment were in.

Called "the most flamboyant lady in American letters," Amy Lowell slept till 2:00 P.M., ate breakfast in bed, followed by her first cigar of the day. Being the sister of the president of Harvard, Lowell kept her cigar smoking a secret until she was discovered puffing away on the deck of a ship late one night by another passenger. Word spread. Lowell decided stogies might help her growing image as an eccentric and boost sales of her next volume of poetry. So, at a time when women didn't smoke anything, Amy Lowell smoked little Manilas in public. (She ordered 10,000 at the outbreak of World War I, lest her supply be cut off by German U-boats.) She attended to business and correspondence in the afternoon, entertained or lectured in the evening (never on time; punctuality was not required of a bohemian—or an heiress, for that matter). When she made her entrance from one room to another, it was usually in the company of a pack of sheep dogs (at one time they numbered 15). She enjoyed her role as a major influence on, and arbiter of, literary taste. If anything, she hungered for more of it. "Being a soldier," she once announced, "I should wish to be a general!" Some thought she was. At midnight, when the staff of 14 and Russell retired, Lowell wrote. She preferred writing poetry far into the night, when the estate was still and her sense of communing with the spirit and nature was at its peak.

In 1916 Lowell injured her abdominal muscles in a car accident and two years later suffered a hernia. Between 1918 and 1921 she had four unsuccessful operations, after which, any movement was difficult and hazardous to her health. Nevertheless, the lady of boundless energy managed to conceal her injuries in bandages and, with a cane, faced her audiences with the apparent health and vitality they had come to expect of her.

In 1921 Lowell was invited to give the Keats centenary address at Yale. Having been a student of Keats since she was 15, Lowell had acquired the largest collection of his manuscripts in existence. She accepted, and the lecture led to her beginning a massive work on the romantic poet. She often worked 18 hours a day. By 1925 the 1,200-page *magnum opus* was complete. Immediately a best-seller, it established for the first time a sound chronology for Keats's poems and writings, as well as a credible account of his day-to-day activities. Lowell's work is still used as a reliable source by today's Keats scholars.

But the tremendous outpouring of energy took its toll. Lowell's weight went down to 159, which was thin for her. Several months after its publication, she was seated at her mirror, fixing her hair, Russell behind her to help as always. The poet felt a numbness in her hand; in the mirror, she saw one side of her face slump. "Pete," she whispered, "a stroke." She died later that day.

Lowell left the literary world one more volume, *What's O'Clock*, published posthumously that same year. It won the Pulitzer Prize. To Harvard she left her library and manuscripts. The grand estate, along with a trust fund to care for her the rest of her life, was left to Ada Russell, of whom she wrote in *Sword Blades:*

> . . . *the cup of my heart is still,*
> *And cold, and empty.*
>
> *When you come, it brims*
> *Red and trembling with blood,*
> *Heart's blood for your drinking,*
> *To fill your mouth with love*
> *And the bitter-sweet taste of a soul.*

GERTRUDE STEIN
1874–1946

It remains a small, unremarkable studio tucked away in a courtyard of 27, rue de Fleurus, near the Luxembourg Gardens in Paris, but for 35 years it stood at the crossroads of early-twentieth-century arts and letters. Here the intelligentsia of Europe and America could feast their eyes on the greatest private collection of Cubist and Fauvist paintings in the world. What mainly drew them to this address, however, was not the walls covered with the latest works of Pablo Picasso, Henry Matisse, and Georges Braque, but the woman who sat within the walls.

From 1903 to 1938, Gertrude Stein lived, wrote, and held court at 27, rue de Fleurus. In appearance she was as potentially intimidating as many of the artworks that surrounded her. She had close-cropped hair and a massive body, usually clothed in a dark robe. Her friend Jacques Lipchitz, the famous sculptor, once described her as "a sleek Buddha with a topknot." What attracted people to her were the vast reserves of intellect, courage, honesty, and humor that lay beneath this monumental façade. Through sheer force of personality she commanded the attention and respect of all who visited the Saturday at-homes she hosted with her lover, Alice B. Toklas; and her startling originality as a collector, critic, and prose stylist inspired an entire generation of painters and writers to experiment with fresher, more personal forms of self-expression.

Although Stein is so closely identified with France, she never stopped considering herself an American. "And so I am an American," she said in a 1936 lecture, "and I have lived half my life in Paris, not the half that made me but the half in which I made what I made." She was born in Allegheny, Pennsylvania, on February 3, 1874, and raised in Oakland, California. The youngest child of five in an upper-middle-class German-Jewish family, she was the object of much love and much expectation. She was pressured to excel in school, and she did. In 1893 she entered Radcliffe College, where she studied psychology under William James. Profoundly influenced by James's philosophy of pragmatism, she decided to become a psychologist herself. James urged her to acquire a strong clinical background first; and so, after graduating from Radcliffe in 1897, she enrolled at Johns Hopkins in Baltimore.

Neither the medical profession nor America was destined to offer a haven for Stein's restless spirit. In 1902 she dropped out of Johns Hopkins to accompany her brother Leo to Europe. When her school friends expressed their shock at her change in plans, her reply was characteristically blunt: "You don't know what it is to be bored." Provided with independent incomes by their generous and wealthy older brother Michael, Gertrude and Leo were soon settled at 27, rue de Fleurus in Paris, free to follow the dictates of their hearts. Leo had already launched a career as a collector and painter of modernist art; indeed, he chose their somewhat cramped studio because it offered ample northern light. Gertrude decided that she would become a modernist writer.

She based her first novel, Q.E.D., on an event that had helped to precipitate her move to Paris: her failed love affair with a Baltimore woman named May Bookstaver. In Q.E.D., Adele

(Stein) finds herself becoming more and more passionately involved with Helen (Bookstaver). At first Adele is too strait-laced to acknowledge her feelings. When Helen gives Adele a kiss "that seemed to scale the very walls of chastity," Adele is repulsed. By the end of the book, Helen has turned to another woman just as Adele has grown to love her. In a final, desperate letter to Helen, Adele makes virtually the same plea that Stein once made in a letter to Bookstaver: "I don't want you ever to deny that you care for me. The thought of your doing it again takes all the sunshine out of the sky for me. Dear I almost wish sometimes that you did not trust me so completely because then I might have some influence with you for now as you know you have my faith quite absolutely and as that is to you abundantly satisfying I lose all power of coming near you."

Perhaps Stein considered *Q.E.D.* a strictly private, therapeutic exercise, or perhaps she was reluctant to be labeled a "lesbian writer." Whatever the case *Q.E.D.* remained unpublished until after her death. Her first published work was her next novel, *Three Lives*, which appeared in 1909. *Three Lives* consists of three stories profiling two German servants and a black woman named Melanctha. In the latter story the relationship between Helen and Adele in *Q.E.D.* is recast as the heterosexual love affair between Melanctha and Jefferson Campbell (respectively). While *Three Lives* failed to attract a large popular audience, it was a resounding critical success. Her halting, repetitious style won general praise as a bold new way of capturing the rhythms of thought and experience.

Stein's distinctive style grew directly out of her association with the newly emerging coterie of abstract painters that she and her brother Leo patronized and entertained. Chief among these was Pablo Picasso, who credited Stein with engineering his early fame and who remained her devoted friend for the rest of her life. Stein, in turn, considered Picasso to be a "fellow genius" and claimed that she would "transform the novel for the 20th century as Picasso transformed painting." With the favorable reception of *Three Lives*, she seemed to be heading in the right direction.

Stein had another reason to be joyful at this time in her life. She had fallen in love with a shy, witty, and resourceful woman named Alice B. Toklas. A native of San Francisco, Toklas visited Stein in 1907 at the urging of mutual connections. Instantly the two women felt a rapport. Stein later said that Toklas had heard bells, signaling her encounter with the first of the "three unheralded geniuses" she was to meet (the other two being Picasso and the philosopher Alfred North Whitehead). According to Toklas, Stein had been struck by *"un coup de foudre"* or love at first sight.

Toklas lingered in Paris, typing Stein's manuscripts and performing other secretarial duties. In 1910 she moved in with the Steins on a permanent basis. Three years later Leo Stein moved out. The studio in the rue de Fleurus was now the happy home of a couple whose mutual care and affection continued undiminished until Stein's death. They called each other "Lovey" and "Pussy"; and while Stein was ever the dominant partner (occasionally referring to Toklas, who cooked and managed the household, as "my wife"), Toklas's constant and wondrously self-effacing support was critical to her career.

Together Stein and Toklas carved a legendary life for themselves in the years that followed—a life that was chronicled in magazines and newspapers on both sides of the Atlantic. During World War I they purchased a Ford van and distributed supplies to hospitals throughout France (Stein always drove). After the war their salon became a principal meeting place of such expatriate American writers as Ernest Hemingway, F. Scott Fitzgerald, and Sherwood Anderson, who shared Stein's interest in experimenting with literary style. Stein dubbed these Americans "the lost generation" and tutored them to be less affected and more declarative in their prose. Her informal lessons were especially instrumental in assisting Hemingway to develop the blunt, journalistic style that made his subsequent work so compelling.

Stein's personal literary efforts during this period were not widely appreciated. Since *Three Lives* her style had become increasingly unorthodox. Readers of her poems and short "word portraits" (analogous to Cubist paintings) accused her of practicing "automatic writing," citing passages such as the following fragment from her word portrait of Picasso: "This one had something being coming out of this one. This one was working. This one always had been working. This one was always having something that was coming out of this one that was a solid thing, a charming thing, a lovely thing, a perplexing thing, a disconcerting thing, a simple thing, a clear thing, a complicated thing, an interesting thing, a disturbing thing, a repellent thing, a very pretty thing."

Stein insisted that her style was not "automatic" but required a great deal of concentration and thought. Calling it "process writing," she explained that she sought "to fuse the being with the continuous present." Contemporary critics were not sympathetic. William Rose Benét of the *Saturday Review of Literature* compared her 1925 novel *The Making of Americans* to "conversations in the Tower of Babel." Edmund Wilson, reviewing the novel for *The New Republic*, complained: "With sentences so regularly rhythmical, so needlessly prolix, so many times repeated and ending so often with present participles, the reader is all too soon in a state, not to follow the slow becoming of life, but simply to fall asleep."

Everything changed with the publication of *The Autobiography of Alice B. Toklas* in 1933. Adopting a more conventional style in keeping with her pretense to be Toklas, Stein wrote about her own life and art in a frank and engaging manner that captivated her audience. By 1935 the book had run through four printings in the United States, selling almost 12,000 copies, and had reached a large popular audience through serialization in the *Atlantic Monthly*. To the American public Gertrude Stein, the celebrated eccentric, now assumed the character of an admirable, even lovable individualist.

In October 1935 Stein, accompanied as always by Toklas, embarked on a seven-month lecture tour of the United States that won her legions of new fans. She spoke on subjects ranging from art and literature to crime and newspapers with such intelligence and clarity that her previously skeptical critics were taken aback. "Why don't you write as well as you talk?" one asked. "Oh, but I do," Stein replied. "After all, it's all in learning how to read it." Defending her most famous repetitive line, "Rose is a rose is a rose is a rose," Stein said: "I'm no fool. I know that in daily life we don't go around saying 'is a . . . is a . . . is a . . .' Yes, I'm no fool; but I think that in that line the rose is red for the first time in English poetry for a hundred years."

Returning from their triumphant trip to America, Stein and Toklas resumed their pleasant life of winters in Paris and summers at their country home in Bilignin, a village near the Swiss border. Two of Stein's works, *The Geographical History of America* (1936) and *Picasso* (1939), received favorable critical attention but earned very little in sales. Her experimental style was still too rarefied to appeal to a broad spectrum of readers. During World War II, Stein and Toklas forsook Paris and took up full-time residence in Bilignin, where they patiently awaited what they called "the liberation of Gertrude Stein." It came in 1944. Stein wrote about her wartime experiences in two popular short novels, *Wars I Have Seen* and *Brewsie and Willie*, both published later that year.

After the war things were not the same. American G.I.'s who spotted Stein on the streets of Paris would shout "Hiya, Gertie!" and ask for her autograph, but she no longer had the physical stamina to entertain. On July 27, 1945, she checked into a Paris hospital to be operated on for cancer. Lying on her bed, heavily sedated, Stein turned to Toklas and murmured: "What is the answer?" Toklas, too choked up to reply, remained silent. "In that case," Gertrude said at last, "what is the question?" Shortly afterwards, she lapsed into a coma and died.

E. M.
FORSTER
1879–1970

Visitors came to Edward Carpenter's rural cottage in Derbyshire, England, to hear the "apostle of the simple life" speak on the blight of industrialization, the inadequacies of modern education; on vegetarianism, mysticism, and yoga; on the virtues of wearing sandals, and the need for sexual diversity. As the major advocate of "Whitmanism" in England, the handsome, Cambridge-educated Carpenter lived openly with his working-class lover, George Merrill. In 1912 the shy and dowdy E. M. Forster visited Carpenter.

"I was perhaps too intellectualized and mentally fidgety quite to suit him," Forster admitted. When Forster tried to answer Carpenter's questions brightly and intelligently, Carpenter replied, "Oh, do sit quiet." To Forster, Carpenter embodied the values and courage that Forster lacked, and he had come to Derbyshire for enlightenment about the love of men for men.

But ironically it was the rough-tough George Merrill who provided the flash of insight when he playfully swatted Forster's behind. "The sensation was unusual," Forster explained much later, "and I still remember it. . . . It seemed to go straight

141

through the small of my back into my ideas, without involving my thoughts. If it really did this, it would have acted in strict accordance with Carpenter's yogified mysticism, and would prove that at that precise moment I had conceived." The revelation that came with Merrill's touch was overwhelming. Suddenly Forster realized the joyful possibility of sexual love between men and the free and easy comradeship that could exist between the middle and lower classes.

Forster went home feeling that a fog had been lifted from his eyes, that a seed, planted in the womb of his imagination, was ready to sprout. What Forster had conceived was *Maurice*, his only homosexual novel, which he wrote over the next year and showed only to a few friends. Some of them criticized the impossibly euphoric ending, in which the upper-middle-class protagonist, Maurice, falls in love with Alec, a gamekeeper, and gives up his urban respectability to live with his lower-class lover in rural bliss. But Forster refused to tinker with the ending, even though he continued to rewrite sections of the novel up to his death. After all, he figured, Carpenter and Merrill stayed together for life, as did Forster's friend the writer William Plomer and his working-class lover. Lacking the courage to go public about his gay identity, Forster believed that *Maurice* would have to remain unpublished "until my death or England's."

The world of Maurice was the world Forster had dreamed about since childhood. He grew up in a confining female world of wealthy aunts, spinsters, and, most important of all, his mother, with whom he lived until she died in 1945. He longed to unite his two obsessions of sex with boys and the spontaneous emotions of the lower classes. His only outlet was the one day a week he was allowed to play with the garden boys. His favorite, Ansell, lent his name to a character in Forster's later novel *The Longest Journey* and to the title of a 1902 short story whose theme prefigured *Maurice*.

Forster's public-school days were a nightmare. He was constantly mocked and bullied by other boys because he was a day student. As late as 1933 he was still bitter about the English educational system. "School was the unhappiest time of my life," he wrote. In a mock speech to students, he promised: "My last words to you are: 'There's a better time coming.'" For Forster, the English public-school system bred snobbery, philistinism, and racial and class consciousness, and did nothing to heal "the undeveloped heart," a major theme of Forster's work.

At Cambridge he became a member of the Apostles, an elite society of freethinking students, and later he participated in the Bloomsbury group of writers, artists, and intellectuals. In both groups he discovered how liberating open-ended discussion and verbal sparring could be in a stuffy age that refused to talk openly about so many topics, especially sex and any opinion deemed unorthodox.

From 1901 to 1912 Forster found his identity as a writer. On a journey to Italy with his mother, he had his first literary epiphany, which resulted in "The Story of a Panic," an allegory about Forster's own sexual awakening. He also soaked up impressions of scenery, personalities, and customs for his novel *A Room with a View*. In the same decade he served as a tutor for a countess in Germany; and later, in England, he tutored the wealthy Indian Syed Ross Masood, with whom he became close friends. Tutoring, he found, gave him time to develop the ideas that were soon to flower in a series of successful novels: *Where Angels Fear to Tread* (1905), *The Longest Journey* (1907), *A Room with a View* (1908), *Howards End* (1910); and *Maurice* (1914), which he wrote for his own enjoyment.

Throughout these years Forster searched for the "ideal male friend," a search that would color his affectionate longings for most of his life. Although he had plenty of literary friends and admirers, their own sexual preferences were heterosexual or simply did not extend to E. M. Forster. With the exception of a few casual acquaintances, Forster's friends did not provide outlets for his sexual needs.

In 1912 he went to India, where Masood now lived, and while visiting him he was shocked by the festering Anglo-Indian conflict. He began writing about it on his return, but he did not understand it sufficiently until his second trip to India in 1921. During World War I he worked for the Red Cross in Egypt, where he also encountered the condescending British attitude toward colonial peoples, an attitude resulting in exploitative, bungling policies that destroyed the native population's spirit and dignity. After he returned from his second trip to India, his ideas crystallized and he was able to finish his masterpiece on the subject, *A Passage to India*.

After *A Passage to India*, Forster stopped gathering material for fiction. When asked by his friends why he was not working on something, he replied: "I have nothing more to say." He felt that England and the world had changed so enormously that he could no longer understand them imaginatively. But Forster's voice was not silenced. Instead he turned to essays and articles and other forms of nonfiction (radio broadcasts, reviews, speeches), which undoubtedly influenced more people than did his novels.

Between the wars Forster became a sage, a voice speaking for humanism and decency, an advocate for human rights, and a literate foe of hypocrisy and injustice. "We can't build as we like or drink when we like or dress as we like. . . . We can't say what we like—there is this legend of free speech but you try it on: free speech and saying what you want to say are very different things," he argued boldly, keenly aware of all the things he would have liked to say, especially about himself, but lacked the courage to say them.

In 1928 the government suppressed the lesbian novel *The Well of Loneliness* by Radclyffe Hall, not because of obscenity, but simply because of its theme: love between women. Forster agreed to be a witness at the trial. With Virginia Woolf he wrote a letter decrying the government's attempt to prevent writers from writing about a subject solely because the literary censors did not approve. In the end the magistrate refused to call any witnesses and, on his sole authority, pronounced the book obscene. Later, in 1960, Forster got a second chance to appear in an obscenity trial when he spoke as a witness for D. H. Lawrence's *Lady*

Chatterley's Lover, a test case under a new publications law that required the court to hear expert witnesses. Forster testified with other literary figures, and the court found that the novel had redeeming interest and therefore should not be banned.

In 1927 Forster joined P.E.N. (International Association of Poets, Playwrights, Editors, Essayists, and Novelists) and became very active in the organization over the next few decades, crusading for the notion that "the creative impulse . . . existed before nationality was invented and . . . will continue to exist when that dubious invention has been scrapped." Forster's defense of human and civil rights led him in 1946 to speak out even against P.E.N., however, when the organization wanted to blacklist writers who had supported the Nazis. Forster knew personally the threat of blacklisting, having been on the Nazis' blacklist.

Throughout the middle of the twentieth century, Forster raised his voice for decency, human liberty, and the recognition of honest emotion as opposed to accepted behavior. He spoke out against Stalinism, Nazi Germany, the curtailing of civil liberties in Britain during the war, and the destruction of the English countryside by spreading urbanization. When confronted with the postwar movement to impose secrecy in public affairs on the pretext of national security, he asked: "How can we try to improve the world when we do not know what the world is like?"

In 1934 and in 1942 he was president of the National Council for Civil Liberties; he also served as president of the Humanist Society. On his last visit to India for P.E.N., in 1945, he warned Indian writers about becoming subservient to political agendas. He recalled: "When I spoke about the necessity of form in literature and the importance of the individual vision, their attention wandered. . . . Literature, in their view, should expound or inspire a political creed."

Throughout the latter half of his life, Forster enjoyed the friendship of Bob Buckingham, a policeman whom he had met in 1929, when he was 51, and Bob was 28. In Buckingham he found the working-class companion he had long dreamed of. Even after Buckingham's marriage, Forster stayed on friendly terms with the Buckinghams, shared important holidays with the family, stayed with them on many occasions, and contributed financially to their only son Rob's education. When Rob died of Hodgkin's disease in 1962 at age 29, he left behind a young wife and two sons who had each been given Morgan as a middle name, in honor of their grandfather's best friend, Edward Morgan Forster.

In the 1960s, *A Passage to India*, *A Room with a View*, *Where Angels Fear to Tread*, and *Howards End* were successfully adapted for the stage. In the 1980s critically acclaimed film versions of *A Passage to India* and *A Room with a View* were produced.

Forster suffered a series of strokes in his later years and died peacefully in 1970 at the Buckinghams', where his ashes were scattered over their rose garden. The following year *Maurice* was published. In 1987 it became a motion picture: one of the biggest and boldest film productions ever made that dealt with the theme of homosexuality.

VIRGINIA WOOLF

1882–1941

"Who's afraid of Virginia Woolf?" asks Edward Albee in the title of his 1962 play. During her lifetime almost everyone around Virginia Woolf was afraid of her at one time or another. She was a shrewd judge of character, and the satirical portraits that she worked into her writings frequently embarrassed their models. "I am alarmed by my own cruelty with my friends," she once confessed in her diary. Today it's her readers who are inclined to be afraid of her. They're intimidated by the sheer originality of her writing style— a poetic and highly allusive style that defies all narrative conventions. Yet, despite her sharp wit, Virginia Woolf was a very caring and vulnerable human being. And shining through her demanding literary technique is an extraordinary sensitivity to the human heart.

In polite Victorian English society a woman risked being fearsome if she displayed any independence at all, and Virginia Woolf was raised to be independent. Her father, Leslie Stephen, was a distinguished man of letters (among other accomplishments he edited the *Dictionary of National Biography*) and was an

147

outspoken agnostic. Rather than send his clever younger daughter Virginia to school, he gave her the run of his enormous library, and she read voraciously throughout her childhood and adolescence. It was her joy as well as her solace: Virginia was a shy, gaunt girl who craved far more affection than she received. She grew up in the shadow of her beautiful older sister, Vanessa, and her mother's death in 1885 dealt the awkward 3-year-old a blow from which she never recovered. Thereafter she turned to her sister and various other women for emotional reinforcement, and most of her novels extol the maternal figure as a source of goodness and power.

Difficult as it had been for Virginia Stephen to accept her mother's death, the loss of her father in 1904 caused an even more severe trauma. He had been an incredibly forceful presence in her life: a stern critic, a setter of high standards, and a man of strict working habits that she imitated slavishly. When he died she suffered a complete nervous breakdown and remained, as her doctor termed it, "neurasthentic" for the rest of her life. Her sister, Vanessa, and her two brothers, Thoby and Adrian, nursed her through her breakdown, and then all four of them moved out of the family home in fashionable Kensington to Gordon Square, Bloomsbury.

Moving to Bloomsbury was a bold act, especially for a woman whose mental health was frail, for Bloomsbury was considered a shabby and disreputable area of London. Her relatives were aghast, and they were shocked even more by the unconventional social life that the Stephen children began to conduct a year later. Thoby Stephen was in the habit of inviting his friends from Cambridge to use the Bloomsbury house as a second home. Eventually a regular crowd of visitors dubbed themselves the "Bloomsbury group" and set each Thursday as a day for discussing all sorts of topics that were controversial at the time, from new art forms to radical politics to sexual freedom.

Over the years the Bloomsbury group grew to encompass a host of influential young talents. In addition to Virginia Stephen herself, who started gaining fame in 1905 as a book reviewer for the *Times Literary Supplement*, and Vanessa, who was a promising avant-garde painter, the group included the writers Lytton Strachey and E. M. Forster, the painters Duncan Grant and Roger Fry, the economist and Cambridge don John Maynard Keynes, and, on the outer fringe, the poet T. S. Eliot, whom they all liked but found faintly ridiculous for his pedantry.

Another member of the Bloomsbury group—indeed, one of its founders—was Leonard Woolf, a longtime friend of Thoby Stephen. Recognizing an especially strong intellectual kinship, Virginia and Leonard married in 1912. For all their compatibility on a mental level, however, their marriage was not destined to be successful on a physical level. After a disastrous honeymoon Virginia Woolf declared herself to be "sexually frigid" and wrote to one of her women friends: "I might still be Miss S. Why do you think people make such a fuss about marriage and copulation?" In 1913 her despair over her self-described "sexual problem" led her to attempt suicide with a lethal dose of Veronal. Recuperating from the attempt, she resolved to make the best of things. Leonard Woolf was willing to accept a marriage without sex, and so they settled into a mutually supportive partnership that made up in domestic affection what it lacked in passion.

In 1917 the Woolfs founded the Hogarth Press, a modest enterprise designed to publish works of unusual merit that might not attract the more established houses. It was a phenomenal success, and after a few years the profits enabled the Woolfs to entertain more extensively, sponsor struggling artists, travel frequently in Europe, and buy a country house at Rodmell in Sussex. More and more the Woolfs became arbiters of literary taste in the English-speaking world between the wars; and their main residence, still in Bloomsbury, served as a virtual clubhouse for the most creative minds of the time.

As the Hogarth Press flourished, Virginia Woolf gained stature as a writer. Her first two novels, *The Voyage Out* (1915) and *Night and Day* (1919), were well received but did not generate much excitement—they were, after all, very traditional in form. Her 1921 sketches *Monday or Tuesday*, on the other hand, caused a sensation. She had found her own voice: an impressionistic one that speaks mainly of the interior consciousness of her characters rather than of the exterior events in their lives. Over the next 20 years she produced an extraordinary series of novels that gave vent to that voice: *Jacob's Room* (1922), *Mrs. Dalloway* (1925), *To the Lighthouse* (1927), *The Waves* (1931), *The Years* (1937), and *Between the Acts* (1941). Many critics have traced a similarity between Woolf's literary voice and the shimmering pointillism of her sister Vanessa's painting style, citing such passages as the following one from her last novel, *Between the Acts:*

> The little boy had lagged and was grouting in the grass. . . .
> The flower blazed between the angles of the roots. Membrane after membrane was torn. It blazed a soft yellow, a lambent light under a film of velvet; it filled the caverns behind the eyes with light. All that inner darkness became a hall, leaf smelling, earth smelling, of yellow light. And the tree was beyond the flower; the grass, the flower and the tree were entire. Down on his knees grubbing he held the flower complete.

In addition to book reviews, novels, and sketches, Woolf's literary output was prodigious. She had a compulsive need to record her thoughts and feelings in writing, and the result is a wealth of fascinating essays, diaries, letters, and miscellaneous nonfiction works. Many of these writings directly discuss the feminist movement that came into being during Woolf's lifetime. Outraged at being labeled a "bluestocking authoress" by the predominantly male literary establishment, Woolf actively supported women's rights and a general social liberation from male and female stereotypes. Her 1929 essay *A Room of One's Own* is perhaps her strongest single feminist statement, but the spirit of feminism informs all of her major writings, particularly her novels, which argue for "complementary" rather than "role-divided" unions between men and women. For this argument alone her novels are unique in their era.

One of Woolf's works, however, stands apart from all the others in terms of its novelty: the fantastical entertainment *Orlando* (1928), which she wrote as a celebration of her love for a woman, Vita Sackville-West. Woolf first met Sackville-West at a social gathering in 1922 and immediately became enchanted with the person and the history behind the person. Sackville-West had grown up at Knole, the largest and, in many respects, one of the noblest houses in England still in private hands. Like Woolf, she was a free spirit intellectually and was comfortably married to a man with whom she did not have sex (her husband, Harold Nicolson, was a homosexual, and they ceased to have sexual relations after the birth of their son, Nigel). Unlike Woolf, she was an extrovert who reveled in the more robust aspects of life. As Woolf admitted in her diary:

> I like her and being with her and the splendour—she shines in the grocer's shop in Sevenoaks with a candle lit radiance, stalking on legs like beech trees, pink glowing, grape clustered, pearl hung. . . . What is the effect of all this on me? . . . There is her maturity and full breastedness; her being so much in full sail on the high tides, where I am coasting down backwaters; her capacity to take the floor in any company, to represent her country. . . her being in short (what I have never been) a real woman.

The sexual aspect of Woolf's relationship with Sackville-West was over within a year, but the emotional ties remained in place until Woolf's death. *Orlando* is a mythical epic inspired by Sackville-West (with her picture on the original dust jacket) that her son, Nigel Nicolson, describes as

> the longest and most charming love letter in literature, in which she [Woolf] explores Vita, weaves her in and out of the centuries, tosses her from one sex to the other, plays with her, dresses her in furs, lace and emeralds, teases her, flirts with her, drops a veil of mist around her, and ends by photographing her in the mud at Long Barn, with dogs, awaiting Virginia's arrival next day.

As happy and productive as Woolf's relationship with Sackville-West was, it could not prevent Woolf from succumbing to fits of rage, melancholy, and depression with increasing frequency as she grew older and the world around her grew more bellicose. When the Battle of Britain began in 1940, she retreated to Rodmell and seldom ventured out. On March 28, 1941, the "monstrous agony of the world" was too much for her to bear any longer. She loaded her pockets with stones, walked into the river Ouse, and drowned.

JOHN MAYNARD KEYNES
1883–1946

John Maynard Keynes and Duncan Grant spent two months in the summer of 1907 in the Orkney Islands off the coast of Scotland. Grant sketched and painted; Keynes wrote about the theory of probability. Their Bloomsbury friend Lytton Strachey called the holiday their "honeymoon." Strachey, who was also in love with Grant, hoped the affair would cool. It didn't. Keynes and Grant remained on intimate terms until 1914.

After they returned from their "honeymoon," professional duties frequently kept the two lovers apart. Contrary to the common folk wisdom, Keynes's obsession with his absent lover did not inspire or facilitate his dissertation on probability. He wrote Grant: "I seem to be getting very little work done, which is a pity, as I tend to spend almost the whole day being in love with you. Probability, I find, will not drive you out of my mind and does not occupy it jointly very well." In 1909 they took an apartment in the Bloomsbury area of London, where Grant, fast becoming a major figure in the English Postimpressionist movement, set up his studio and where Keynes could stay when he came down from Cambridge University.

Always a man of feeling and intellect, Keynes was usually able to unite the two. The philosopher Bertrand Russell, who knew him at Cambridge, noted: "Keynes's intellect was the sharpest and clearest that I have ever known. When I argued with him, I felt that I took my life in my hands, and I seldom emerged without feeling something of a fool. I was sometimes inclined to feel that so much cleverness must be incompatible with depth, but I do not think this feeling was justified." In spite of the distractions of a separated lover, Keynes managed to complete his thesis on probability. It won him a fellowship at King's College in 1908, whereupon he resigned the position at the India Office in Whitehall that he had held for two years after graduating from Cambridge.

Maynard Keynes was always at home in Cambridge. His father, John Neville Keynes, a logician and economist, was registrar at Cambridge. His mother, Florence Ada Keynes, was one of the first women to graduate from Cambridge and later became mayor of the town. Keynes, a gifted child, pursued the typical educational route of the upper middle class. At Eton, the educational symbol of the British ruling class, he won a reputation among his peers for managing student organizations with great efficiency. He wrote his father from Eton: "I am finding that, like you, when I am appointed to a committee, I am inevitably made to do all the work." And he did it well.

At King's College he became a member of the Apostles, a secret undergraduate society of 12 students dedicated to truth, unworldiness, and self-development through an association with each other marked by absolute candor. Here he met the writer Lytton Strachey and, through him, the famous "Bloomsbury group" of young intellectuals. In a 1905 letter to Strachey, he wrote: "I find economics increasingly satisfactory, and I think that I am rather good at it. I want to manage a railway or organize a trust. . . . It is so easy and fascinating to master the principles of these things."

Keynes valued his friendships in the Bloomsbury group and shared their interests throughout his life. He also shared their sense that they were different from others, more open and honest about their feelings and less inhibited about expressing opinions on any range of topics from one's personal sexuality to politics. Within this creative atmosphere he learned to appraise critically the widespread cant and hypocrisy within the major institutions of English life: the monarchy, the church, the educational system, the army, the stock exchange. Years later Keynes would continue to use members of the group as sounding boards and sources of creative ideas on the important issues of the day.

When World War I broke out, Keynes was working in the British Treasury, where his duties eventually included the economic management of the war. During these years he met and made friends with the highest officials in the government and came to know many prominent members of society. By the end of the war, he was facilitating foreign exchange arrangements and negotiations with the Allies. As a delegate from the British Treasury to the Paris Peace Conference, he opposed the controversial reparations clauses attached to the Versailles Treaty. He wrote his father that the reparations demanded of Germany would constitute "the devastation of Europe." He called the war debts "a menace to financial stability everywhere." Because of these objections he resigned from the peace commission in 1919.

The same year, he published *The Economic Consequences of the Peace*, which argued for the economic unity of Europe, exposed the selfishness on the part of the Allies in framing the reparations, and demonstrated how the enormous sum involved was not only unrealistic but devastating to world economic stability. Keynes predicted accurately that the reparations would never be paid. He also drew scathing character sketches of the Big Four: Woodrow Wilson, David Lloyd George, Georges Clemenceau, and Vittorio Orlando. The work became a best-seller in economics and brought Keynes international fame. Throughout the 1920s he wrote on the dire effects of the treaty, the need for revising it, and the vital issue of reconstructing Europe. He also dealt with the origins and effects of high unemployment and the problems of deflation in postwar currencies.

But the twenties weren't all devoted to the "dismal science" of economics. Keynes found time to court and marry Lydia Lopokova, a Russian ballerina who was currently enjoying a successful career in Europe and America. Promoted by the Russian impresario Sergei Diaghilev, Lopokova performed in England, where she met Keynes in 1918. Keynes began taking her to Bloomsbury parties and in time began advising her financially, making investments for her, and negotiating dance contracts. Called a "will-o'-the-wisp dancer" by the *New York Times*, Lopokova impressed audiences and friends with her dainty, exuberant charm. Although many of Keynes's Cambridge associates thought her nothing but a "chorus girl"—and a Russian, to boot!—friends who knew him well thought marrying Lopokova in 1925 was "the best thing Maynard ever did." Lopokova continued to act and dance after they were married, and, sharing her interests in theater, Keynes was instrumental in 1936 in establishing and promoting the Cambridge Art Theater.

In the 1930s Keynes published two monumental works on economics, comparable in importance to Adam Smith's *Wealth of Nations*, in which he devised a new economic framework for twentieth-century capitalism. His *Treatise on Money* (1930) and *The General Theory of Employment, Interest and Money* (1936) revolutionized economic theory and practice in western democracies. Keynes's proposal was that income and employment levels depend directly on private and public expenditures. This was a radical departure from the classical economic theory, espoused by Adam Smith, that had ruled since the eighteenth century. Basically, Smith advocated a laissez-faire policy on the part of the government. He argued that the collective effort of individuals seeking their own gain would assure the best use of resources and best meet consumer needs. In other words, if government kept hands off a nation's economy, time and nature would assure prosperity.

In the darkest days of the Depression, it became clear to government officials, economists, and the average man and woman that these traditional policies were bankrupt. Lowering wages and slashing prices did not restore the western democracies' economies. New explanations and policies were urgently needed to preserve the capitalist system and promote economic recovery.

Keynes offered two major propositions. First, existing theories of unemployment were no longer applicable. Lower wages would not eliminate unemployment. Second, the origins of unemployment and the Depression were to be found in the aggregate economic activities of consumers, business investors, and public agencies. When the aggregate demand was low, sales and jobs suffered; when aggregate demand was high, sales and jobs would bounce back. This was a new view of economic behavior. Keynes argued that, contrary to traditional theory, consumers had relatively little power to influence business cycles; hence, consumer activity—or lack of it—was not responsible for economic slumps or recoveries. The major influences on economic cycles were business investors and government policies. Keynes suggested that easier credit and lower interest rates might stimulate business investment and restore the aggregate demands for goods and services. In very hard times governments might inaugurate more severe remedies, such as public works and subsidies to the groups hardest hit by the Depression.

In a relatively short time Keynes convinced his colleagues and the international economic community of the value of his proposals. By World War II the western democracies had become committed to the goal of maintaining high employment. In 1946, for example, the United States passed the Employment Act, which mandated that Congress and the president maintain prosperity by governmental policies. To many critics the terms "Keynesian" and "New Deal" became odiously synonymous, but President Roosevelt was always a "reluctant Keynesian." By 1940, however, Keynesian economics had swept the field of younger economists, who would in time become part of the decision-making circles at the highest levels of government.

During World War II, Keynes was made a member of the House of Lords and given the title Baron Keynes of Tilton. Lord and Lady Keynes made six trips to the United States on which Keynes worked for Anglo-American cooperation and the creation of international monetary alliances to prevent financial chaos after the war. In 1944 Keynes participated in the Bretton Woods meeting in New Hampshire, which created the International Monetary Fund and the International Bank for Reconstruction and Development, commonly called the World Bank. Keynes was later appointed a governor of these institutions.

After a heart attack in 1937, Keynes was never again in perfect health. The trips to America and the intense negotiations overstrained him—as did the Washington social circuit. He wrote in a letter: "In the first five weeks here I lunched and dined out forty-seven times, which really is service at the front and certainly not more dangerous than the blitz. However, health stands up to it, and indeed I haven't felt so well for years. . . . Yet I shouldn't have survived without Lydia, who provides constant rest, discipline, and comfort." However, after an exceptionally frustrating meeting in Savannah, Georgia, in March 1946, Keynes suffered a heart attack on the train leaving the conference. Back home in England he suffered another heart attack after breakfast on Easter Sunday, and died.

In spite of his close marriage, Keynes remained a member of the Bloomsbury group, open about his bisexuality, and dedicated to tolerance and acceptance of each individual's uniqueness. Along with the men and women of Bloomsbury, whose goals blended service and reform with enjoyment and gaiety, Keynes could always see through the self-important poses in others as well as in himself. In the true spirit of Bloomsbury, he admitted late in life that he had only one regret: that he hadn't drunk more champagne.

T. E.
LAWRENCE
1888–1935

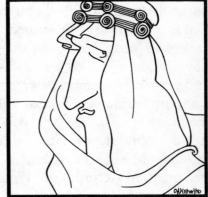

During the Paris Peace Conference following World War I, T. E. Lawrence was asked about his presence there and what his motives were. He answered: "Personal. I liked a particular Arab, and I thought that freedom for the race would be an acceptable present." The particular Arab whom Lawrence liked, however, was dead. Working as a spy for Lawrence behind enemy lines, the young boy, Dahoum, disappeared in 1916; and his fate remained unknown until 1918, when he died of typhoid fever.

Lawrence met Dahoum in 1911 while on an archeological study of Hittite settlements on the Euphrates River. The Middle East had fascinated Lawrence since his student days at Oxford, where he had studied medieval military architecture. In 1909 he visited Syria and Palestine to study castles constructed during the Crusades to liberate the Holy Land from Moslem control. From 1911 to 1914 Lawrence traveled in the Arab world, learned the languages, and studied the peoples and their customs. Later he wrote: "The Arab appealed to my imagination. It is the old, old civilization which has refined itself clear of household gods, and half the trappings which ours hastens to assume."

One of the water boys on the Hittite excavation was the 15-year-old Dahoum. According to Sir Leonard Woolley, with whom Lawrence explored the Sinai Desert, Dahoum was "not particularly intelligent . . . but beautifully built and remarkably handsome." Everyone seemed to agree on Dahoum's physique and good looks; many disagreed on his lack of intelligence. In time Dahoum worked his way up to being Lawrence's houseboy and personal assistant. Lawrence taught him photography, and Dahoum became invaluable to Lawrence on archeological and intelligence missions. The two became inseparable and wandered around the desert together, exploring terrains, studying the magnificent scenery and vistas that captivated Lawrence's imagination. According to Woolley, even the Arabs, who take intimate male friendships in stride, were mildly amused by the intense relationship of the young Englishman and his Arab friend.

In 1914 Lawrence and Dahoum accompanied Woolley on an exploration of the Sinai along the Turkish frontier, a trip sponsored by the Palestine Exploration Fund. Ostensibly a mapping expedition, the team was actually engaged in espionage, noting Turkish strongholds and preparing a military map to be used in the event of hostilities. The cover study, however, was jointly published by Woolley and Lawrence in 1915 as *The Wilderness of Zin*.

Lawrence took Dahoum back to England with him. When war broke out in 1914, Lawrence found himself in the map department of the London War Office; in December he and Dahoum returned to Egypt, assigned to Intelligence. Lawrence's knowledge of languages, customs, and the terrain qualified him to work behind enemy lines (Turkey, which controlled the Arab world at that time, was allied with Germany). Drawing from his espionage activities, Lawrence prepared a handbook on the Turkish army for British forces.

In 1916 he went to Arabia, then in revolt against Turkish oppression. He met with the Emir Feisal, son of Sherif Hussein, and persuaded his own superiors to aid Feisal's efforts against the Turks around the city of Medina, a Turkish stronghold. It was Lawrence's belief that the British could capitalize on the Arabs' desire for independence as part of the British strategy against Turkey. Soon he joined Feisal's army as a political and liaison officer with the British operating in the Middle East.

Lawrence's major role was that of military technician for the Arab uprising. He supervised hit-and-run missions behind enemy lines, mining bridges and destroying supply trains. His major goal was to obstruct the Hejaz railway, the primary supply line between Damascus and Medina. Among the many names he was given by his Arab friends was Emir Dynamite. In the course of the operations, Lawrence received 32 wounds. His personal heroism inspired others, as did his kingmaker's vision of an Arab nation. In addition to winning support by his personal bravery, he garnered Arab support with promises of British aid and money.

In July 1917 Lawrence's Arab forces seized Aqaba. In November, while operating behind Turkish lines near Der'a disguised as a Circassian, Lawrence was captured and brutally tortured. He was flogged, knifed, and sodomized by Anatolian peasant soldiers, an experience that never ceased to haunt and disturb him. But he never revealed his true identity, and he finally managed to escape and return to safety. In October 1918, in joint maneuvers with General Allenby, Lawrence and his troops marched to Damascus, arriving ahead of the British forces. For the first time in 400 years, the ancient city was freed from Turkish rule.

Lawrence, however, was physically and emotionally exhausted. In his student days he had practiced torturous physical self-discipline to toughen his body, fasting for two or three days, marching cross-country in the winter, climbing or swimming every obstacle he encountered, riding his bicycle nonstop until he collapsed by the roadside. During his military operations he displayed remarkable self-confidence, will power, and physical strength. But he pushed himself to the breaking point too often.

At the end of the war, Lieutenant Colonel Lawrence was offered the Distinguished Service Order. But at a royal audience with King George V, he refused the award along with an earldom on the grounds that since the British were not upholding their promises to the Arabs, it would not be right for him to accept the honors. King George was shocked at Lawrence's refusal and claimed that the famed desert soldier left him "holding the box in my hand."

At the Paris Peace Conference, Lawrence wore Arab dress and served as interpreter for King Feisal. Caught in the postwar bickering over mandates in the Middle East, Lawrence was continually frustrated in arguing the Arabs' cause. The Middle East was not much more than a sideshow in the western nations' attempts to redraw the map of Europe. Lawrence lobbied in vain against detaching Syria and Lebanon from the Arab hegemony and turning them into a French mandate. British interests, however, in Palestine and elsewhere, required that they appease the French, and so the Arab interests were given short shrift. Some observers mistakenly thought Lawrence was favoring a united Arab state, a plan which he called "a madman's notion for this century or the next probably." But caught as a double agent, expecting to represent both British interests as well as those of his Arab friends, he found the negotiations increasingly frustrating. Disillusioned, he left feeling that both sides had let him down and that he, in turn, had let his friends down.

At the end of the war, Lowell Thomas, an American correspondent operating in London, launched an illustrated lecture series on the Middle East, which in a short time became a one-subject show: the romantic exploits of Lawrence of Arabia. The war lectures inaugurated the "selling" of T. E. Lawrence as a modern hero. British audiences were amazed and wondered why they had not heard of this hero before. Why did an American know about him, and not the British? Amused, Lawrence himself went to the lectures several times, both embarrassed by the spectacle that was being made of him, and secretly fascinated by the romantic aura that was quickly growing up around his name. On some level he realized that he was as much responsible for the romantic myth as was the American journalist.

The last 15 years of Lawrence's life are puzzling and enigmatic. He never married; he preferred the company of men. He had a circle of friends, but no one seemed to hold a special place in his life. He did not handle fame gracefully. "I am trying to accustom myself to the truth," he wrote, "that probably I'll be talked over for the rest of my life; and after my life too." And he was not happy about it. He returned to the Middle East as a consultant to Winston Churchill, who was colonial minister, during the ensuing rebellions and political disorders that erupted in the wake of the peace treaty. Growing increasingly bitter that the wartime promises to the Arabs were not being kept, Lawrence rejected all further government positions and tried to disappear into obscurity.

He enlisted in the Royal Air Force under the name John Hume Ross, giving up his £1,200 salary in the Colonial Office for the aircraftsman's wage of two shillings and ninepence a day. The London press discovered his whereabouts and revealed his presence at the air base where he was stationed. Later he again tried to disappear into the ranks and, with the help of a friend, enlisted in the Royal Tank Corps under the name T. E. Shaw, which he legalized in 1927. He was based at a camp in Dorset, where he continued to live for the rest of his life in a cottage called Clouds Hill.

His autobiographical account of his exploits in the desert, *The Seven Pillars of Wisdom*, a 330,000-word history, was published in a lavishly bound and illustrated volume in 1926. An action-packed narrative filled with colorful incidents and spectacles and rich character portrayals of the individuals Lawrence knew, the work also dealt with the author's own personal transformation. *The Seven Pillars* is as much the story of one man's spiritual journey as it is of the repeated journeys he made from one end of the desert to the other. The following year, to defray the cost of the work, Lawrence followed the advice of his postwar friends E. M. Forster and George Bernard Shaw and brought out a shortened edition, only 130,000 words, titled *Revolt in the Desert*.

He also wrote *The Mint*, a fictionalized account of the problems involved in his RAF training, a work that embarrassed and horrified the government, and did an English translation of the *Odyssey*, which he published in 1932 under the name Shaw. He wrote a friend shortly thereafter: "Have I done my best, do you think? . . . May I rest now? All the heat in me is gone out, and the endurance that was tougher than other men's." During his final years, living quietly at Clouds Hill, he designed, tested, and wrote technical manuals for high-speed naval boats for the RAF. He occasionally entertained a circle of friends that included E. M. Forster, the artist Eric Kennington, George Bernard Shaw, and Shaw's wife, Charlotte, who was his most trusted confidante over the last 13 years of his life.

He retired at 46 and wondered what he would do with the rest of his life. To Lady Astor, an old friend, he wrote: "There is something broken in the works . . . my will, I think." The artist man-of-action who withdrew from politics and the world to live a life of relative obscurity was demoralized and dejected. His final years were filled with self-doubt, shame, and a sense of guilt. In 1929 he wrote: "I have done with politics, I have done with the Orient, and I have done with intellectuality. O Lord, I am so tired! I want so much to lie down and sleep and die. . . . Die is best because there is no reveille. I want to forget my sins and the world's weariness."

In May 1935, while riding his motorcycle, Lawrence swerved to avoid hitting two delivery boys on bicycles, was flung over his handlebars, and landed on the road. He lingered in a coma for six days and died. About a week before, he had written to Eric Kennington: "What I have done, what I am doing, what I am going to do, puzzle and bewilder me. Have you ever been a leaf and fallen from your tree in the autumn and been really puzzled about it? That's the feeling."

Later, at the unveiling of Kennington's bust of Lawrence in Saint Paul's Cathedral, Lord Halifax speculated: "I cannot doubt some deep religious impulse moved him . . . some craving for the perfect synthesis of thought and action which alone could satisfy his test of ultimate truth and his conception of life's purpose."

LUDWIG WITTGENSTEIN

1889–1951

Ludwig Wittgenstein was living in seclusion in a cabin he built for himself in Skjolden, Norway, when World War I broke out. The brilliant philosophy student had studied with Bertrand Russell at Cambridge University from 1911 to 1913. Russell claimed that knowing the wealthy young Austrian was "one of the most exciting intellectual adventures" of his life and that Wittgenstein "soon knew all that I had to teach." And then Wittgenstein tired of the intellectual atmosphere of Cambridge and wanted to distance himself from the sexual temptations of the university town. Versed in the psychological theories of the day that attributed promiscuous sexual activity to a decline in intellectual energy and genius, Wittgenstein hoped that a remote cabin in Norway would prevent him from frequenting the homosexual haunts to which he was attracted all his life. In the spring of 1914, G. E. Moore, the popular professor who dominated philosophy at Cambridge and whose chair Wittgenstein would fill in 1939, visited him in his hut. Wittgenstein talked; Moore took notes.

After the outbreak of hostilities, Wittgenstein returned to Austria and enlisted in the army. He served on the Russian front, where he won several decorations for bravery. Later, trained as an artillery officer, he was transferred to the Italian front, where he was captured and imprisoned. Throughout the war he carried a notebook in his rucksack and jotted down ideas whenever time allowed. He sent the slim, 75-page manuscript to Bertrand Russell, whose influence got it published in 1921 as *Tractatus Logico-Philosophicus*. It was a strange little book, destined to revolutionize philosophy.

The *Tractatus* consisted of remarks and observations, ordered and numbered by a decimal system, covering such topics as the nature of language, logic, ethics, philosophy, causality, the self and the will, mysticism, death, good and evil. But Wittgenstein's primary concern was the nature of reality and language. How is it, he asked, that language is possible, that human beings speak sentences and can be understood?

He suggested that the world is made of simple objects and that a sentence is a picture made up of the names that stand for those objects in the external world; and because each sentence and that to which it refers are understood as being related, they must each have the same form. In other words, the "form of reality" and the "form of representation" in language are one. Wittgenstein went on to posit that the limits of language are the limits of thought. There are some things that the human mind cannot imagine and of which it cannot speak. There are, in other words, "unsayable things" which include, surprisingly, logic, ethics, aesthetics, religion, and philosophy itself!

Clearly the *Tractatus* was a gauntlet hurled before the academic community, challenging the very nature of academic thought. Wittgenstein felt that metaphysics (one of the "unsayables") was a "mental cramp" and that much of traditional philosophy was the attempt to say the unsayable, to push language beyond its limits into metaphysical realms where both language and logic break down. Stated simply, the philosophical profession must deal with the issue of whether or not "unsayable things" exist. The final sentence of the *Tractatus* states: "Whereof one cannot speak, thereof one must be silent."

While in an Italian war prison, Wittgenstein made a momentous decision. Influenced by reading Leo Tolstoy on the Gospels, he gave away his inheritance as the son of the leading Austrian steelmaker. He did not want to spend his life defending himself from friends who were attracted to him for his money; and as an admirer of Tolstoy, he believed in leading the simple life, stripped of ease and luxury. When Bertrand Russell proposed that Wittgenstein meet him in Holland, Wittgenstein did not have enough money for a train ticket. Russell, not wanting to embarrass the young man with a handout, bought some of Wittgenstein's Cambridge furniture that was still in storage and sent him the proceeds to pay for his fare.

Wittgenstein also decided while in prison to study for an elementary-school teacher's certificate. In 1920 he took up his teaching duties in a small Austrian village, where he was a hit with his students but found it hard to make friends with their parents and other villagers. Discouraged, he contemplated suicide. His only friend was a priest. He gave up teaching, and in 1925 he worked as a gardener for a monastery and seriously considered taking vows himself.

In 1927 Wittgenstein met with the so-called Vienna Circle, a group of philosophers who would later inspire the school of logical positivism, a movement which repudiated traditional philosophical methods that did not acknowledge the need to study language. Following many of Wittgenstein's original concepts, logical positivists claim that all genuine philosophy is, in effect, a critique of language. The Vienna Circle invited Wittgenstein to join them, but he declined. For ten years—from 1919, when he was back in civilian life, until 1929, when he returned to Cambridge as a fellow at Trinity College—he pursued no formal philosophical studies.

Wittgenstein's enormous influence on philosophy in the English-speaking world paralleled his lively influence at Cambridge. Students found his lectures original and stimulating; he used the Socratic dialogue, posing spontaneous questions to his students, whom he then badgered into answering. In the course of this intellectual sparring, students came to understand the concepts Wittgenstein was teaching. His intense personality and novel discussions attracted students to philosophy; but because he held such a low opinion of contemporary philosophy, he would usually talk them out of making it a profession. He hated university life, despising the affectation, superficiality, and complacency typical of university faculties; eventually he stopped dining at their table. He was fond of saying that it was nearly impossible to teach and be honest.

Wittgenstein published only the *Tractatus*, but he was a voluminous writer his entire life, pouring his thoughts and theories into journals and notebooks, or dictating them to students. When his second great work, *Philosophical Investigations*, was published posthumously (1953), it set the philosophical world spinning, for in it he retracted the major premises of the *Tractatus*. Specifically he withdrew his former theories that language and reality are composed of simple objects, that there is a logical form or an *a priori* order to the world, and that all representations share a common, logical form. He also denied the concept of the "unsayable."

Philosophical Investigations reflected Wittgenstein's growing impatience with academic philosophy. He argued that much traditional philosophical thinking was faulty in assuming that there was an essence underlying concepts and ideas. He suggested that there is no essential nature to thinking, language, or representation; that each of these has many diverse forms. Wittgenstein's new arguments backed philosophers up against the wall, challenging the very methodology of philosophy, which considers concepts as they exist in the mind rather than in the give-and-take of daily life. Language, he argued, must be studied where it is being used, at work in the real world, not where it is "idling." The academic reaction to *Philosophical Investigations* was mixed. Some critics thought it was inferior to the *Tractatus*; others found it represented a more mature position. In any event, the later work, like its predecessor, transformed philosophical thinking and methodology.

At the outbreak of World War II, Wittgenstein left the chair of philosophy at Cambridge to serve as a porter in a London hospital and then as a laboratory assistant in the Royal Victoria Infirmary. In neither position did he let it be known that he was a university professor. He returned to Cambridge in 1944, ever more convinced that being a professor of philosophy was "an absurd job" and "a kind of living death." Three years later he resigned, claiming that he needed time for "thinking alone, without having to talk to anybody."

As he had in his youth, he retired to a remote cottage, this time on the west coast of Ireland, where he made quite a reputation among the local fishermen with his ability to tame birds. He stayed there until his health failed, then lived with friends in the United States and England. In 1949, when he learned that he had cancer, he seemed relatively unconcerned, claiming that he had "*no* wish to live on." Nevertheless, he continued to work hard on his notebooks and meet with students and disciples who visited him. He died at the home of his doctor in April of 1951.

"One wonders what philosophy would have been like in Britain and the United States had it not been for the accident of Wittgenstein, for he might not have been on the scene at all," mused one admirer. Had it not been for Bertrand Russell and Cambridge University's efforts to keep the reluctant professor available, his definitive influence on twentieth-century philosophy might have been considerably less, or not have been exerted at all.

In his early life Wittgenstein was not even drawn to philosophy. After studying mathematics, science, and mechanical engineering, he chose aeronautical research at the University of Manchester, England, where he developed a prototype of a jet engine. But being curious about the foundations of mathematics, he read Bertrand Russell's *Principles of Mathematics* and decided to leave Manchester to study under the great philosopher at Cambridge.

Maintaining his own commitment to life was not easy. Three of Wittgenstein's four brothers committed suicide, and he himself contemplated it on many occasions. A lonely man, Wittgenstein had a great need for friendship and affection, but was able to develop only platonic relationships with young male students who had, in his words, "nice faces." He feared losing himself in the rougher homosexual haunts of Vienna, Manchester, and London. Resolved to follow Tolstoy's example of self-imposed celibacy, he was often dispirited by his lifelong lapses from his rigorous attempts to repress his sexual needs. And yet many who knew him thought those very lapses kept him from the brink of madness—and kept him alive.

Ultimately Wittgenstein despaired of ever perfecting his philosophical treatises. He believed that his work would probably not "bring light into one brain or another" because of its imperfections and what he called "the darkness of this time." But perhaps to console himself, he added, in the Socratic spirit for which he was famous, that he did not want his writing "to spare other people the trouble of thinking" for themselves, but rather, "if possible, to stimulate someone to thoughts of his own."

JEAN
COCTEAU
1889–1963

"**A**stonish me!" Sergei Diaghilev, the impresario of the Ballets Russes, commanded Jean Cocteau as they stood one night in the Place de la Concorde. The 22-year-old poet approached him later with the scenario for a daring new ballet, *David*. Diaghilev was impressed. So was Igor Stravinsky, who told Cocteau he was interested in composing the music for it. Then, suddenly, Diaghilev turned cold on the project. Jealous over "Jeanchik's" amorous advances toward his protégé and star Vaslav Nijinsky, he snatched Stravinsky away from Cocteau to score *The Nightingale* instead. Nevertheless, Diaghilev's challenge changed Cocteau's life. Beginning at that moment in the Place de la Concorde, Cocteau set out to astonish the world; and he succeeded, not only in ballet but also in art, film, theater, poetry, fiction, journalism, and design.

Cocteau's virtuoso career extended from the *belle époque* to the New Wave era. He came into being in the same year, 1889, as the Eiffel Tower; and, like that monument, he was destined to become a world-wide symbol of French style and invention. Marcel Proust enshrined him in *Remembrance of Things Past* as the

172

dramatist Octave, writing: "People well qualified to judge considered his works highly important, almost works of genius, and I, moreover, agree with them." The American novelist Edith Wharton, marveling at his gift for epigrams, gushed: "Every subject touched upon—and in his company they were countless—was lit up by his enthusiasm." Such innovative film directors as Orson Welles, François Truffaut, and Steven Spielberg have claimed him as their hero. He was commissioned to create postage stamps for the French government, stained-glass windows for churches, and fashions for the house of Schiaparelli. His accomplishments are so many and so polymorphous that he eludes easy definition; but in his own mind he was always a poet in the root meaning of the word: a "maker" (in Greek, *poiētēs*) of wondrous images, whether they be visual, literary, auditory, or kinetic.

As a youth, Cocteau relied on his wit, nerve, and family connections to gain entry to the most important salons and artistic circles in Paris. One of his first mentors was the actor Edouard de Max. At the age of 16, Cocteau caused a sensation when he accompanied de Max to a grand Paris ball dressed as the Roman emperor Heliogabalus, with mascaraed eyes, red curls, a tiara, a jewel-embroidered train, anklets, and painted nails. He even managed to upstage the actress Sarah Bernhardt, who chided him: "If I were your mother, I'd send you to bed!" Three years later de Max sponsored the first public reading of Cocteau's poetry by some of Paris's most famous actors. Another early patron was the salon hostess and poet Anna de Noailles, granddaughter of the Comtesse de Chevigné, a model for Proust's Duchesse de Guermantes. Cocteau adapted de Noailles's ornate literary style for his first three published books of poetry: *Aladdin's Lamp* (1909), *The Frivolous Prince* (1910), and *The Dance of Sophocles* (1912).

A far more potent influence on the young Cocteau was André Gide. When they met in 1912, Gide was 20 years older than Cocteau, an established writer, and a founding power at the *Nouvelle Revue Française*, a huge enterprise that included a publishing house, a literary journal, and an experimental theater. Gide was intrigued by Cocteau's public persona but ambivalent about his talent. Much more drawn to sober, intellectual discourse, Gide seized on Cocteau's title "The Frivolous Prince" and accused Cocteau of being frivolous. However subjective that judgment may have been (Gide considered Proust "shallow"), it carried weight in French literary circles. Eager to prove himself, Cocteau took Gide's advice, "simplify your writing," to heart. Ultimately he won Gide's respect but never his friendship. Apart from their stylistic differences, they fought for the affections of a young man named Marc Allégret. The three-sided affair evolved into the central plot of Gide's famous 1926 novel, *The Counterfeiters*.

While Cocteau was under Gide's literary spell, he was also attending to a revolution in the worlds of music and art, thanks to his growing friendships with Diaghilev, the composer Erik Satie, and the artist Pablo Picasso. Cocteau's 1917 ballet *Parade*, which he derived from the *David* scenario he had written to astonish Diaghilev, gave the four of them a chance to work together. Diaghilev produced it, Satie scored it, and Picasso created the sets and costumes (including the huge drop curtain, which survives as his largest work). Cocteau's sprightly story of a circus sideshow was unconventional enough to allow each artist involved with the production to express himself freely. The result was a turning point in the development of modern ballet. It was also Cocteau's first triumph, inspiring a whole new aesthetic for which the poet Guillaume Apollinaire coined the word "sur-realistic." When some critics complained that *Parade* was too shocking to be called art, Cocteau replied: "Beauty is always born invisible."

Shortly after the premiere of *Parade*, Cocteau fell deeply in love with a 15-year-old fan of his poetry, Raymond Radiguet. Because of Radiguet's minority their relationship was guarded and tentative at first, but with each passing year it grew more intimate. Cocteau's happiness with Radiguet inspired one of the most creative periods in his life. He turned out hundreds of drawings, three volumes of verse, two novels (*The Great Split* and *Thomas the Impostor*, both in 1923) and a series of "spectacle-concerts" combining music and drama, such as *The Ox on the Roof* in 1920 (whose title became the name of a popular bar where the first Surrealists gathered) and *The Wedding on the Eiffel Tower* in 1921. Radiguet was also quite productive, publishing two immensely popular and highly acclaimed novels, *The Devil in the Flesh* (1923) and *The Ball of Count Orgel* (1924).

In 1923 Radiguet died of typhoid fever, and Cocteau was devastated. "I've lost something winged, noble, mysterious," he wrote his mother. "I see Raymond's face the last night, his difficulty in speaking, his heavenly eyes. Tears and sorrow tear me apart." In his grief Cocteau turned to opium. He never completely recovered from the loss of "the pupil who became my master," nor did he go for very long without his opium until he was well past middle age.

Whatever his private problems, Cocteau the artist continued to astound the world. In 1925 his play *Orpheus*, a recasting of the Greek myth, amazed critics with its clever mix of fantasy and reality. Filled with startling images from Cocteau's dream life (as were many of his other works), *Orpheus* also featured clothes designed by Cocteau's close friend Coco Chanel that set new standards for stage costuming. In 1927 Cocteau once again reclaimed ancient mythology for the modern stage with his oratorio *Oedipus the King*, scored by Stravinsky. And in 1929 he wrote his most famous work of fiction, *The Holy Terrors (Les Enfants Terribles)*, a shocking portrait of rebellious adolescents that has since become a classic of twentieth-century literature.

Among all Cocteau's *succès de scandale*, however, nothing matched the impact of his 1930 experimental film *The Blood of a Poet*. With its disjointed plot, ingenious special effects (such as a girl flying up to a ceiling), and bizarre symbols (such as a mouth speaking out of the palm of the Poet's hand), the film transformed the way artists regard the cinema. No longer was this relatively new medium dismissed as a vehicle for popular amusement. Cocteau had demonstrated that it offers a unique outlet for creative expression or, as he claimed, "a descent into oneself, a way of using the mechanism of the dream without sleeping, a crooked candle, often mysteriously blown out, carried about in the night of the human body."

Cocteau went on to produce other drawings, ballets, novels, poems, and plays (most notably *The Human Voice* in 1930 and *The Infernal Machine* in 1932), but it was his imaginative film work during the 1940s that has earned him his most lasting fame, particularly *The Eternal Return* (1943), *Beauty and the Beast* (1946), and *Orpheus* (1949). Each of these films and many others starred the dashing French leading man Jean Marais, who became Cocteau's lover in 1937 and remained with him until his death. In 1947, while still very much attached to his "Jeannot," Cocteau formed another close "father-son" relationship with his handsome chauffeur, Edouard Dermit, and gave him a leading role in his 1949 film *The Holy Terrors*.

By the time he reached his 60s, Cocteau was a living legend. In 1949 Harvard University offered him a chair as Charles Eliot Norton Professor of Poetry, which he declined in order to stay in France. In 1953 he was invited to preside over the Cannes International Film Festival. In 1955 the Royal Academy of Belgium and the French Academy inducted him as a member. But all these honors came with a heavy price. During the last few years of his life, he was deluged with requests for appearances, prefaces, reviews, articles, translations, poems, spectacles, and sketches. The more he labored to meet these requests, the more he taxed his health and the more he risked tarnishing his reputation by commercializing his talent.

Cocteau's 1959 film *The Testament of Orpheus* was his last major artistic endeavor. Described as "an active poem" by its creator, it presents Cocteau's own personal mythology in a series of visually remarkable scenes featuring Cocteau himself and such friends as Dermit, the matador Luis Dominguin, and Jacqueline and Pablo Picasso. In the closing scene of the film, Cocteau dissolves into a rocky landscape. It is fitting that this scene served as his final public act. Four years later, on October 11, 1963, he died of cardiac arrest after learning of the death of another French legend and dear friend, the chanteuse Edith Piaf.

BESSIE SMITH

1894–1937

Bessie Smith was once thrown out of an all-black chorus line by the manager, who was also black, because she was *too* black. The fashionable color for black entertainers in the 1920s and '30s was tan. Bessie Smith also had other liabilities: she was large-bodied, full-lipped, coarse, bad-mannered, raucous, obscene, and rough. She drank a lot and fought with her fists. She frequently ended up in jail. Lacking self-restraint, Smith was not the demure, light-skinned, slender, willow-waisted black singer that entrepreneurs were promoting among both white and black audiences.

And yet Bessie Smith was proud of who she was. Born in the ghettos of Chattanooga, Tennessee (in 1894, according to her marriage certificate), she was one of seven children. Her father, a part-time Baptist preacher, died soon after her birth; her mother died when she was eight. At age nine she began singing on the street corners for nickels. Smith's older sister, Viola, raised her younger brothers and sisters; and years later, when Smith was making good money singing in the major cities in the South, the Midwest, and along the East Coast, she banked part of her salary in Viola's name, so her sister could continue to support their apparently shiftless and unambitious siblings.

Bessie Smith was black, southern, poor, and ill-mannered and did not apologize for who she was. The money she did not send back to her family, she spent on clothes, jewelry, and gifts. She never owned a home, because she preferred to live on the road. Traveling in a brightly painted railroad car, she heartily embraced the uprooted, gypsy life of tent shows and the whole raucous carnival world they encompassed. She refused to polish up her act, or her personality, in order to please the world of white respectability, as so many black entertainers were doing to break into the big time. Bessie Smith made her own big time.

Eventually Smith became an embarrassment to successful black show people who lived out on Long Island, frequented the homes of wealthy white New Yorkers who backed and supported them, and entertained in glamorous nightclubs. To them, Bessie Smith represented everything they had escaped: poverty, street life, southern roots, hard liquor, wild parties, and ghetto language. In time, both middle-class and poor blacks referred to the rough language of the ghetto as "Bessie Smith talk." The typical expression was: "Why, I never heard such Bessie Smith!"

Smith's early recording for Columbia records, "T'Aint No-body's Biz-ness If I Do," says it well:

> There ain't nothin' I can do, or nothin' I can say, that folks
>   don't criticize me.
> But I'm going to do just as I want to anyway and don't care if
>   they all despise me.

When she was 18, her brother Clarence, a dancer and comedian for Moses Stokes's traveling show, got Smith an audition and she joined the troupe. Among the cast was Ma Rainey, the "Mother of the Blues." A lesbian who had no children of her own, Rainey took Smith under her wing, treated her like a daughter, and introduced her to the world of professional singing. Rumors had it that Ma Rainey kidnapped her, but Smith was so eager to escape the slums of Chattanooga that she would not have needed much coercion.

In 1923 Frank Walker's studio cut Smith's first record for Columbia. It was the heyday of the Jazz Age. The Harlem literary renaissance brought the southern black experience into the mainstream of American culture."Slumming" became fashionable among middle-class whites who ventured into Harlem for a night of jazz and blues in black nightclubs. White and black audiences wanted recordings. Smith's records sold for 75 cents each, and each sold 20,000 copies or more. Unfortunately, without her knowing it, Frank Walker had struck out the royalty clause in her contract, so Smith received only a fraction of the money she could have earned.

In addition to Columbia's "race" records, Bessie Smith's career rode on the fortunes of the Theater Owners' Booking Association (TOBA) in the South. Known to less successful black entertainers as "Tough on Black Artists," TOBA sponsored and booked black singers and musicians in cities and towns where there was an audience. The organization thrived throughout the 1920s and Smith traveled widely, performing in nightclubs across the South.

A Bessie Smith performance could raise good money. TOBA promoted her well, and her shows were often mobbed, patrons standing in line for hours waiting to get in. Her repertoire included powerful blues songs she wrote herself, as well as the great classics which she sang in her own memorable style. As pianist Art Hodes recalled: "There's no explainin' her singing, her voice. She don't need a mike; she don't use one. . . . As she sings, she moves slowly round the stage. Her head, sort of bowed. . . . I'm not sure whether she even has her eyes open. On and on, number after number, the same hush, the great performance, the deafening applause."

Smith's act included young chorus girls, some of whom became her lovers. She was a demanding employer, and expected loyalty from them, even to the extent of becoming jealous when they showed too much interest in young men. Through Smith, however, young and inexperienced showgirls got their first professional start. Smith could be gallant when she wanted to be. In 1935, for example, when her show was asked to replace Louis Armstrong at the Apollo Theater in Harlem, the owner thought the chorus girls were too dark and would look gray under the lights. He wanted them replaced with lighter-skinned women. Smith fought with him and threatened to pull out if he didn't change the lights to amber to accommodate the women's dark skin. But on other occasions she could let them down. She got drunk and landed in jail, and the show would have to go on without her. Audiences felt cheated, and the chorus girls were embarrassed.

In 1922 Smith met Jack Gee, a strong, handsome night watch-man, who fell in love with her. He was wounded in a shooting incident on their first date and spent five weeks in the hospital recuperating. They were married the following year. Gee always traveled with a loaded gun and became a manager-bodyguard for Smith and her troupe. He didn't enjoy drinking and partying as his wife did and tried to provide a little balance in her life. But Smith did not hanker after a balanced life. She continued to have affairs with women or men she met on the road; she would disappear for weeks at a time; she would end up in jail and need Gee to bail her out. She claimed the excitement of young people and parties kept her going, that it was part of her life "on the road" and that it wasn't any of his business.

Smith's closest relationship, outside the members of her immediate family, was with Ruby Walker, Gee's niece, who danced in her show. Although 20 years younger than Smith, Walker admired her aunt and hoped her association with Smith would help launch her own career. The two were fond of each other, even though Smith could be jealous of Walker's interest in young men, and on some occasions attacked her physically. Ruby Walker's job was often to cover for Smith so that Gee would not know when she was drinking or partying too much. On many occasions Gee caught Smith in bed with other women or men. There were many fights, and Gee had several nervous breakdowns. But Smith never reformed her ways. She showed little restraint or concern for others' feelings, including Ruby Walker's. At one point she even had a passionate affair with one of Walker's girlfriends.

Smith resented Walker's desire to become a star on her own, and she let the younger woman know in no uncertain terms who was boss. Walker, however, enjoyed living vicariously through her aunt, and Smith was generous with money and gifts to hold her loyalty. However, when Smith and Gee broke up, Ruby Walker sided with her uncle and left her aunt with yet another reason to sing the blues.

Smith never had any children of her own, but she adopted the six-year-old son of one of the women in her show and named him Jack, Junior. Jack Gee never liked the arrangement, but it seems he was appeased when Smith bought him a Cadillac for which she paid $5,000 cash.

The Depression years were hard for Smith. In 1929 she was offered her first part in a Broadway show, *Pansy*, but it closed after three performances. In 1930 TOBA folded, and theaters began closing their doors. Vaudeville was singing its swan song. Records became a luxury, and sales plummeted. In 1931 Columbia records did not renew Smith's contract.

The 1930s did hold some bright spots, however. After separating from Jack Gee, Smith latched onto Richard Morgan, a Chicago bootlegger, who provided a financial cushion for her. In 1932 she organized a new show, ironically titled *Broadway Revue*, that played to enthusiastic audiences far from the Great White Way. As the swing era began, Smith's strong, powerful voice was ideal for the big bands. She sang with Jack Teagarden on trombone and Benny Goodman on clarinet. Okeh Records offered her a contract to start recording again. And she managed to beat up Jack Gee's girlfriend, Gertrude Saunders, twice.

Mystery still surrounds the death of Bessie Smith. At 3:00 A.M. on a fateful Sunday in September, 1937, Bessie's car, driven by Morgan, ran into a Nabisco truck, parked with its lights off on a highway about 70 miles south of Memphis. Seven hours later, at 11:30, she died in a black hospital in Clarksdale, Mississippi, from internal and external hemorrhaging.

According to Edward Albee's play *The Death of Bessie Smith*, the singer died because a black ambulance driver took her to a white hospital where she was refused admittance. But the events surrounding the incident are still confusing. Pieces of the puzzle include: a white doctor going fishing who stopped immediately after the accident, attended to Smith, but did not drive for help; Morgan's account that he walked ten miles to send an ambulance; a second car of white people that ran into Morgan's car and received help before Smith; a second ambulance sent by the guilty truck driver, who drove off after the accident; the improbability that a black ambulance driver would take a black woman to a white hospital in the Jim Crow era; and the fact that the black hospital where the singer was eventually admitted and died was only a mile from the white hospital that refused her.

Whatever twist of fate prevented Bessie Smith from receiving prompt medical treatment, the woman who had been victimized by white racism all her life died a death laced with the tragedy she had known and sung about so often. As the great blues singer Alberta Hunter said: "Bessie had a sort of tear—no, not a tear, but there was a *misery* in what she did. Even though she was raucous and loud, Bessie was the greatest of them all."

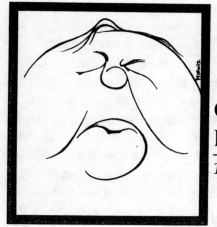

CHARLES
LAUGHTON
1899–1962

Nero was a homosexual, and Charles Laughton wanted to play him as one. He knew from research and his own background in the classics that Nero was a self-indulgent, petulant, childish, flamboyant "queen." Cecil B. DeMille, the director of the movie, was notoriously homophobic and wanted the Roman emperor played as an old-time villain, reminiscent of vaudeville—safe and corny. Laughton won out. Although he had only a few scenes in *The Sign of the Cross,* he played them with outlandish effeminacy worthy of the lecherous and debauched emperor.

It took Laughton a long time to know what he wanted in life. As a child growing up in Scarborough, England, where his parents operated a hotel, young Charles had a flair for make-believe and dressing up. A fat boy who saw himself as ugly, he retreated into the world of fantasy, partly as escape, partly because he was good at it. At age 18 he turned down a commission in World War I to enlist as a private. On the battlefield he bayoneted and killed German soldiers. He was gassed shortly before the armistice and suffered from outbreaks of rashes on his back the rest of his life. After the war he enrolled in the Royal Academy of Dramatic Arts in London. His father was the only member of the family who supported his precarious choice of a career. He made his London debut in 1926 in a series of student performances and was given the academy's award for the finest actor of that year.

In spite of his extremely poor self-image, Laughton rose steadily in his stage career, a result of his enormous talent and perseverance. Being overweight, homely, and often looking as if he were approaching 50 rather than 30, he realized that he would never land the romantic leads. Nevertheless his fine characterizations soon became the talk of the London theater world. As a fellow cast member in Sean O'Casey's *Silver Tassie* put it: "In the late 1920s when any male star in London was inevitably tall, slim, handsome, debonair, . . . how could a character actor like this one, patently built to support the stars, short, fat, moon-faced—how could *he* be a star? But he was, and he became the talk of London."

Charles Laughton was a new phenomenon in the age of matinée idols: the character actor as star. He had fortuitously appeared in the right place at the right time. The English theater was embarking on a period of naturalism, and Laughton's acting style, coupled with the massive research that he put into preparing important roles, resulted in fine naturalistic performances. Laughton's career also coincided with the end of silent films and the emergence of talkies; and producers were looking for actors with a strong screen presence who had the rich vocal skills that could be translated onto the screen.

Being heavy, Laughton was cast, not surprisingly, as a heavy. A London *Times* theater critic praised his first role as a villain in *A Man with Red Hair*: "Mr. Laughton has made so subtle, so revoltingly brilliant a study of sadistic obsession that the man, and through him the play, is well nigh intolerable. Mr. Laughton by face, by voice, above all, by imaginative bodily movement, compels suspension of disbelief." Throughout his career, Laughton would play many villains, among them Captain Bligh in

Mutiny on the Bounty, the police chief in *Les Misérables*, Dr. Moreau in *Island of Lost Souls*, the father in *The Barretts of Wimpole Street*, the Devil in George Bernard Shaw's *Don Juan in Hell*. For his Capone-like character in *On the Spot*, a *New York Times* critic said what was true of all of Laughton's serious roles as villain: "Charles Laughton's study of evil is extraordinarily accomplished."

What made a Laughton villain so memorable was the pitiable humanity that he brought to it. He understood the essential loneliness of evil, and his rogues' gallery of villains is understandable because he presents them with such authority. Laughton wrestled with every role, went through intense periods of soul-searching and agonizing, and drew on his own feelings of worthlessness, guilt, and remorse. By exploring and struggling with his own terrors and fears, he came to each part with an honesty and credibility not often found in other actors of his day.

In the 1920s and '30s, many of the most popular and sought-after stars on stage and screen portrayed stock, black-and-white characters. But Laughton needed to understand the essence of the men he portrayed and understand the meaning of a scene, not merely recite lines. His research and study of a part were legendary. For example for *Mutiny on the Bounty* he read everything on Captain Bligh in print. When he discovered the name of the tailor who designed special water-resistant uniforms for Bligh and learned that the shop was still in existence, he visited it. He asked if they, in fact, had had a customer named Bligh. The clerk asked what year that would be. Laughton replied, "Seventeen eighty-nine." The clerk disappeared to check the records and returned with the exact measurements, material, and cost of Bligh's uniforms. Laughton ordered the same.

For his role as the hunchback of Notre Dame, Laughton read Victor Hugo's novel four or five times and visited all the locations in Paris. For his role in *Rembrandt* he studied the master's works, traveled through Holland, and read everything he could on the artist. He did the same for his role as Galileo in Brecht's drama on the Renaissance scientist, and for the title role in *The Private Life of Henry VIII.* He knew whom he played.

Laughton's personality could be trying for his fellow cast members. A perfectionist, he would demand to read the same line dozens of times. Director Billy Wilder said of Laughton's rehearsal for *Witness for the Prosecution:* "We would have fifteen or more readings and each time the interpretation of the lines was different. He was like a musician looking for variations in a theme." If he felt that he was not performing a scene particularly well on a certain day, he would wander to another set and ask to film a scene there instead. Zoë Caldwell, who played Cordelia to Laughton's Lear, remembered him as "a very talented child." She said: "He wanted the complete devotion of all of us in the cast. I found him abrasive. There was tension on the stage both in rehearsal and full performance. But his abrasiveness was exciting and stimulating."

Some of his colleagues could be cruel. Tallulah Bankhead, who played his wife in *The Devil and the Deep,* called him "a big, fat slob" at a party in front of everyone, and Carole Lombard had it written into her contract for *They Knew What They Wanted* that she wouldn't have "to kiss his fat lips." Laurence Olivier, who worked with Laughton on the film *Spartacus,* was kinder. He realized that the iciness between himself and Laughton stemmed partly from Laughton's resentment that he would never get to play the dashing roles offered Olivier. Olivier knew that he would never be Laughton's equal. "I really did not believe that he and I would get on as I never could really understand what he said to me—which meant that I was not intellectually his equal. I never really felt on quite the same level as he."

Like many actors, Laughton made atrocious films, such as *Captain Kidd,* to make money to maintain his standard of living and to allow him to do stage work, which was his first love. He always bounced back with new stage roles or new projects. In 1948 he began teaching acting in California to select students whom he could handpick from hundreds of applications. Jane

Wyatt, Shelley Winters, Robert Ryan, Denver Pyle, and Arthur O'Connell were among some of his first students. He always emphasized that studying acting was "discovering among friends" the right way to read a part. In a day when so many young actors merely imitated the stars, Laughton encouraged them to draw a part out of their own experience—to be the part, not merely perform it.

In the late 1940s he began traveling with a one-man show of dramatic readings. Playing colleges and small-town theaters for one-night stands, he read such diverse authors and pieces as James Thurber, Thomas Wolfe, Charles Dickens, Lincoln's Gettysburg Address, the Book of Daniel from the Old Testament, and Shakespeare. At first the notion of one-night stands appalled him, but when he learned that he could command $2,000 a night, he warmed to the idea. On returning from a long tour, his wife, Elsa Lanchester, told him: "You look exhausted—and ten years younger."

He also produced, scripted, directed, and sometimes starred in unique theatrical projects such as *Don Juan in Hell*, a dream sequence often omitted from productions of Shaw's *Man and Superman*, and Stephen Vincent Benét's *John Brown's Body*. Brooks Atkinson, theater critic for the *New York Times*, said of Laughton's production of *John Brown's Body* that it "was not stage literature until Judith Anderson, Raymond Massey, and Tyrone Power [Laughton's cast] took hold of it. But it is stage literature now. It brings into the theater the brooding beauty of a literary masterpiece." Laughton worked with Bertolt Brecht on his *Galileo*, and brought Herman Wouk's best-seller *The Caine Mutiny* to the stage with Lloyd Nolan and Henry Fonda. He also directed Robert Mitchum and Shelley Winters in *The Night of the Hunter*, which has become an American film classic.

In London in the 1920s, he had met Elsa Lanchester, the daughter of vegetarian, pacificist, socialist parents who never married. She had attended Isadora Duncan's school of dance in Paris, founded a dance magazine at age 11, run a children's theater at 15, and in her late teens opened a nightclub called the Cave of Harmony, which offered plays, cabaret, music-hall songs, but no alcohol. Later she lived in Bloomsbury Square and became friends with many of the celebrated Bloomsbury group of creative people. Clearly, she was Laughton's intellectual and creative match. They hit it off immediately, and married in 1929. Throughout their careers and marriage Charles and Elsa became the mainstay in each other's life. Neither wanted children, but their mutual support of each other's careers, their love of flowers, houses, and the books and paintings they collected provided a strong bond for their relationship.

Early in their marriage, Lanchester learned that Laughton was gay. She understood it and accepted his male lovers, even as he accepted hers. Years later she recalled the first homosexual incident that she learned about two years after their marriage. "He told me he was with this fellow on our sofa. The only thing I could say was, 'Fine, O.K. but let's get rid of the sofa.'"

Laughton preferred lovers who were simple, uncomplicated fellows, such as his masseurs. He was never attracted to intellectual, tormented personalities like his own. His partners were always young, handsome men through whom he could vicariously enjoy the beauty and virility he would never know in himself. He frequently played a fatherly role with them, advising them on their acting careers, or encouraging them to marry. In 1941 he met David Roberts, a young actor with whom he had a close friendship for over two decades, even after the initial sexual attraction became platonic. Lanchester heartily approved of the relationship because she claimed Laughton tended to hate himself less and take better care of himself physically when he was around Roberts.

In 1961 Laughton was offered a key supporting role in *Advise and Consent*, a movie about a young senator plagued by a homosexual incident in his past. Laughton was eager to do the film. As Lanchester put it, he wanted to stop being so closety about his homosexuality at this point in his life, and "be with his own kind." He relished the role of the bigoted, contemptuous southern senator who epitomized everything that Laughton had always hated. It was one of his best performances, and it was his last.

On December 15, 1962, he died of cancer of the bone at his Hollywood home.

In his eulogy for Laughton, his friend and neighbor Christopher Isherwood said: "He was such a powerful person. . . . Most of the great parts he played were power figures of one kind or another . . . but you felt about him that he was not only powerful, but a vehicle of power, something through which power passed, and was transmitted."

NOËL COWARD

1899–1973

A week or two before World War II broke out in Europe, Noël Coward asked Winston Churchill's advice on what role he could play in the war effort. The prime minister's suggestion was for the actor-singer-playwright to "Go out and sing 'Mad Dogs and Englishmen' while the guns are firing." Entertaining the troops was not what Coward had in mind. He preferred something in Intelligence, where he could use his brain. He did, in fact, serve in a Paris propaganda office until the fall of France in 1940. But in a later bid for espionage work, the government turned him down on the grounds that, as one of the most famous entertainers of his day, he was too well known to be a spy. In the end he followed Churchill's advice and entertained British troops around the world.

"I behaved through most of the war with gallantry tinged, I suspect, by a strong urge to show off," he later claimed. His war efforts did not go uncriticized. In spite of the fact that he often performed solo, for an hour and a half, four or five times a day, some Britons resented his relaxing by a swimming pool with a cocktail. But in spite of the suntan lotion and martinis, the Nazis had Coward on their hit list.

In 1942 Coward wrote, directed, and starred in the war-propaganda film *In Which We Serve*. The story of a torpedoed destroyer and the people who served her (Coward playing the role of the captain) won an Academy Award the following year. Churchill admitted that the movie brought tears to his eyes.

To many of his generation, Coward epitomized the beauty and glamor of youth. Coming of age in the 1920s he represented the new force called "youth" or, as some mocked them, the "bright young things." His brazenly sophisticated lifestyle centered around the nightclubs and the automobile, new symbols for a new age. He became a spokesman for a new generation, perhaps "lost," as Gertrude Stein would say, but hell-bent on having a good time. "Were we happy in the Twenties?" Coward later reminisced. "On the whole I think most of us were but we tried to hide it by appearing to be as blasé, world-weary, and 'jagged with sophistication' as we possibly could. . . . Taken all in all, the Twenties was a diverting, highly exciting decade in which to live and I wouldn't have missed it, not—as they say—for a King's Ransom."

As a playwright, Coward held the mirror up to his age, revealing what the critics called "decadence" and "depravity," but what Coward and his generation hailed as the relaxing of the stiff moral code that had prevailed since Victorian times. In a period when national goals were questioned and postwar disillusionment encouraged many to give up the progressive reforms of the previous era, Coward argued that his age was "no more degenerate or decadent than any other civilized age." The only difference, he said, is that "the usual conglomeration of human vices have come to the surface a little more lately, and there is mercifully a little less hyprocrisy about." Comparing human vices to rocks submerged beneath the surface of the water, over which "the sluggish waves of false sentiment and hypocrisy have been washing," he maintained that it was the artist's responsibility to reveal them since they are "infinitely more dangerous" when hidden.

Coward updated the drawing-room drama for the twentieth century, turning it into what has been described as "comedy of bad manners" about affluent young men and women indulging their individualities and egos, totally fascinated by their own self-importance. For his time, Coward democratized the stage by allowing actors to speak in the average idiom of the day, as they bantered back and forth, usually about their relationships, their need to be light-hearted, their bizarre ways of pursuing pleasure in the modern world.

As the character Amanda says in *Private Lives:* "I think very few people are completely normal really, deep down in their private lives. It all depends on a combination of circumstances. If all the various cosmic thingummys fuse at the same moment." For Coward the thingummys fused in an extraordinary way. Talent, genius, charm, looks, and sexuality. The "talent to amuse" that became his hallmark was a hybrid, a major element being his homosexuality, with its ability to perceive the world as an outsider, value the transitoriness of human relationships, and see through the masks and disguises which everyone wears, especially the homosexual himself.

In the truest sense of the word "gay," Coward, like many of his characters, realized the need to be lighthearted in the face of adversity. He believed in the strength needed to live in the shallow world of appearances and come to terms with superficiality. As Elyot in *Private Lives* puts it: "Let's be superficial and pity the poor Philosophers. Let's blow trumpet and squeakers, and enjoy the party as much as we can, like very small, quite idiotic schoolchildren. Let's savour the delight of the moment."

In 1926, at age 26, Noël Coward had his first Rolls-Royce. By age 33 he had his first biography. But his rapid rise to stardom began even earlier. He made his stage debut at age 10 in *The Goldfish:* "A Fairy Play in Three Acts with a Star cast of Wonder Children." A review claimed: "Great success is scored by Master Noël Coward as Prince Mussell." Coming from parents who were both musical and avid theatergoers, Coward appeared as a child actor in *Peter Pan* and *Charley's Aunt*, and had a walk-on part, pushing a wheelbarrow, in D. W. Griffith's film *Hearts of the World*." By age 20 the "wonder child" had been on the stage for ten years.

After the First World War, Coward consciously cultivated the rich and famous and the right social circles that would promote his acting-writing career. In 1919 he attended a meeting of the Tomorrow Club, a prestigious organization that included the literary lions of the day. Not knowing the proper protocol, Coward arrived in evening dress, surprised to discover everyone else in day clothes. With the poise and aplomb worthy of any number of his future characters, he covered his faux pas with, "Now, I don't want *anybody* to feel embarrassed!"

In 1920 his first play to be produced in London's West End, *I'll Leave It to You*, opened with Coward playing a leading role. In 1922 and 1924 *The Young Idea* and *The Vortex* opened to standing ovations. "I made my usual self-deprecatory speech with a modesty which was rapidly becoming metallic," he admitted, "but which had the desired effect of lashing the audience to further ecstasies." *Hay Fever*, *Easy Virtue*, and *Private Lives* were further successes in the 1920s. His plays seemed to gush from his pen. He wrote *Hay Fever* in five days, *Private Lives* in four days, *Present Laughter* and *Blithe Spirit* (both produced in the 1940s) each in six days.

In the early days of the Depression, Coward lifted the nation's spirit with an extravaganza called *Cavalcade*, a program that traced the fortunes of two English families from 1899 (the year of his birth) to 1930. It required 22 sets, hundreds of costumes, a cast of 250. Whipping up patriotism to a fever pitch, it became a national sensation. When called to step forward on the stage after opening night, Coward announced, "I hope that this play made you feel that, in spite of the troublous times we are living in, it is still pretty exciting to be English." The audience went wild. Two weeks later the entire Royal Family attended, an event which made front-page headlines. In spite of Coward's sincere faith in duty and love of country, he admitted to his producer that a primary motive for writing the spectacle was "to test my producing powers on a large scale."

Those powers prevailed into the 1950s, when suddenly, almost overnight, Coward became old-fashioned. As British theater critic Kenneth Tynan called for a "new theater," playwrights responded with "new wave" plays about disillusionment and disenchantment. Heroes had become common blokes: cab men, grocers, politicians. Coward's sophisticated, charming characters seemed passé, and the faithful audiences that had grown up with him were dying off. Coward replied to the "new wave": "I am aware that two major wars are apt to upset the world's equilibrium but I still cannot quite blame the two wars for this dreadful cult of 'Boredom' which seems to have the French, American, and English theater so sternly in its grip." He railed against a theater that was anti-style, what he called the "scratch and mumble" school of acting, the actors who were "so dreadfully scruffy." He said: "I remember the excitement of driving up to rehearsal in my best suit." But that day had passed.

Undaunted, he vowed, "They can slam my plays as hard as they like and I shall continue trying to entertain, charm, touch and amuse the public." In 1960 he wrote *Waiting in the Wings*, a play about retired actors in a nursing home called The Wings. Audiences loved it; critics gave it scathing reviews. At age 60, it was his fiftieth production. Coward was hurt by the critics' response, and felt "time's wingèd chariot goosing me." What was waiting in the wings, of course, was death.

His cabaret performances, however, continued to please both audiences and critics. He performed at such diverse establishments as the Café de Paris in London, the Desert Inn in Las Vegas, and Carnegie Hall in New York. Each performance created an elegant retreat from what he saw as the grubbiness of the modern theater. "I don't care for the present trends in literature or the theater. Pornography bores me. Squalor disgusts me. Garishness, vulgarity, and commonness of mind offend me. . . . Subtlety, discretion, restraint, finesse, charm, intelligence, good manners, talent and glamour still enchant me."

In 1965 he wrote *A Song at Twilight*, about a writer who concealed his homosexuality all his life by maintaining a frustratingly heterosexual appearance for the sake of his career. Coward seemed to be dealing with his own dilemma. But even though he could write that "Homosexuality is becoming as normal as blueberry pie," he could not doff the sexually ambiguous persona he had maintained so faithfully over 60 years. For him it was as important as the proper evening dress. He told a reporter from the *New York Times:* "If you're a star, you have to behave like one. The public are very demanding. They have a right to be."

And so did Noël Coward. Friends and acquaintances knew him as very demanding, often selfish, temperamental, difficult to get along with. He fell in love about four or five times in his life, but his relationships were always marked by possessiveness and jealousy that led to bickering and fights. "Hey ho," he once wrote as a whimsical, lyrical refrain, "if love were all." But it was not. He admitted that he hated the loss of control that went with being in love. "To me, passionate love has always been like a tight shoe rubbing blisters on my Achilles heel," he wrote at age 58, having fallen in love with a man half his age.

In 1970 knighthood was bestowed, and he became Sir Noël Coward. In honor of his 70th birthday, the BBC ran commemorative programs for seven straight nights. He called it Holy Week. In the early 1970s, after a long tour, an enormously successful revue of his songs, *Oh! Coward*, opened on Broadway. In March 1973, after suffering a heart attack, Coward died peacefully at his home, Firefly Hill, in Jamaica.

The author of *Blithe Spirit* had often been preoccupied with death. He had once written somewhat flippantly, "Death is very laughable really, such a cunning little mystery. All done with mirrors." Ultimately, he hoped that his songs and plays would give him a kind of immortality. As he put it:

> *I'm here for a short visit only*
> *And I'd rather be loved than hated;*

Eternity may be lonely
When my body's disintegrated
And that which is loosely termed my soul
Goes whizzing off through the infinite.
By means of some vague, remote control
I'd like to think I was missed a bit.

MARGUERITE YOURCENAR
1903–1987

$\mathbf{E}$lection to the prestigious French Academy, a society of 40 designated "Immortals" in French literature, seldom comes as a surprise to the honorée, whose stature as a writer must be lofty enough to make the election logical, or to the general public, which has usually come to regard such a writer as a cultural hero. In 1981, however, the academy surprised everyone. For the first time in its 350-year history, it inducted a woman, Marguerite Yourcenar. Although the literary excellence of Yourcenar's work certainly entitled her to the accolade, she and her readers had assumed throughout her career that her gender disqualified her. After all, the academy had previously ignored such illustrious Frenchwomen as Madame de Staël and Colette. And although Yourcenar was widely admired in France, she was virtually unknown elsewhere. The year 1981 changed all that. Suddenly the fiercely reclusive intellectual felt a global spotlight beating down upon her.

Yourcenar managed her newfound fame with grace and humility. Speaking about her induction, she said: "This uncertain, floating me, whose existence I myself dispute, here it is, surrounded, accompanied by an invisible troupe of women who perhaps should have received this honor long before, so that I am tempted to stand aside and let their shadows pass." She also exonerated the academy from any direct blame for not admitting a woman sooner. "One cannot say," she remarked, "that in French society, so impregnated with feminine influence, the academy has been a notable misogynist. It simply conformed to the custom that willingly placed a woman on a pedestal but did not permit itself to officially offer her a chair."

In referring to social history, Yourcenar was well within her field of expertise. Most of the novels and stories that helped her earn a chair in the academy take place in bygone eras—second-century Rome, Renaissance Flanders, Habsburg Austria—but they are imbued with a painstaking authority and a passionate imagination that set them far above other historical fiction. She was also not afraid to tackle complex themes. Eschewing what she called "drugstore psychology," Yourcenar concentrated instead on exploring the universal aspects of power, interpersonal as well as political, and love, homosexual as well as heterosexual. "The books I like best," she once said, "are those where there is intelligence, goodness, and no injustice. They are very rare indeed. I think that the reason there is so much bad literature . . . is that the average person who sets out to be a writer goes around looking for subjects to write about, and editors have the effrontery to ask you: 'Could you not possibly write a novel about X or an essay on Z,' to which I always reply that I never write anything I have not chosen myself."

Yourcenar's life was an independent one from the very beginning. Her mother died shortly after Yourcenar's birth in Brussels, Belgium, on June 8, 1903; and so her upbringing was supervised entirely by her free-spirited father, the aristocratic Michel de Crayencour (she assumed the name Yourcenar, an imperfect anagram of Crayencour, in the 1920s). Her father gave her the best private tutors available and left her free to use his library at any hour. As an eight-year-old she was already infatuated with the works of the seventeenth-century dramatist Racine, and by her mid-teens she had published two volumes of verse. After her 18th birthday, her personal wealth not only enabled her to travel extensively and thus to acquire a cosmopolitan outlook, but also gave her the freedom to pursue whatever literary enterprises she wished.

Initially, Yourcenar confined her writing efforts to poems and essays, but she was irresistibly drawn to the novel. "In our time," she claimed, "the novel devours all other forms; one is almost forced to use it as a medium of expression." She used her first novel, *Alexis* (1929), as a medium for expressing her thoughts on homosexuality. The text consists of a long letter written by Alexis, a young musician, to his wife, Monique, explaining that he must leave her because he is gay. Apart from its mellifluous prose style, the novel is remarkable for presenting homosexuality as a viable, even honorable lifestyle. "Alexis does not feel self-hatred," Yourcenar wrote to a critic. "Why should he? Being very young and living in a period even more conventional than ours, he undergoes a period of anguish and fear in the presence of inclinations which his milieu thinks reprehensible and which could have led him to serious *social* troubles. He gets over these states of anxiety at the end of his story. Self-hatred is a feeling that does not interest me."

Yourcenar repeatedly chose male homosexuality as subject matter for her future writings; and she always presented it in a positive light, as a source of vitality, inspiration, and self-fulfillment for both partners, including Erick and Conrad in her novel *Coup de Grâce*, Zeno and his male lovers in her novel *The Abyss*, and Yukio Mishima and Masakatsu Morita in her extended essay, *Mishima: A Vision of the Void*. Her most fascinating treatment of homosexual love, however, occurs in her 1951 masterpiece, *Memoirs of Hadrian*, a triumph of classical research and narrative skill that immediately placed her in the front rank of the world's writers. An imaginary autobiography of the emperor based entirely on historical evidence, *Memoirs of Hadrian* chronicles the profound love Hadrian shared with the beautiful youth Antinous and the overwhelming grief he felt when Antinous died—a grief that inspired him to arrange for Antinous's deification, to found cities in Antinous's name, and to spread Antinous's likeness throughout the Roman empire on coins, in paintings, and in statues.

Memoirs of Hadrian is a monumental work in more ways than one. Despite the fact that it is not a lengthy book, Yourcenar took more than two decades to complete it. Commenting on the genesis of the novel, she wrote:

> In turning the pages of a volume of Flaubert's correspondence . . . about the year 1927, I came again upon this admirable sentence: "Just when the gods had ceased to be, and the Christ had not yet come, there was a unique moment in history, between Cicero and Marcus Aurelius, when man stood alone." A great part of my life was going to be spent in trying to define, and then to portray, that man existing alone and yet closely bound with all being.

While her enthusiasm for the project never flagged, she worked on it only intermittently over the years, mindful that it was a "life's challenge" which demanded much more time spent in reflection and incubation than in the actual labor of composition. In 1937, for example, it dawned on her that the journeys of T. E. Lawrence ("Lawrence of Arabia") in Asia Minor crossed and recrossed the tracks of Hadrian, and the realization sparked a pivotal new direction in the book's development. Explaining this direction, Yourcenar wrote:

> The more I thought of these two men, the more the adventure of one who rejects life (and first of all rejects himself) made me desirous of presenting, through Hadrian, the point of view of the man who accepts all experience. . . . It goes without saying, of course, that the asceticism of the one and the hedonism of the other are at many points interchangeable.

In addition to novels, poems, essays (notably *The Dark Brain of Piranesi*) and short stories (such as *Oriental Tales* and *Two Lives and a Dream*), Yourcenar wrote plays and translated into French the lyrics of American spirituals as well as works by James Baldwin, the Greek poet Constantine Cavafy, Henry James, Thomas Mann, Yukio Mishima, and Virginia Woolf. Thanks to her strong individualism, her eclectic interests, her flair for languages, and her studious approach to source materials, she was able to handle virtually any literary task she gave herself with insight, compassion, and objectivity. "I am rootless," she told an interviewer in 1979. "To steal from Hadrian, 'I am at home everywhere and nowhere.'"

Intellectually Yourcenar may have been rootless, but her personal life was deeply committed for over 40 years to Grace Frick, an American woman whom she met in 1938. Inseparable from the start, they visited the United States in 1939 to wait out World War II. As the months stretched into years, they decided to stay. Yourcenar taught comparative literature at Sarah Lawrence College for the next decade, and in 1947 she acquired U.S. citizenship (she was later reinstated as a citizen of France). In 1951 she and Frick purchased the house in Northeast Harbor, on Mount Desert Island off the coast of Maine, that became their final home. Frick, who translated *Memoirs of Hadrian* and other works by Yourcenar into English, died there in 1979.

Yourcenar always protected her relationship with Frick from public scrutiny, even after her induction to the French Academy, when she was hounded by the news media. Nevertheless, in an afterword to *Memoirs of Hadrian*, she pays this moving tribute to her life companion:

> This book bears no dedication. It ought to have been dedicated to G. F. . . . and would have been, were there not a kind of impropriety in putting a personal inscription at the opening of a work where, precisely, I was trying to efface the personal. But even the longest dedication is too short and too commonplace to honor a friendship so uncommon.

When I try to define this asset which has been mine now for years, I tell myself that such a privilege, however rare it may be, is surely not unique; that in the whole adventure of bringing a book successfully to its conclusion, or even in the entire life of some fortunate writers, there must have been sometimes, in the background, perhaps, someone who . . . bolsters our courage and approves, or sometimes disputes, our ideas; who shares with us, and with equal fervor, the joys of art and living . . . someone who is neither our shadow nor our reflection, nor even our complement, but simply himself [sic]; someone who leaves us ideally free, but who nevertheless obliges us to be fully what we are.

In keeping with her rational, disciplined temperament, Yourcenar commissioned a tombstone for her eventual gravesite, complete up to the last two digits of the year of her death. A friend was horrified by this action and complained to her: "Why should you not live till the year 2000?" Yourcenar replied: "I have absolutely no desire to live till the year 2000. The year 2000 is not for me." Indeed it was not. Yourcenar died peacefully on December 17, 1987.

CHRISTOPHER ISHERWOOD

1904–1986

^{66}**W**ith me, everything starts with autobiography," Christopher Isherwood once said of his writing career. Fortunately, Isherwood's life involved him intimately in some of the most significant political and social developments of the twentieth century, and his clear, incisive prose style served well to make his experiences palpable to three very different generations of readers.

The beginning of Christopher William Bradshaw-Isherwood's life on August 26, 1904, offered no hint of the rootlessness and controversy to follow. His father's ancestors, the Bradshaw-Isherwoods, were among the oldest and most distinguished landowners in Cheshire, England, and his mother was descended from a long line of wealthy wine merchants. Isherwood's formative years at Marple Hall and Wyberslegh Hall, the two family homes, were as steeped in convention as an upper-class English childhood can be. In 1914 he entered Saint Edmund's, an ultraconservative preparatory school in Surrey. A year later, however, his peaceful world was shattered. His father, a lieutenant colonel in the British army, was killed in action near Ypres, Belgium. From that point on Isherwood became disillusioned with England and the English way of life—a feeling he shared with a precocious 13-year-old cynic, W. H. Auden, during his last year at Saint Edmund's.

Isherwood continued his studies at Repton and Cambridge, but more and more he was attracted to literature as the proper vehicle for his discontent with English society. In 1925 he deliberately wrote facetious answers to his Cambridge exam questions and was asked to leave. Immediately he began writing novels and leading a life that moved, in his words, "according to the needs of my spirit." He declared E. M. Forster to be his literary hero and frankly acknowledged his homosexuality to himself, his family, and his friends.

A handsome and gregarious fellow, Isherwood maintained many contacts in the English academic world; and his early unpublished writings soon attracted the attention of his prep-school friend Auden, who was then an undergraduate at Oxford. Auden set up Isherwood as his self-proclaimed "senior literary advisor" and introduced him to his classmate Stephen Spender. The three friends went on to form the inner circle of the so-called Auden gang—angry young men who ruled the English life of letters during the 1930s.

Isherwood's first two published novels, *All the Conspirators* (1928) and *The Memorial* (1932), offered scathing indictments of British hypocrisy and stodginess; but in consolidating his reputation as the most gifted young novelist of his generation, Isherwood drew his most intriguing subject matter, not from England, but from Germany. He moved to Berlin in 1929, both to witness the political turmoil of Germany at closer range (he had "leftist" sympathies) and to enjoy more sexual freedom in the city's bohemian underworld. There he tutored English and, as a result, met Berliners of all social classes and philosophical persuasions. He transposed these acquaintances into unforgettable characters in his famous Berlin stories.

Consisting of two novels, *The Last of Mr. Norris* (1935) and *Goodbye to Berlin* (1939), the Berlin stories manage to tread a fine line between comedy and tragedy in depicting the adventures of touchingly vulnerable human beings caught in a monstrously inhumane system. According to critics and readers alike, what makes the stories so successful is the engagingly smooth, playful, and nonjudgmental voice of Isherwood's alter-ego narrators. This voice helps to domesticate personal histories that might otherwise appear too grotesque or too overladen with symbolic messages. In *Goodbye to Berlin* the narrator claims he is merely "a camera with its shutter open, quite passive, recording, not thinking. Recording the man shaving at the window opposite and the woman in the kimono washing her hair. Some day, all this will have to be developed, carefully printed, fixed."

The "photographic" style of the Berlin stories became an Isherwood trademark and inspired such future writers of journalistic fiction as Norman Mailer, Gore Vidal, and Truman Capote. It is a style, critics have remarked, that permits the writer to communicate personal experience and yet leaves the reader free to interpret its significance. It is also a style that translates well into other artistic media. John van Druten adapted the Berlin stories into a highly successful 1951 play, *I Am a Camera*; and John Kander and Fred Ebb used them as the basis for their enormously popular 1966 musical and 1972 film, *Cabaret*.

During the time Isherwood was recording material for his Berlin stories, he was also deeply involved in a love affair with a German working-class youth whom he later identified as "Heinz." After Hitler's rise to power in 1933, Isherwood and Heinz fled from Germany to avoid Heinz's possible conscription into the Germany army. Together the lovers wandered furtively through Europe for the next four years. Finally Heinz was compelled to return to Germany, where he was sentenced to prison for homosexual activities with Isherwood and then to service in the *Wehrmacht*.

Heartbroken and disgusted, Isherwood immigrated to the United States with Auden shortly after Germany invaded Poland. Auden settled in New York, but Isherwood and a new American lover named Vernon journeyed to California. On their arrival in Los Angeles, the writer Aldous Huxley introduced Isherwood to Swami Prabhavananda, a Hindu monk who was head of the local Vedanta Society. "The electricity between the two men," Huxley later reported, "was visible and affirming to everyone in the swami's community." Inspired by the serenity and wisdom of Prabhavananda, Isherwood wholeheartedly embraced Vedantism, a nondogmatic philosophy that does not consider either homosexuality or heterosexuality to be an obstacle to spiritual growth. He gave serious thought to taking monastic vows but decided instead to use his writing skills to spread the Vedantic message to the public at large. The first product of this pledge was an important translation of the sacred Indian epic, the *Bhagavad-Gita*, in 1944.

On a more worldly level Isherwood inaugurated a lifelong association with Metro-Goldwyn-Mayer as a scriptwriter. Through the powerful studio he met many influential people in the arts who evolved into steadfast friends, including Charles Laughton, Greta Garbo, Igor Stravinsky, Tennessee Williams, and the painter David Hockney. During America's involvement in World War II, he worked briefly as a conscientious objector with the American Friends Service. After the war, he published his first novel written in America, *Prater Violet* (1945), a fictional account of his work in the English film industry during the 1930s that was also informed by his experiences in Hollywood and his conversion to Vedantism. American critics unanimously praised it, which made him all the more enthusiastic about his adopted country. In 1946 he became a naturalized U.S. citizen and entered into a comfortable life of working on films, lecturing at the University of California, and writing books.

During the winter of 1953 Isherwood's placid existence was stirred by passion. He fell in love with Don Bachardy, an 18-year-old student he'd first encountered two years before on a Santa Monica beach. In 1954, at Bachardy's suggestion, they set up housekeeping together. Although his friends and associates were scandalized by the 30-year difference in their ages, Isherwood acknowledged: "I myself didn't feel guilty about this, but I did feel awed by the emotional intensity of our relationship, right from the beginning; the strange sense of a fated, mutual discovery. I knew that this time, I had really committed myself. Don might leave me, but I couldn't possibly leave him, unless he ceased to need me. The sense of responsibility which was almost fatherly made me anxious but full of joy."

Over the years the unwavering strength and affection of Isherwood's and Bachardy's relationship silenced all criticism. Bachardy successfully established himself as an artist; and the two lovers collaborated on a number of projects, including a 1972 dramatization of Isherwood's novel *A Meeting by the River* (1967) and a 1981 book, *October*, in which each page of Isherwood's prose is balanced by one of Bachardy's portraits. Talking about *October* to the press, Isherwood described Bachardy as "the ideal companion, to whom you can reveal yourself totally and yet be loved for what you are, not for what you pretend to be."

Throughout the 1950s and '60s, Isherwood continued to promote Vedantism in translations of sacred scriptures as well as in such nonfiction works as his 1965 biography *Ramakrishna and His Disciples*. His efforts helped to fuel a growing interest in eastern religions among westerners, especially among young people who grew up in a "global village." He also produced a number of popular novels, including *The World in the Evening* (1954), which contains his famous explication of the homosexual aesthetic, "High and Low Camp"; *Down There on a Visit* (1962); *A Single Man* (1964); and *A Meeting by the River* (1967). Of these works, *A Single Man* is considered by many critics to be his masterpiece and a unique contribution to world literature, because of its technical precision, its haunting spirituality, and the light it shed on the then seldom-discussed subject of homosexuality.

In the final 15 years of his life, Isherwood allied himself more and more publicly with the gay-rights movement. His 1971 memoir of his parents, *Kathleen and Frank*, includes a blunt admission of his own homosexuality; and as he appeared on television shows to discuss the book, he repeatedly emphasized the central role that a gay sensibility had played in his life and his craft. Almost overnight he became a media spokesperson for homosexuality, assisting mainstream Americans and Europeans to understand and respect the values involved in gay lifestyles. His 1975 address to the annual convention of the Modern Language Association, "Homosexuality and Literature," was a major catalyst in persuading many American colleges to incorporate gay literary materials in their curricula. At a press conference Isherwood insisted: "In taking up the cause of one minority, that of homosexuals against the dictatorship of heterosexuals, I have spoken out for all minorities."

Isherwood's death of prostate cancer on January 4, 1986, was mourned by legions of admirers: gay and straight, young and old, artistic and spiritual, European and American. An exceptionally warm, gifted, and brave individual, Isherwood championed humanism in an age threatened by totalitarianism and materialism. Throughout his life he remained true to the poetic plea made to him by his friend Auden in 1937, as they felt the western world falling apart around them: "Use your will. We need it."

TENNESSEE WILLIAMS

1911–1983

 $\mathbf{I}$ n 1943 M-G-M studios informed one of their screenwriters that they were not interested in a script based on one of his short stories. After the immensely successful *Gone With the Wind,* studio moguls reasoned, it would be at least a decade before moviegoers would want another film about southern women. So they turned down the movie rights to Tennessee Williams's *Gentleman Caller.* Two years later the play opened on Broadway as *The Glass Menagerie.* Remembering that historic night, Arthur Miller called it "a revolution" in the New York theater: ". . . in one stroke [it] lifted lyricism to its highest level in our theater's history." The following week it won the New York Drama Critics Circle's Award for best play.

The Glass Menagerie was based on what Thomas Lanier Williams called his "anguished familial situation" as a young boy in Saint Louis. From those tortured days of living with a rowdy, alcoholic father who saw no value in his son's literary pursuits, a beloved sister slowly sinking into an inner world of phobias and obsessions from which she would never emerge, and a strong-willed mother continually regretting being uprooted from the genteel southern background from which she drew a sense of identity, the young Williams found his own sanity in a portable typewriter that he called "my place of retreat, my cave, my refuge." By the time he was 15, Williams had lived in 16 different homes.

Williams's college days were equally nomadic. He attended the University of Missouri in Columbia, Washington University in Saint Louis, and the University of Iowa, interrupting his course of studies to return to Saint Louis when the family needed him during the dark days of the Depression. Yet he thrived artistically on his disrupted life. A work habit he developed during these years would persist into later life: He would begin with an idea for a poem, write it, then expand it into a short story, and ultimately transform it into the dramatic dialogue that would leave audiences breathless or, as on the opening night of A Streetcar Named Desire, applauding for a half-hour. From his earliest days Williams's life never settled down; neither did his work. Even in his mature years he would often revise and reshape scenes or bits of dialogue, working with the cast, reading new lines for them, attending rehearsals right up to opening night.

While at the University of Iowa, he realized that plays, not poems or stories, would be his major field of writing. It was there also that he began going by the name Tennessee. Several reasons have been given for the name change, all of them equally good. He acquired the name either because his family had fought Indians several generations before in Tennessee; or because his fellow students wanted a nickname for this boy born in a southern state with a long name and (due to the vagaries of nicknaming) latched onto Tennessee rather than Mississippi, his actual birthplace; or because a high point of his youth was the summer he spent at his maternal grandparents' home in Memphis, recovering from a nervous breakdown. It was also in Memphis that one of his early plays was first performed by a nonacademic theater group.

In 1938 Williams moved to New Orleans, a welcome relief from his painful memories of the Midwest. In the "city that care forgot," he discovered the liberating decadence of the French Quarter and had his first homosexual experience. (At the University of Missouri, he had fallen in love with his roommate but, as he said later, "neither of us knew what to do about it.") From then on, Williams's life was dominated by two obsessions: writing and sex.

In 1939 he sent four one-act plays to a contest sponsored by the Group Theatre organization in New York and then left New Orleans to travel through the Southwest. One of the readers, Molly Day Thacher, told her husband, the director Elia Kazan, "There's a wonderful young playwright riding around southern California on a bicycle." She sent Williams's plays to Audrey Wood, a literary agent who took Williams under her wing and began to promote and manage his career. Although he did not win the $500 prize, he came to New York, and the New School for Social Research produced his play *The Long Good-bye*, his first New York production.

It was Wood who arranged Williams's six-month contract with M-G-M in 1943 as a scriptwriter. When he arrived in Hollywood, the 32-year-old writer had written ten long plays, 12 short plays, 17 one-acts, 19 short stories, and over 250 poems. He could not, however, buckle down to producing a script for Lana Turner or the child star Margaret O'Brien. Finding him uncooperative, M-G-M dropped him.

But beginning in the mid-'40s, Williams's career proved that he did not need Hollywood. In 1944 he appeared for the first time in a book, *Five Young American Poets*, and he received a grant from the American Academy of Arts and Letters for his dramatic work. The following year *The Glass Menagerie* opened, and the next 15 years witnessed one dramatic success after another: *A Streetcar Named Desire* and *Cat on a Hot Tin Roof* (both of which won Pulitzer Prizes), *Summer and Smoke*, *Suddenly Last Summer*, *Sweet Bird of Youth*, *Orpheus Descending*, and *The Night of the Iguana*, in addition to the movie screenplay for *Baby Doll* and a novel, *The Roman Spring of Mrs. Stone*.

Williams maintained that all his characters were based on himself. "I can't draw a character unless I know it within myself," he said. His own neurotic personality and lifestyle served him well in creating the disturbed characters teetering on the brink of insanity, trying to reconcile the pull of the flesh with the higher aspirations of the spirit. A hypochondriac, Williams constantly feared either a physical collapse or a mental breakdown (in 1937 his sister, Rose, was one of the nation's first patients to undergo a prefrontal lobotomy). He also suffered from an almost unrelenting persecution complex, which grew exceedingly severe after poor reviews of his plays. "I have an unfortunate inability to believe in people's admiration or even their acceptance," he once said, referring to his inability to accept love and friendship, as well as to the difficulty he had accepting himself as a major artist.

In 1948 he began living with Frank Merlo, a 26-year-old navy veteran whom Williams met in Provincetown, Massachusetts. Merlo managed Williams's household and finances and gave him the love and support his erratic, gypsy life needed, even though Williams himself found it hard to reciprocate. As Tennessee's longtime friend, actress Maureen Stapleton, put it, "Frank Merlo was a man everyone adored. . . . He loved and protected Tenn and did everything for him." Williams's younger brother, Dakin, said, "Frank was the best person Tom ever lived with. . . . He cared for Grandfather equally well [when the retired Episcopal minister, then in this nineties, lived with Williams and Merlo]. Frank was a unique man."

But in spite of the stabilizing influence of Merlo, Williams's life was bent on the self-destructiveness that found its artistic expression in his many leading heroes and heroines. Eventually he became dependent on drugs, alcohol, and a restlessness that constantly drove him from New York to Key West to Europe, from city to city, from lover to lover, never staying more than a few months in any one place. Williams never matched the loyalty shown him by Merlo in their 15 years together. A character in *Orpheus Descending* could well be talking to Williams himself when she says, "You and me belong to the fugitive kind. We live on motion. . . . Nothing but motion, motion, mile after mile, keeping up with the wind."

And yet his pain was the source of some of the most powerful moments on the American stage. In *Summer and Smoke* Alma Winemiller's conflict between fantasy and reality, between spirit and flesh, was his own. The breakdown of Blanche DuBois in *A Streetcar Named Desire* prefigured the bouts of mental and physical collapse that would plague his own life. In *Cat on a Hot Tin Roof*, Williams portrayed the debilitating effects of alcohol which he knew only too well. *Suddenly Last Summer*, a searing drama of a woman fighting for her sanity, was written while he was in psychoanalysis. In *The Night of the Iguana*, Williams presents an alcoholic, sex-driven minister realizing that he has reached the end of his rope. Although he was only 38 years old when he wrote *The Roman Spring of Mrs. Stone*, his own midlife anxieties became the material for the 50-year-old Mrs. Stone. The novel also drew on his own sexual infidelities during a stay in Italy with Frank Merlo.

In 1963 Frank Merlo died of lung cancer, and Williams's own life teetered on the edge of extinction. His dependency on drink and drugs left him with slurred speech and an unsteadiness on his feet. He feared falling down in public and dying alone at night. By 1964, 12 films had been made based on his plays, and three more would be produced before the decade was over. Yet his own sense of accomplishment was greatly impaired by his growing paranoia and fear that he would slip into total unreality, as had his beloved sister. In 1969 his brother, Dakin, forced him into Barnes Hospital in Saint Louis and literally saved his life. But celebrity drug clinics were a thing of the future, and Tennessee hated his brother's interference; he never admitted that he had needed such drastic treatment.

Throughout the '70s Williams continued to work on new poems, stories, and plays. He called his studio a "madhouse," and on the surface he seemed to be healthy, in spite of incessant worries about his health. The countercultural forces of the 1960s and '70s gave the nation new standards and tastes, and, as the nation binged on novelty for novelty's sake, Williams seemed somewhat old-fashioned. He tried to keep up, but reviews of newer works, when kind, would point out that his failures should be judged as minor exercises or experimental pieces, and that since he had already established himself as one of America's greatest playwrights, it was unfair to expect him to continually live up to himself.

In the heady days of the gay liberation movement, Williams acknowledged his homosexuality, as did a few other celebrities, such as the writer Christopher Isherwood, but he never felt comfortable with the movement, possibly because he never felt entirely comfortable with his own homosexuality, even though it was a major driving force in his life and his art. It became especially troublesome in his later life, when he was buffeted by the media and plagued by a following of young, insincere gay men who used him as an entry into the world of fame and celebrity. Yet through his last years it was only by writing that he continued to find meaning in the light and shadows of his life and some semblance of order. As a character in *Orpheus Descending* says, "You know we live in light and shadow—that's what we live in, a world of light and shadow—and it's confusing."

In 1983 he was found dead in a New York hotel room, ironically having choked on a plastic safety bottle cap (which he may have used as a spoon to take two capsules of Seconal). A life which had created so many lives—and had endured professionally over four turbulent decades—had come to an end. As Williams had told an interviewer after opening night of *The Glass Menagerie*, "It's human valor that moves me. The one dominant theme in most of my writings, the most magnificent thing in all human nature, is valor—and endurance."

ALAN
TURING
1912–1954

              The boys at Sherborne School in Dorset, England, recited a little ditty when Alan Turing, one of their alumni, was awarded a fellowship at Cambridge when he was only 22 years old.

> *Turing*
> *Must have been alluring*
> *To get made a don*
> *So early on.*

More to the point was that Turing's dissertation on topology, a branch of mathematics, impressed the fellowship committee. While he was alive and for several decades after his death, even those who thought they knew him well had difficulty understanding the brilliant young English mathematician whose team of experts broke the Nazi war code, Enigma, during World War II and whose far-ranging theories about mathematics, machines, and intelligence led to the development of computers.

    Turing had not always impressed his teachers. As a student in a private boarding school, he was considered sloppy and uninterested in most academic subjects. He did, however, excel at mathematics and its applications in related areas, such as astronomy. For Turing, a boy of strong independent character, school days were as important for homoerotic experiences as for academic study.

At Cambridge, Turing's interests were drawn to recent developments in mathematics and physics that shaped his thinking for later important breakthroughs in what would become known as computer science. Discoveries in quantum physics indicated that an electron could jump from orbit to orbit without transgressing the space in between. Turing wondered how this fact might be applied to machines. A second field of inquiry was the possibility of mechanizing mathematical logic. Putting the two together, Turing began his research into the possibility of a machine that could move from one state to another under instructions fed to it in the form of mathematical propositions. Could such a machine be built?, he wondered.

Turing's studies led him to reflect on the precise nature of machines—an issue of relatively little importance to most lay people, for whom a machine is something to be used, rarely understood, hardly ever questioned. His inquiries resulted in what has come to be called a "Turing machine," a core contribution to the development of computers. In 1937 his published paper *Computable Numbers* succeeded in explaining the concept of a machine by means of a precise mathematical definition.

Turing's work at Cambridge was interrupted by the outbreak of war on the Continent. Along with other intellectuals and mathematicians, he was enlisted to work at Bletchley Park, a Victorian country mansion near Oxford, where around-the-clock research was underway to break the German war code. Using a machine called the Enigma, the German high command sent instructions to its submarine fleet (as well as its land forces) by means of a numerical code. In the early years of the war, British shipping, which was crucial for the island nation's survival, was being sunk at an alarming rate.

The British already knew how the Enigma was constructed, but what they didn't know was how its internal state was adjusted before encoding any given set of instructions. By means of several independently turning rings, the code could vary from message to message. When Turing arrived at Bletchley Park, British intelligence believed that the problem was unsolvable. And by current modes of thought regarding cryptanalysis, it was. Turing, however, brought a unique set of insights into the mathematical principles underlying the Enigma's functioning.

Turing used high-speed searching machines to decode intercepted messages. At first he and his colleagues discovered the Enigma's internal state and deciphered messages within a couple of weeks after receiving a coded message. By that time, of course, the information was useless. But soon they reduced the search-and-decipher time to a few days, and eventually they could decode messages in a matter of minutes. The result was a striking decrease in the number of British ships sunk.

Surprisingly, in spite of their mathematical wizardry, the Germans did not put two and two together and realize that the British had cracked the code. Convinced that the Enigma, like the Third Reich, was inviolable, German experts attributed the rising number of British ships escaping submarine patrols to an improvement in British espionage efforts, so they responded by stepping up their own counterspy operations. Occasionally they did alter the Enigma's program, but Turing and his associates would feverishly search for new formulas. They always found them, and the Allied powers could regularly rely on the decoded messages to elude or counteract Nazi strategies.

Throughout the war Turing never thought of himself as a national hero, and he was never honored as one. After Germany was defeated, cold-war tensions convinced the British government to keep the Bletchley Park project classified as top secret. Even Turing's mother had no inkling of the crucial role he had played. Her son's physical appearance was always that of a befuddled professor, slightly shabby, unkempt, lost in a world of his own, spinning out theories and propositions that were indecipherable to the average lay person. That Alan, whom she considered "brilliant but unsound," had been entrusted with state secrets would have astounded her.

Turing enjoyed the quiet life of an ordinary mathematician. He had no grandiose beliefs that his work fell into the same category as that of more active spies whose life-and-death exploits would be dramatized in best-selling thrillers. The fact that his work had denied the sea-lanes to Nazi submarines and secured them for the Allies was not something that Turing would have thought merited public recognition. That a 600-page biography of his life should be published in 1983 and two plays about his career should run concurrently on Broadway in 1987 would have astounded him. In 1945 he was glad to return to the erudite mathematical studies that had occupied him before the war. He also resumed his lifelong sport of running, at times spending several hours a day when training for a marathon.

After the war Turing's interests turned to the possibility of creating a "universal machine" that could be programmed to perform all the functions of any other machine. He began thinking about a way to perfect a "tape" on which such instructions could be stored. In other words he began thinking about computers. Turing was not the first to ponder the use of universal machines, nor was he the first to consider using the latest developments in electronics to power such machines. Turing's contribution (he never actually invented a computer) was to pull together a set of crucial ideas which in time became the basis upon which modern computer science was built.

Turing's mind roamed through the maze of possibilities regarding human intelligence that have intrigued thinkers throughout the centuries. What is intelligence? Where does it reside? Can it be embodied in organic, mechanical, and electronic substances? Can a machine think? Could it have emotions? Will a machine ever predict its own behavior?

Turing argued that there was no reason in principle that a machine could not take over the work of programming itself in such a way that it could be accurately described as intelligent. He also suggested that if a random element could be introduced—something like a roulette wheel—it would approximate human thought even more closely. In a 1946 speech he even suggested to an astounded audience that instead of programming a machine to give no answer when it was baffled, "we could arrange that it gives occasional wrong answers." In other words, he reasoned, "if a machine is expected to be infallible, it cannot also be intelligent" in terms that human intelligence is understood.

Turing proposed that we should not expect more from a machine than we do from human intelligence, adding that no thinker adds very much to the body of knowledge he or she already possesses, but simply reuses what he or she has been trained to do. The same, he felt, could be expected from a machine. Although the immediate response to many of Turing's ideas was disbelief, his papers and speeches are now widely acknowledged as the beginnings of research into the field of artificial intelligence.

In 1952 Turing's home was burglarized, and in filing a police report he related that he suspected a former lover had been involved. He thought the information would help, but events took an unexpected turn. The police put together a case against Turing, accusing him of having violated a criminal statute involving "gross indecency," as homosexuality was then defined by the courts. Pleading guilty at his trial, Turing faced either two years in prison or a new "therapy" then in vogue of "chemical castration" by means of hormone injections. He submitted to the injections of sex hormones, a torment that left him physically and psychologically scarred.

Over the next two years he appeared to recover—not from homosexuality, as the courts had foolishly hoped, but from the indignities he had suffered at the hands of a state that tried to control certain citizens by chemical means. He seemed happy, in good health, free of financial worries. But on June 7, 1954, at the age of 41, he bit into an apple that had been dipped in cyanide, and died. His death was officially declared a suicide.

The truth had always been important to Alan Turing. Although he was a shy and retiring man, he never felt his homosexuality was something that needed to be hidden. He expected his colleagues to know and accept the fact that he was gay, and he did not refrain from dropping a comment about a good-looking man in the presence of heterosexual associates. He had even told Joan Clarke, to whom he was briefly engaged during the war, that he was gay. In Stanley Kubrick's film *2001: A Space Odyssey*, the character of HAL, the computer based on Turing's ideas, is destroyed by the logic built into it by its planners. In the book based on the film, Arthur C. Clarke and Stanley Kubrick wrote: "The twin gods of Security and National Interest meant nothing to HAL. He was only aware of the conflict that was slowly destroying his integrity—the conflict between truth, and the concealment of truth." In a sense, that is what destroyed Alan Turing.

BENJAMIN BRITTEN
1913-1976

World War II was at last ending, and London's Sadler's Wells Opera Company was planning to move back into its home theater. Greatly excited about the reopening as well as the imminent victory, the managers decided to do something special. Instead of playing it safe by mounting a popular repertory opera for their first postwar production, they chose a new work, *Peter Grimes*, by the relatively unknown musician Benjamin Britten. The story took place in England, the composer was English, and the music had astounded all of them. The premiere on June 7, 1945, is now regarded as a legendary event in opera history. Aside from being a resounding success in its own right, *Peter Grimes* launched the career of one of the greatest British composers who ever lived and signaled a flourishing new era in English music.

Based on an 1810 poem by the Suffolk poet George Crabbe, *Peter Grimes* concerns a fisherman who is blamed by his community for the death of a young apprentice. Some experts claim that Grimes's status as a pariah is meant to comment on Britten's own outcast situation as a homosexual. Whether or not this is true, the opera does evoke the background of its creator—a Suffolk boy who grew up loving the sounds and the sights of the sea.

Britten relished the fact that he was born on the feast day of Saint Cecilia, patron saint of music: November 22, 1913. His mother taught him to play the piano, and he was already composing at the age of five. Entranced by the many musicales held in his home, he was one of the last composers to be brought up exclusively to the sound of live music, and one of the first to learn the idioms of twentieth-century music as a child. By the age of 14 he had written numerous instrumental and vocal works reflecting the styles of his favorite composers: Gustav Holst, Maurice Ravel, and Frank Bridge.

When Bridge attended the premiere of his orchestral suite, *Enter Spring*, at the 1927 Norwich Festival, Britten was there to meet him; and for the next six years Bridge served as Britten's "prime mentor." Recalling Bridge's "mammoth lessons," Britten said: "Bridge insisted on the absolutely clear relationship of what was in my mind to what was on the paper. He taught me to think and feel through the instrument I was writing for. It was just the right treatment for me."

In 1930 Britten won a scholarship to the Royal College of Music in London. Academically it was not the productive experience he'd anticipated; but he did manage to diversify his skills, becoming an accomplished conductor, viola player, researcher, and editor in addition to gaining even more proficiency as a pianist and composer. Far more meaningful than his days at the RCM were his evenings in London's concert halls. There he developed a keen interest in the "12-tone" works of Alban Berg, Anton von Webern, and Arnold Schoenberg. After graduating in 1933 he threw himself into composition and within a year wrote *A Boy Was Born* (a choral piece), *Simple Symphony*, and *Friday Afternoons* (a group of children's songs). His first important public exposure was a concert performance of *A Boy Was Born* in 1934. The influential *Observer* critic A. H. Fox-Strangways led a chorus of praise in the reviews the next morning: "[The music] has endless invention and facility. He rivets attention from the first note onwards: without knowing in the least what is coming, one feels instinctively that this is music it behooves one to listen to and each successive moment strengthens that feeling."

A Boy Was Born also brought Britten good luck in his personal life. When it was broadcast by the BBC earlier that year, he met the tenor Peter Pears, who was then with the BBC Singers. Despite their mutual attraction, they were little more than acquaintances for the next three years: Pears already had a lover; and, more to the point, Britten had yet to accept his own homosexuality. In 1935 Britten began collaborating with the poet W. H. Auden on films for the Government Post Office Film Unit; and Auden, an unashamed homosexual, provoked Britten into coming to terms with his feelings. Auden even extended his campaign into his poetry: "For my friend Benjamin Britten, composer, I beg / That fortune send him soon a passionate affair." Auden's plea was answered. In 1937, after the death of Pears's lover in a plane crash, Britten and Pears cast their fates together. Britten resisted discussing his homosexuality throughout his lifetime; but in a 1980 television biography of Britten after his death, Pears felt free to describe their 40-year union as one of "passionate devotion, faith, and love."

Besides triggering Britten's sexual awareness, Auden also encouraged his pacifist tendencies. When Auden and the writer Christopher Isherwood fled to the United States at the onset of World War II, Britten and Pears followed. Once settled in Amityville, New York, Britten continued to solidify his reputation as a brilliant and daring musician with such works as *Les Illuminations* (a song cycle based on Rimbaud's poems); *Sinfonia da Requiem* (a tribute to the non-Fascist heroes of the Spanish Civil War); and *Seven Sonnets of Michelangelo* (a song cycle written for, and dedicated to, Pears).

During most of 1940 Britten and Pears lived with Auden in an artists' colony in Brooklyn Heights. Their housemates included the writers Carson McCullers and Paul and Jane Bowles, the poet Louis MacNeice, the artist Salvador Dali, and the entertainer

Gypsy Rose Lee. In many respects the commune's bohemian atmosphere made the reserved Britten uncomfortable, but it inspired him to produce his first modernist opera, *Paul Bunyan*. As a composer he was always eager to experiment with different cultural perspectives, and *Paul Bunyan* gave him the chance to work with New World music and mythology. Unfortunately the premiere at Columbia University in 1941 was not a success. Critics found Auden's libretto "awkward" and Britten's new format "unsettling": It was neither the "separate numbers" classical model nor the "through-composed" Wagnerian style that they associated with opera. The general audience was more enthusiastic, possibly because it instinctively responded to the natural intonations and rhythms of American speech that lie behind Britten's orchestration.

The critical failure of *Paul Bunyan* added to the depression Britten had been feeling ever since coming to America. Both Britten and Pears found solace in Crabbe's poetic evocation of the Suffolk coast, and in 1942 it prompted their return to England, as well as the opera *Peter Grimes*. Britten's other accomplishments during the last years of the war include several acclaimed church pieces, such as *Hymn to St. Cecilia* and *Rejoice in the Lamb*. He and Pears also traveled through Britain in a series of piano-and-tenor concerts. For the next three decades Britten held to this pattern of composing and touring with Pears—one activity feeding the other.

Within four years after the success of *Peter Grimes*, Britten wrote three well-received chamber operas: *The Rape of Lucretia*, *Albert Herring*, and *The Little Sweep* (based on William Blake's *Songs of Innocence*). The latter opera, one of many works that Britten composed especially for children, is perhaps his most frequently staged creation. He also wrote *The Young Person's Guide to the Orchestra* during this period. Originally the sound track for an educational film, it has evolved into a popular record and a staple in concerts for young audiences.

In 1947 Britten joined art historian Kenneth Clark and theatrical director Tyrone Guthrie in founding the English Opera

Group, an organization committed to sponsoring the works of English composers. The group thrived; but the very next year he shifted his attention to a project even closer to his heart—the formation of an annual music festival at Aldeburgh, where he and Pears now lived. It got off to an impressive start with the premiere of his cantata *Saint Nicolas*. The writer E. M. Forster was moved to comment: "It was one of those triumphs outside the rules of art which only the great artist can achieve." The critic Donald Mitchell remarked: "I was so confused by its progressively overwhelming impact that all I could find to say was: 'This is too beautiful.'" The festival itself came under the patronage of the Queen Mother and survives as one of the most engaging musical events in the European calendar.

Britten was now ready to attempt a third large-scale opera, and once again he chose a male-oriented story with a solitary hero: Herman Melville's *Billy Budd*. With Forster as librettist and Pears in the role of Captain Vere, *Billy Budd* premiered at Covent Garden in 1951 and raised howls of protest. Some complained that the comparison of Billy Budd's hanging to Christ's crucifixion was sacrilegious. Others objected to the work's homosexual overtones, dubbing it "The Bugger's Opera." Only in years to come did the intensity of the music earn the respect it deserves. For the coronation of Elizabeth II in 1953, he was commissioned to write yet another large-scale opera. The result, *Gloriana*, is a portrait of Elizabeth I that, like *Billy Budd*, combines grand spectacle with intimate psychological drama; but, also like *Billy Budd*, it did not charm its opening-night audience, which consisted of conservative courtiers clustered around their new monarch. It too became much more popular as the years went by.

With rare exceptions Britten's subsequent works drew immediate praise from critics and audiences alike. They include *The Turn of the Screw*, an opera based on Henry James's novella (1954); *Noye's Fludde*, a children's opera (1957); *A Midsummer Night's Dream*, an opera based on Shakespeare's play (1960); *War Requiem*, a vocal and orchestral piece based on the antiwar poems of Wilfred Owen (1961); and *Owen Wingrave*, an opera based on another Henry James story (1971).

Britten's last opera, *Death in Venice* (1973), is by all accounts his most personal creation. Taken from a novella by Thomas Mann, it tells the tale of an aging artist, Aschenbach, who is obsessed with the beauty of a 13-year-old boy, Tadzio. Again Britten chose a text with homosexual undercurrents, and again he wrote the principal role expressly for Pears. Commenting on the extra devotion Britten brought to each detail of the production, Colin Graham, the stage producer, said: "Of all his works, this one went deepest into Britten's own soul." Pears himself remarked: "Aschenbach asks what it is he has spent his life searching for. Knowledge? A lost innocence? And must the pursuit of beauty, of love, lead only to chaos? All questions Ben constantly asked himself." The premiere at the Aldeburgh Festival in 1973 was a triumph.

Sadly, Britten himself could not attend the premiere: He was recuperating from heart surgery performed earlier that year. Knowing that his days of conducting, playing the piano, traveling around the world, and making personal appearances were over, he nevertheless refused to stop composing. On December 4, 1976, he died peacefully in Peter Pears's arms. He had spent his last moments gazing at the North Sea that he loved so much and that had inspired some of his greatest works.

PIER PAOLO PASOLINI

1922-1975

In October 1962, Pier Paolo Pasolini was sitting in his guest room in Assisi, Italy, waiting out a tumultuous reception for Pope John XXIII occurring outside. Killing time until the streets cleared, he read the Gospel according to Saint Matthew, and felt "an immediate need to 'do something'—a terrible, almost physical energy." Struck by the poetry of the Gospel, he decided to make it the basis of his next film.

Pasolini's subsequent trips through Africa and the Middle East convinced him that his Christ must be a Third World peasant and rebel. As usual he chose faces unknown to the public, selecting a young Spanish student to play Christ. When moviegoers around the world viewed *The Gospel According to Saint Matthew* (with the Gospel itself as its only script), the actors portraying angry young apostles burning for a moral and social upheavel left them stunned with the truly revolutionary character of the Gospel message.

The Gospel According to Saint Matthew was dedicated "to the dear, happy, familiar shade of John XXIII," and Pasolini liked to think that he had turned the cinema into what he called the

"Bible of the poor." But when the film opened at the 24th International Film Festival in Venice in 1964, right-wing fascist elements created an uproar. How a communist and an atheist like Pasolini could produce an honest film on the Christian Gospels required an explanation. Pasolini was never at a loss for words: "To put it very simply and frankly, I don't believe that Christ is the son of God, because I am not a believer—at least not consciously. But I believe that Christ is divine . . . in him humanity is so lofty, strict, and ideal as to exceed the common terms of humanity."

The Gospel According to Saint Matthew was not the first Pasolini work to attract sharp criticism. His first film, *Accattone* (1961), divided critics and public alike. The actors were not beautiful by current film standards. They had pimples, scratches, and broken teeth. With his lover's brother, Franco Citti, a raucous boy of the streets, playing the lead, the rough, crude world of the subproletariat came to life in language expressing the incontestable religious anguish of its inhabitants. The background music, by contrast, was from Bach. Government censors banned the film because of obscenity.

Pasolini's later film piece *La Ricotta* (one of four sequences in a movie featuring four directors) portrayed religious scenes in terms that government censors found blasphemous. The film was seized on the grounds that it was an insult to the state religion, even though professor-priests at the Pontifical Gregorian University in Rome disagreed. Pasolini was found guilty and sentenced to four months in prison, but an appeals court in Rome overturned the decision.

Along with other film directors in the early 1960s, such as Godard, Truffaut, Bertolucci (who began as Pasolini's assistant), Antonioni, and Fellini (who gave Pasolini his start as a scriptwriter for *Nights of Cabiria* and *La Dolce Vita*), Pasolini pioneered a new concept in cinema: the *auteur* film. In an *auteur* film the entire project from conception through writing, casting, directing, and editing is under one individual's control. The *auteur* director has complete freedom; and Pasolini used that freedom to create a cinema that didn't need words, presenting the immediacy of raw, unadorned life in visual images. His films are free of the type of contrived dialogue usually written for mass-market films. He also used "natural" actors, free from the affectations of professionals. As a poet, revolutionary, communist, antifascist, atheist, and homosexual, Pasolini made films that bore his undeniable stamp, which can be traced back to his childhood.

Pasolini was born in Bologna in 1922, the same year Mussolini came to power. His father became an officer in the Italian army and would always represent for Pasolini the authoritarian spirit. His mother came from simple peasant stock more congenial to his temperament. Growing up in a fascist environment, Pasolini identified with the peasants of the "little homelands" in northern Italy who struggled not only against the centralizing power of the national government but also against Yugoslavian expansionism. As a young boy he championed the peasant communities' efforts to maintain their own dialects, traditions, and heritage. By their distinctive dialects, peasants broke the rule with their lips. Pasolini did the same; his first poems were written in the dialect of his native Friuli.

During World War II Pasolini and his younger brother, Guido, worked in the resistance movement—Pasolini was arrested for distributing antigovernment pamphlets; Guido was murdered by a rival Communist faction. Nevertheless, Pasolini remained in the local Communist party, seeing in its philosophy the only hope of "furnishing a 'real' new culture . . . a culture that will represent both morality and a full interpretation of life." Later, when he was expelled from the party because of the scandal surrounding his work and his sexual life, he maintained that he would always remain a communist "in the most genuine sense of the word," for he believed that in communism was the will to survive and the instinct for self-preservation that could rebuild Italy.

Pasolini's early adult years were busy ones. He founded a school for peasant children, studied philology, wrote poetry, and received an arts degree with honors. In 1950 he and his mother moved to Rome, where he worked as a copy editor and she as a maid. He continued his political and literary activities and developed a wide circle of friends with similar interests. He also met the *ragazzi di vita*, the boys of the street, who would fascinate him for the rest of his life. Among them he found his actors and his sexual partners. Two young boys in particular, Sergio Citti and Ninetto Davoli, remained his closest friends until his death.

Pasolini's poetry and articles won such praise that eventually he was compared to the great Italian soldier-poet Gabriele D'Annunzio. Later in the 1950s he founded periodicals and wrote poetry and film criticism for newspapers and journals. His "dialogue with readers" in *Vie Nuove*, from 1960 to 1965, allowed him to respond to reader questions on topics as diverse as baptism, Soviet military strength, Italian family laws, and Marxist ideology. Many of his works won prestigious awards.

Pasolini's presence and comments always brought notoriety. Caught in a street brawl in a ghetto area of Rome, he explained to a judge that he was there to "gather impressions about a neighborhood" that he wanted to use in a film. He was released. Right-wing students physically attacked him once in a theater. A 23-year-old teacher claimed that Pasolini picked him up late one night, threatened him with a pistol, and stole a manuscript from him. He retracted the story two weeks later, admitting it was a ruse to seek publicity for his own literary career! Brought to trial for his first novel, *Ragazzi di Vita* (1955), because it was deemed obscene, Pasolini was acquitted on the grounds that the novel had redeeming "religious values" and showed "a compassion for the disinherited."

The 1968 film *Teorema*, a story dramatizing a single family's reactions to a visit from God, won an award from the International Catholic Cinema Office (as had *The Gospel According to Saint Matthew*), although the Vatican protested the award. The controversial issue was the fact that the Godlike figure, as played by the beautiful young Terence Stamp, sexually seduces each member of the family, both male and female, in a scenario that includes several nude scenes. The film was confiscated by the public prosecutor's office in Rome for obscenity. Pasolini argued that the film was a blending of eros and religiosity that celebrated the sacredness of the human form. The trial ended in an acquittal. The film was judged to be a work of poetry.

Pasolini's versions of *Oedipus the King* and *Medea* (which starred the famous soprano Maria Callas) showed that the versatile film director could rework the Greek classics for 1960s audiences. But Pasolini's greatest box-office success was his trilogy— the *Decameron,* the *Canterbury Tales,* and the *Arabian Nights*— which allowed him to do what he did best: tell stories through the stark faces, broken smiles, and terse dialogue of relatively unknown actors. With the release of each film and its immediate confiscation, obscenity trials became part of the promotional campaigns. In the process, Pasolini's fight against censorship established the principle that art can triumph over pornography.

In the aftermath of the world-wide student revolutions of 1968, Pasolini continued to be a disturber of the peace, siding with the younger generations that were calling for greater participation in the lives of their nations. But he grew increasingly disillusioned with the consumer society that young people were fighting to join. He found the "economic miracle" of postwar democracies to be "irreligious, totalitarian, violent, falsely tolerant—indeed more repressive than ever—corrupting, and degrading."

In the flight from the countryside to the city, Pasolini witnessed a movement away from dialect and the "little homelands" that create the cultural mosaic necessary for diversity and freedom of expression. He denounced the standardized Italian that was fast becoming the bland, technological language of bourgeois bureaucrats. The increase in right-wing terrorist attacks appalled him, and he felt that a state of emergency existed for everyone, "especially the masses." He called for "total commitment" to a revolution that would humanize the emerging world culture.

His final film, *Salò, or the 120 Days of Sodom*, an allegory set in a Nazi-fascist society, dealt with the theme that power is anarchy. The brutally graphic rituals and symbols based on the Marquis de Sade's posthumously published novel of the same title disturbed many audiences, but Pasolini's message was clear: the passivity of victims who waver between refusal and consent is terrifying. The "final solution" of the film is that the prisoners, all young boys and girls, are sadistically killed.

In the dawn of November 2, 1975, Pasolini's body was discovered in the port town of Ostia, crumpled on a dirt road near a makeshift soccer field and a row of shanties. His face was disfigured, one ear was almost torn off, and there were deep wounds in his skull. His hands were scraped and his fingernails crushed. He had been beaten, kicked in the groin, and run over by his own car. The young boy who later confessed to the murder was a typical *ragazzo di vita*, the same type who had appeared in so many of his films. In spite of the fact that the boy confessed to having acted alone, the judge concluded that "some other person . . . had participated in the assault." It is still a mystery whether his death was a political execution, a sexual escapade that got out of hand, or a suicide by proxy.

JAMES BALDWIN

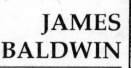

1924–1987

In May 1963 James Baldwin's portrait appeared on the cover of *Time* magazine. The story about the black writer did not appear in the literature section, but under "National Affairs." That same month Baldwin took a group of black leaders to meet with Attorney General Robert Kennedy. The delegation was not politely quiet; it was angry. Baldwin explained that he wanted "to give [Kennedy] an actual experience—the kind of mixed, emotional rap session that was close to the heart of the civil rights movement and the black experience." In December of that year Baldwin was invited to Africa as a guest of honor for a celebration marking Kenya's independence as a nation.

As the fiery decade of the 1960s drew to a close, Baldwin received phone calls from around the world. "As the weather began to be warmer [each spring], my phone would ring," Baldwin said. He would pick it up and find that "Washington was on the line," inviting him to lunch. In the course of the meal "someone would say . . . 'Say, Jim. What's going to happen this summer?'" And Baldwin would recite his by then familiar list of black grievances, cataloging the seething frustrations of ghetto life and the demoralizing effects of poverty and joblessness on black youth. Nothing would be done, as usual, and the summer would erupt in riots.

Baldwin's litany of ghetto problems came from personal experience. He was born illegitimately in New York's Harlem on August 2, 1924. His mother later married David Baldwin and had eight other children by him. Young Baldwin grew up hating the rigid, Bible-thumping, white-hating preacher from New Orleans who was his stepfather. He always felt that his stepfather hated him because of his ugliness (children at school nicknamed him "Froggie" and "Popeyes"). For all the abuse suffered from landlords, pawnbrokers, teachers, grocers, and the two white policemen who beat him up when he was ten, Baldwin claimed that his stepfather was the only person he ever truly hated. He continually argued with the older man about the possibility of having white friends. A sympathetic white teacher planted the notion in Baldwin that, despite his father's prejudices and daily evidence to the contrary, a black man could have white friends in America.

Baldwin later said that he never had time "to go jumping off the roof, or become a junkie or an alcoholic." He spent most of his time caring for his eight younger siblings, protecting them "from rats, roaches, falling plaster, and all the banality of poverty." He spent a lot of time telling them what to do and spanking them. Years later, meeting with leaders like Robert Kennedy, Medgar Evers, Martin Luther King, Jr., college administrators, leaders of CORE (Congress of Racial Equality), senators and congressmen, and the heads of foreign nations, Baldwin claimed he was still playing the older brother, "telling people what to do and spanking them."

By age 13 Baldwin had read his way through the two Harlem branch libraries and began going to the main library at Forty-second Street. The following year he became a junior preacher in his Pentecostal church, delivering sermons to the dispossessed men and women of his congregation. Religious conversion and deconversion (he left the church three years later) would be a continuing theme in his best works. He was graduated from high school in 1942. The next year his stepfather died of a debilitating mental illness, his youngest sister was born three days later, and the Harlem riots broke out. Baldwin was 19.

"I wasn't a dancer, I wasn't a boxer, I can't sing. And as it turned out I wasn't very good at carrying a mop. So I wrote." And at age 19 he had already spent two years working on a novel he would continue to revise for the next eight years and eventually publish as *Go Tell It on the Mountain*, which he wrote "in a sense . . . to redeem my father." In the late 1940s, when Baldwin was in his early 20s, he contributed reviews and essays to the *Nation*, the *New Leader*, and *Commentary* magazines. He won two fellowships that provided him with enough money to leave the United States and live in Paris, a move which he said saved his life.

Over the next 40 years he would continue to write novels, plays, and essays that would be controversial, inspiring, courageous, and often received with high critical acclaim. Among them were *Go Tell It on the Mountain* (1953), *The Amen Corner* (1954), *Notes of a Native Son* (1955), *Giovanni's Room* (1956), *Nobody Knows My Name* (1961), *Another Country* (1962), *The Fire Next Time* (1963), *Blues for Mr. Charlie* (1964), *Going to Meet the Man* (1965), *Tell Me How Long the Train's Been Gone* (1968), and *If Beale Street Could Talk* (1974).

James Baldwin was the right man at the right moment in history. Emerging as a young black intellectual in the late 1940s, when Jackie Robinson had barely broken the color barrier in baseball, Baldwin became a vital presence and spokesman for the growing racial problems in America and the emerging black nations of Africa. In 1957 he returned to the United States to become involved in the southern struggle for school desegregation that would eventually spread to all parts of the nation. By the 1960s Baldwin was one of the best-known "angry black men" to challenge white and black Americans to review—or discard—the outworn myths that continued to haunt the national consciousness.

He was one of the first black writers to discuss the connection between the myth of racial superiority and sexuality. America, he argued, had traditionally required a myth of "purity," one that ignored or suppressed the idea of black Americans and sexuality. He pointed out that America wanted a self-concept that blended "a certain kind of New England Puritan virtue linked to a Southern master-slave notion." White Americans, ignoring the realities of race and sex, preferred to view black people and sexuality as something "furtive," as disagreeable realities lurking in the recesses of the national experience, ones that should keep their place, remain hidden, and not threaten the "purity" of American life.

His novels *Giovanni's Room* and *Another Country* dealt openly with homosexuality. As might be expected, both were critically attacked for it, in the sly reportorial style that can conceal an underlying prejudice. Both the *New York Times* and the *New Yorker* magazine denounced *Giovanni's Room*, the latter claiming the book lacked "the validity of actual experience." Baldwin, however, perfectly understood the criticism. Being homosexual, like being black, was not an actual, valid experience for most Americans. "When other races are suppressed, it lends to the myth of white supremacy," he explained. As regards sexuality, he said, "The myth of the stud is what it's all about." The American male is supposed to focus his sexuality exclusively on women. Homosexual experience, by suggesting that a man can be the sensuous, loving partner of another man, attacks that myth. "Being open about homosexuality destroys the possibility of being furtive about sexuality in general. And sexuality in America has always had to be furtive," Baldwin said of an era that was about to erupt in the "sexual revolution" of the 1960s and the gay-rights movement of the 1970s.

The issue of protest became paramount in the postwar era, culminating in the massive demonstrations of the 1960s that shaped music, dance, fashion, movies, journalism, scholarship, and politics. Baldwin and black novelist Richard Wright exemplified the split over the effectiveness of protest fiction. Beginning with an essay in 1949, "Everybody's Protest Novel," Baldwin denied the validity and effectiveness of the blatant protest literature characteristic of Wright. Having helped the young Baldwin win a fellowship in 1945, Wright felt betrayed by this criticism. The rift between the two writers became permanent and exemplified the continuing argument among authors and critics of black literature over protest fiction. When Wright died in 1960, Baldwin wrote: "The man I fought so hard and who meant so much to me, is gone."

And yet Baldwin's protest message was never diluted. He wrote: "To be a Negro in this country and to be relatively conscious is to be in a rage almost all the time." He warned white Americans that "there are in this country tremendous reservoirs of bitterness which have never been able to find an outlet, but may find an outlet soon."

America took note of Baldwin's message. He appeared before a House of Representatives Select Subcommittee on Labor to argue for establishing a National Commission on Negro History and Culture. He was invited to appear on more and more talk shows, debating such diverse personalities as conservative William F. Buckley and Black Muslim leader Malcolm X. After Malcolm X's death, Columbia Pictures hired Baldwin to write a screenplay based on his life. Awards and fellowships continued to pour in: a Ford Fellowship, the National Conference of Christians and Jews Brotherhood Award, a George Polk Award, the foreign Drama Critics Award, an honorary doctor of letters degree from the University of British Columbia, membership in the American Academy and Institute of Arts and Letters and in the French Legion of Honor.

The years of rage and protest took their toll in the lives of many individuals who meant a lot to Baldwin: Emmett Till, a young black murdered in Mississippi in 1956 who became the subject of *Blues for Mister Charlie*; Medgar Evers; four Sunday-schoolgirls killed in Alabama; Malcolm X; Robert Kennedy;

Martin Luther King, Jr. In 1970 Baldwin left America to make his residence in Paris permanent. "I'm the last witness," he explained. "Everybody else is dead." His self-imposed exile, broken only by visits, was for his personal safety. "I intend to survive and get my work done," he vowed.

For the next 17 years he continued to write as the voice of conscience regarding racial and sexual issues, which in his mind were always linked together. His later works continued to explicate and dramatize subjects rooted in his own life—the black family, father-and-son relationships, the child preacher, the menacing city, black writers and artists, heterosexual and homosexual relationships.

Throughout his writings Baldwin returned again and again to the theme of love. It was only because they loved one another, he affirmed, that his large Harlem family survived. "I love America," he said, ". . . and exactly for this reason, I insist on the right to criticize her perpetually." By love Baldwin did not mean something passive; he meant "something more like a fire, like the wind, something which can change you." He predicted that when white people learn to "accept and love themselves and each other . . . the Negro problem will no longer exist, for it will no longer be needed."

When he died at age 63 in 1987, Baldwin left behind a legacy of passion, courage, and conviction. He had confronted issues that most Americans would have preferred to ignore—racism, poverty, sexism, and the fear and oppression of minorities—all of which he believed could be resolved only by love. "The inability to love *is* the central problem," he warned, "because that inability masks a certain terror, and that terror is terror of being touched. And if you can't be touched, you can't be changed. And if you can't be changed, you can't be alive."

YUKIO MISHIMA

1925–1970

The news at midday on November 25, 1970, stunned Japan and sent shock waves rippling around the world. Yukio Mishima, Japan's foremost writer and a three-time Nobel Prize nominee, had taken an army general hostage in Tokyo's Ichigaya military headquarters and was exhorting a forced assembly of 1,500 troops to reject Japan's democratic constitution and restore worship of the emperor. Two hours later the official press reports were even more incredible. Mishima and his devoted young collaborator Masakatsu Morita had committed hara-kiri in the general's office.

Only 45 years old when he ended his life, Mishima was at the peak of his career. He enjoyed fame, fortune, and acclaim as well as a comfortable family life with his wife and two childen. What could have inspired this last, outrageous act? Was he "out of his mind," as Prime Minister Eisaku Sato declared in an interview that evening? Or was his ritual suicide pact with Morita a carefully conceived piece of theater, dramatizing conflicts within the man and his culture, and fulfilling his youthful pledge, "I want to make a poem of my life"?

240

The life of Mishima was, in fact, every bit as mysterious and contradictory as his death. Slight and sickly by nature, he transformed himself through rigorous exercise into a powerful sportsman. A venerator of Japanese traditions, he nevertheless embraced a western style of living and entertaining that scandalized his neighbors. A dutiful husband and father, his main sexual attraction was to male "rough trade." He took on so many roles—novelist, playwright, journalist, actor, designer, model, paramilitary officer—that he was known to the world as "the Leonardo da Vinci of Japan"; and yet he complained: "I slip through life as if I were a ghost, neither dead nor alive, making things up as I go along."

Even the name Yukio Mishima was an invention, a nom de plume he adopted when he published his first story, "The Forest in Full Bloom," at the age of 16. He was born Kimitake Hiraoka on January 14, 1925, the eldest son of an upper-middle-class Tokyo family; and from the very beginning, his life assumed the bizarre character of a fable. Exercising a Japanese mother-in-law's customary power over her son's wife, Mishima's grandmother insisted that she be allowed to raise the delicate child.

Mishima remained under his grandmother's control for the next 12 years. Subject to spells of debilitating weakness (diagnosed as "auto-intoxication"), he was excessively coddled. His grandmother indulged his preference for fancy clothes and quiet activities, and he was dressed and raised as if he were a girl. Speaking of his rare childhood visits to his cousins' house, he recalled: "Like an invalid taking his first steps during convalescence, I had a feeling of stiffness as if I were acting under the compulsion of some imaginary obligation. In this house, it was tacitly required that I act like a boy. The reluctant masquerade had begun."

By the time Mishima was 14, his grandmother had died. He was living with his parents and making a brilliant record as a student at the Gakushuin (the prestigious "Peers School"). He was also awakening to a passion for writing and a far more unsettling passion for the male form. Leafing through a book of Italian Renaissance art, he happened upon a reproduction of Guido Reni's *Saint Sebastian*, and that remarkable painting of a beautiful young body pierced by arrows haunted him for the rest of his life. It symbolized a mystic union of eros and death that would inspire both his literary works and his behavior as an adult.

During this same pivotal year Mishima also fell in love for the first time. The object of his ardor was a well-built upperclassman named Omi. His idolatry of Omi caused him a great deal of suffering over the next year, but it also gave him a clear image of what he wanted. "Because of him," Mishima later wrote, "I began to love strength, an impression of overflowing blood, ignorance, rough gestures, careless speech, and savage melancholy inherent in flesh not tainted in any way with intellect."

Shortly before the outbreak of World War II, Mishima began publishing short stories in magazines. He kept on publishing stories and studying at the Gakushuin until he was graduated with highest honors in 1944. His ill health prevented him from enlisting in the army, but he was finally drafted in February 1945, when the imperial forces were mounting a last-ditch defense of the home islands. Mishima said good-bye to his relatives, certain that he would not see them again. "I shuddered with a strange delight at the thought of my own death," he remarked in a subsequent essay. "I felt as if I owned the whole world." As it turned out he failed his final medical examination and never did see action. Referring to this experience, Mishima wrote: "I now delighted in picturing the agonies of a person who wanted to die but had been refused by Death."

Bowing to his father's wishes, Mishima enrolled in law school at Tokyo University and eventually obtained a position at the Ministry of Finance; but his heart was in his fledgling literary career, now assisted by the patronage of Yasunari Kawabata, the most accomplished novelist in Japan at that time. Impressed by the intensity and beauty of Mishima's prose, Kawabata encouraged him to write a book-length, autobiographical account of his fantasy life. Mishima quit his studies and his job and devoted himself full-time to the project. The result was *Confessions of a Mask*, published in 1949 and immediately hailed by Japanese critics as a work of genius.

Over the next decade Mishima consolidated his literary career with a number of skillfully crafted and exotically plotted novels. Among his most successful books were *Thirst for Love* (1950), *Forbidden Colors* (1951), *The Sound of Waves* (1954), and *The Temple of the Golden Pavilion* (1956). These works and other shorter ones were quickly translated and published in the United States and throughout western Europe, where they excited critics and won him an international reputation. He also branched out into drama. He wrote, produced, and acted in plays for both the modern and the traditional (Nō and Kabuki) Japanese theaters. His plays were often staged abroad, giving many foreign audiences their first exposure to the various themes and formats of Japanese drama.

Meanwhile, Mishima the man was evolving into a colorful national celebrity. In 1955 he began a highly publicized program in body building, which remained a hobby for the rest of his life. Pictures of him boxing, lifting weights, and flexing his burgeoning muscles regularly appeared in popular magazines. He was a natural exhibitionist; and the Japanese public grew increasingly fascinated with the notion of a respected writer who was also a model, posing in loincloths (once as Saint Sebastian) and alternately winking, sighing, or glowering at the camera.

The more public attention Mishima's life and work attracted, the more pressure he received from his family to marry. It is rare for a Japanese man to remain single beyond his twenties. By 1958 Mishima was well into his thirties; and it was becoming much more difficult to cover up his nocturnal visits to the gay bars in Tokyo's Ginza district. Told that his mother might soon die of cancer, Mishima agreed to an arranged marriage with Yoko Sugiyama, a demure young woman who came from a family of artists and had the good fortune to be shorter than the 5'2" Mishima (one of his written requirements).

Mishima and his wife settled in a Tokyo house that he himself had designed to startle his neighbors. It resembled a colonial mansion of the British Empire and was decorated inside and out with Victorian art pieces. In a typically insouciant mood, he told the press: "My ideal is to live in a house where I sit on a rococo chair wearing an aloha shirt and blue jeans." Describing himself in a magazine article at the time, he declared: "I rule my wife at home, act according to common sense, build a house, am fairly cheerful, love speaking ill of others, rejoice when people remark on my youthful appearance, pursue the latest fashions and favor all manner of things in bad taste."

Mishima didn't stop seeking sexual partners in Ginza gay bars, but he was a thoughtful, if distant, husband. Despite his macho posturing he took his wife with him on many of his trips abroad (atypical behavior for a Japanese husband) and gave her plenty of day-to-day freedom. They had two children—a girl and a boy—early in their marriage, and Mishimi took an active part in raising them. But being a family man played an increasingly minor role in his life as the years went by.

Instead Mishima became more and more obsessed with his philosophy of eros and death; and he channeled that philosophy in two directions. One direction was literary. He continued to produce short, best-selling novels, such as *After the Banquet* (1960) and *The Sailor Who Fell From Grace with the Sea* (1963); but he invested most of his energy in the creation of a long novel in four volumes entitled *The Sea of Fertility*. His intention was singularly ambitious. Each volume would feature a protagonist who was a reincarnation of the hero of the previous book, and the novel as a whole would explore issues that dominated his own imagination as well as the collective psyche of modern Japan: the connection between violence and sensuality, and the contrast between self-indulgence and self-sacrifice. It was meant to be (and later proved to be) his masterpiece, and one of the great works of world literature.

The other channel for Mishima's eros-and-death philosophy was more personal and controversial. He decided to form a private army, the Tatenokai, which would allow him and a handpicked host of virile young men to explore the way of the samurai warrior on weekend retreats. Under the spell of his first and most important recruit, the 21-year-old Morita, his quiescent love for ancient militaristic virtues was fanned into a more active imperialism. Thanks to his personal prestige, Mishima managed to convince high-ranking officials in the Japanese army— many of whom had right-wing leanings—to sponsor the Tatenokai as a kind of "mascot" group.

By November of 1970, Mishima had completed three of the four volumes in *The Sea of Fertility: Spring Snow* (1968), *Runaway Horses* (1969), and *The Temple of Dawn* (1970). He had also increased the size of the Tatenokai to 80 members, all primed to follow Mishima in whatever enterprise he might choose. Deeply bound to Morita and resolved to demonstrate the seriousness of his commitment, Mishima finally made a choice. As he left home on November 25 to keep his appointment at the Ichigaya military headquarters, he put the finished manuscript for *The Decay of the Angel*, the last book in his tetrology, on the vestibule table. His life and his work came to a well-planned conclusion on the same day.

ANDY WARHOL
1930–1987

In July 1962 Andy Warhol held the first major showing of his art at the Ferus Gallery in Los Angeles. The entire exhibit consisted of 32 paintings of Campbell's soup cans, each priced at $100. The day after the opening, a gallery dealer next door to the Ferus piled up Campbell's soup cans in his window with a sign: "Buy them cheaper here: 60 cents for three cans." Warhol was delighted. By challenging his audience to question the distinction between what is real and what is art, he had succeeded in doing what he'd set out to do.

Warhol drew much of the inspiration for his paintings, films, and publications from popular culture—from images that are so pervasive in the common experience that people risk never realizing their special beauty and power. While many viewers persist in judging Warhol's efforts as trivial, if enjoyable, put-ons, critics have come to respect his unique talent and message. Banal as a soup-can design may be in any realistic scheme of things, Warhol gives it the status of an icon, forcing the viewer to appreciate not only its aesthetically compelling arrangement of colors, shapes, and lines, but also the extent to which that design is a part of the collective consciousness. "Andy Warhol had the true mark of a genius: the ability to make opposites meet," said Patterson Sims, associate curator of the Whitney Museum of American Art in New York. "In his work, the obvious is rendered mysterious and the bizarre is rendered normal."

Nowhere were all the contradictions embodied in Warhol's art more evident than in his public persona. With his platinum wig, blank expression, androgynous mannerisms, and deathlike pallor (the result of a childhood illness that destroyed his pigmentation), he seemed alternately sensitive or coarse, angelic or satanic, spaced out or brilliant. His cohorts, who reveled in the enigma of his personality, nicknamed him Drella—a composite of Dracula and Cinderella. Truman Capote, who was once barraged with mash notes from Warhol, was less enchanted and called him "a sphinx without secrets."

Warhol was the ultimate Manhattan partygoer during the 1960s, '70s, and '80s; but he never drank, smoked, or did drugs, and was usually in bed by 11 P.M. In his studios he presided over all manner of orgies in the name of amorality, but in his personal life he was squeamishly chaste and withdrawn, a devout Catholic who went to mass every Sunday and a dutiful son who lived with his mother for most of his life. On most occasions his vocabulary consisted of "wow," "gee," "golly," and "great," and he appeared to be little more than a passive onlooker. In fact, his epigrams helped to define a new era in American culture; and although his life and his art championed voyeurism, he was always a creative catalyst to those around him and, above all, an indefatigable worker.

Warhol arrived in New York in 1949, determined to make the most of his artistic skills. The son of Czechoslovakian immigrants (his family name was Warhola), he had grown up in McKeesport, Pennsylvania, where his father was a coal miner. After his father's death, the 13-year-old Warhol helped support his mother by working in a five-and-ten-cent store. In his spare time he drew, constantly experimenting with new ways of sketching suggested by the commercial art that he saw at work and by the movie magazines that were his favorite reading. Somehow he was also able to put himself through the Carnegie Institute of Technology in Pittsburgh and earn a degree in pictorial design.

Once established in a commune of artists at 103rd Street and Manhattan Avenue, Warhol made the rounds of all the major magazines and retailers, carrying his drawings in a brown paper bag from the A&P. The originality of his work, coupled with his waiflike manner, made such a strong impression on the people he visited that he quickly became one of the busiest commercial artists in the city. He designed artwork for *Glamour* and *Vogue* magazines, stationery for Bergdorf Goodman, Christmas cards for Tiffany's, windows for Bonwit Teller, and album covers for Columbia Records.

At the same time that Warhol was accumulating wealth along Madison Avenue, he was also trying to gain fame as a serious painter. His timing was excellent. Modern art was just starting to break away from abstract expressionism and to focus instead on graphic depiction of images from the consumer society. In Jasper Johns's hyperrealistic paintings, Roy Lichtenstein's comic strips, George Segal's plaster casts, and Claes Oldenburg's food replicas, Warhol saw echoes of his own creative sensibility. He followed his Ferus show with an even more sensational exhibit at New York's Stable Gallery, featuring paintings of dollar bills and Coca-Cola bottles, as well as soup cans. Pop art, as it came to be called, was suddenly recognized as the wave of the future; and Warhol was christened the Pope of Pop. For the next three years he turned out hundreds of paintings and sculptures from his studio on East Forty-seventh Street, which he called "the Factory." His silk screens of such famous Americans as Elvis Presley, Marilyn Monroe, James Dean and Jacqueline Kennedy revived portraiture as an art form; and his design pieces—including gaudy flower prints and three-dimensional Brillo boxes—forged a new bond between the world of high art and the worlds of fashion and commerce.

Warhol had transformed himself into the international celebrity he had always yearned to be, but he was not about to relax. In 1965 he moved on to films. His early film works are as cryptically affectless as his early artworks. *Eat*, for example, features the artist Robert Indiana consuming a single mushroom for 45 minutes. Eventually, however, Warhol settled on loosely scripted scenarios in which all the actors could behave as "superstars." Defending this democratic approach to celebrity, he predicted: "In the future, everyone will be famous for 15 minutes."

The Factory soon turned into a 24-hour film happening populated with all sorts of unusual people Warhol collected during his tireless forays into New York night life. They ranged from paragons of mute sexuality (Joe Dallesandro) to transvestites (Holly Woodlawn) to avant-garde intellectuals (Allen Ginsberg) to socialites (Edie Sedgwick) to models (Viva). In shifting ensembles, they created such cinéma-vérité classics as *Lonesome Cowboys*, *My Hustler*, *Chelsea Girls* (which in 1966 became the first underground film to be released commercially), *Trash*, and *Heat*. The writer Norman Mailer praised these films as "invaluable historical documents," and their spontaneous style had significant influence on such innovative directors as John Schlesinger (*Midnight Cowboy*) and Martin Scorsese (*After Hours*).

Warhol also started leaving his stamp on the social scene that he loved so much. He created the Plastic Exploding Inevitable, a multimedia nightclub that introduced the flashing-light effects now standard in every discotheque. He also produced the Velvet Underground, a successful rock group that pioneered the androgynous "punk" style that would later be picked up by such performers as Mick Jagger, David Bowie, and David Byrne.

Given his frenetic schedule, Warhol had little time for a personal life, which evidently suited his rather fey, secretive personality. Although he was distinctly homosexual in orientation, in practice he was almost asexual. "When I got my first TV set," he once told a reporter, "I stopped caring so much about having a close relationship." Speaking of sex in his typically sybilline way, he added: "If you fall in love with someone and never do it, it's much more exciting." True to his word, his love affairs tended to be nonphysical crushes, even if they involved live-in arrangements. The object of his affections may not have been a sexual consort but did become the so-called prime minister of the Factory crowd: an honor enjoyed by Chuck Wein, Gerard Malanga, Rod La Rod and the singer Lou Reed.

In 1968, shortly before Warhol was to be immortalized on the cover of *Life* magazine, one of his erstwhile disciples, Valerie Solanis, shot him at point-blank range, sending two bullets through his stomach, liver, esophagus, and lungs. The founder of SCUM (the Society for Cutting Up Men), Solanis was determined to get rid of the man who she believed "had too much control over my life." Miraculously, Warhol recovered. The assassination of Robert Kennedy that same week robbed him of his *Life* cover and the attention his own brush with death might have received, but far more serious was the effect of the attack itself on his peace of mind. "Since I was shot, everything is such a dream to me," he confessed in *POPism*, his personal account of the 1960s. "Like I don't know whether I'm alive or whether I died. I wasn't afraid before and having been dead once, I shouldn't feel fear now. But I am afraid. I don't understand why."

Warhol closed the Factory a few weeks later, after a stranger walked in and began using a loaded revolver to play Russian roulette. With the help of his saner associates, he installed himself in a far more businesslike work space on Union Square. There he produced paintings that were palpably more mature than his previous ones—notably his "Butterfly" and "Chairman Mao" series—and labored on a number of new enterprises, including a popular magazine, *Interview*; a cable television talk show, "Andy Warhol's TV"; and several books articulating his philosophy of art, life, and celebrity.

The reformed Warhol continued to pursue a vigorous social life, but it lacked the craziness of years past. During the "me" decade of the 1970s, he became something of a court painter, doing portraits of such notables as President Jimmy Carter (the official presidential portrait), the singer-actress Liza Minnelli, and the fashion designer Halston. During the Reagan era of the 1980s, he threw a great deal of his energy into collecting artworks and decorating his mansion on the Upper East Side. He also dropped some of his legendary cool. Every holiday he served food to the needy at the Church of the Heavenly Rest; and in 1986 he permitted several of his works to be shown at a major Philadelphia exhibit devoted to gay and lesbian artists.

By 1987, Warhol could feel his body beginning to fail him. Increasingly concerned about dying, he confided to a friend: "I always thought I'd like my tombstone to be blank. No epitaph and no name." On February 22 he died of cardiac arrest following gallbladder surgery, leaving an enormous blank space in the life and culture of our times.

MICHAEL BENNETT
1943–1987

On August 10, 1987, the musical *A Chorus Line* was slated to give its 5,001st Broadway performance. It had already broken the record for longest-running musical with its 3,389th show on September 29, 1983; but the unflagging box office 12 years after its opening deserved another celebration. To symbolize how great an impact *A Chorus Line* had made on American theater, producer Joseph Papp invited anyone who had ever appeared in a non-Broadway production to apply for a role in the August 10 show, and so 19 winners had their dreams of appearing on Broadway come true. Unfortunately their triumph was not witnessed by the musical's creator, Michael Bennett. He had died of AIDS-related cancer only a month before. "Michael Bennett was the most talented performer in the American stage in the last 50 years," Papp declared in an emotional eulogy. Bernard Jacobs, president of the Shubert Organization, remarked: "I think Michael contributed more to the American theater in his short life than others who had lived far longer."

Bennett himself once said he was "a tap dancer from Buffalo who went all the way." Born April 8, 1943, Michael Bennett DiFiglia, son of a machinist and a secretary, never wanted any other life except in the theater. He started dance lessons when he was three, and by 12 he was proficient in tap, ballet, modern, and folk dancing. At 16 he dropped out of high school to tour Europe in the chorus of *West Side Story*. He returned with the conviction that "only time and hard work stood between me and the top."

It turned out to be not much time but lots of hard work. For six years he was that rarest of creatures—a continuously employed chorus dancer, or "gypsy." He debuted on Broadway in *Subways Are for Sleeping* (1961) and also danced in *Here's Love* and *Bajour*. He remained a gypsy at heart for the rest of his life; but his chorus days ended in 1966, when he choreographed *A Joyful Noise*. The musical closed after 12 shows, but Bennett's work was nominated for a Tony award. The following year history repeated itself: He choreographed *Henry, Sweet Henry*; it flopped; he earned a Tony nomination. With his next project, the choreography for Neil Simon's 1968 musical *Promises, Promises*, his commercial luck improved. The show ran for over a year and brought him another Tony nomination. It also introduced him to the dancer Donna McKechnie, a lifelong friend (and, for a few madcap months in 1976, his wife) whom he often called "my favorite instrument."

Following *Promises, Promises*, Bennett had an incredible five-year string of successes. He choreographed André Previn and Alan Jay Lerner's *Coco* (1969) and Stephen Sondheim and George Furth's *Company* (1970). The latter show featured especially ingenious dance numbers. "What I did in *Company*," Bennett said, "was to choreograph the characters. It was heightened reality. I don't think anyone has demanded of nondancers as much movement as I did." He proceeded to demand the same degree of expression in Sondheim's *Follies* (1971), which he co-directed with Harold Prince. It paid off: He garnered his first two Tonys for choreography and direction. His initial venture as a solo director was Furth's play *Twigs* (1971). A year later he was tapped by Cy Coleman and Dorothy Fields to rescue their musical *Seesaw*. In the first of many stints as a show doctor, he supervised every element of the production. *Seesaw* opened to smash reviews. The show gave Bennett his third Tony (for choreography) and made a star out of his friend Tommy Tune. Flush with this victory, he directed his second nonmusical play, Simon's *God's Favorite*, in 1974.

Bennett's meteoric rise in the theater world took its toll on his personal life. He confessed to friends: "I went to the beach once and exhausted myself worrying about not working." Although openly homosexual he seldom participated in New York's gay nightlife. "He didn't go to bars and things like that," commented Wakefield Poole, producer of the gay erotic film *Boys in the Sand* and a close friend of Bennett since their days on the *West Side Story* tour. "He led a very straight, professional life." In fact his idea of a good time was shoptalk with chorus dancers. Proud of his own gypsy roots, he shared their joys and empathized with their sorrows.

One January night in 1974, while reminiscing with gypsies, he was struck with an idea for a musical in which the chorus line would be the star. After persuading Papp to finance a workshop to develop the show, he hired Marvin Hamlisch to compose the music, Ed Kleban to write the lyrics, and James Kirkwood and Nicholas Dante to write the book. His also recruited McKechnie to play the pivotal role of Cassie.

Like most events in Bennett's life, the progress of *A Chorus Line* from thought to reality was swift. Following ten weeks at Papp's Public Theater, the show opened off-Broadway on May 21, 1975. Two months later, on July 25, 1975, it premiered at the Shubert Theater and caused a sensation. "The conservative word for *A Chorus Line* might be tremendous or terrific," critic Clive Barnes declared. Critic Walter Kerr wrote: "Restless orchestration, expletives over music whenever a misstep occurs, linked bodies cross-kicking forward as rhythms climb to crescendo, all give the sense of a word, a sung note, a sprung dance, an entire show being born on the spot, taking shape as we watch. The accomplishment is brilliant."

A *Chorus Line* redefined musical theater. With its carefully orchestrated suite of monologues, it gave birth to the "concept" musical: a work more concerned about exploring character than unfolding a plot, in which every aspect of the production is seamlessly integrated into a continuously flowing whole. Perhaps most significantly it liberated Broadway from the crippling belief that it had to use star power and lavish production values to attract audiences. Instead *A Chorus Line* relied on the strength of its composition and the talent of its performers. Bennett was rightfully proud. "I think I am now the king of the backstage musical," he boasted. "And you know what? I like it!" So did everyone else. *A Chorus Line* won nine Tony awards, including best direction and choreography for Bennett and best musical. It also captured the Pulitzer Prize and the New York Drama Critics' Circle Award. And it paid back the community that nurtured it: Revenues from *A Chorus Line* soon became the main source of income for Papp's New York Shakespeare Festival.

A Chorus Line pioneered not only a new kind of musical, but also a new way for making theatrical shows—the workshop method. Bennett's goal now was to create the best workshop environment possible, a place where directors, writers, composers, choreographers, and performers could incubate the plays and musicals of the future. In 1977 he bought an eight-story building at 890 Broadway and transformed it into offices and rehearsal spaces. It quickly evolved into a mecca for people in show business. Over the next decade it spawned nearly 100 Broadway shows and an equal number of off-Broadway shows. One of the first musicals to emerge out of 890 Broadway was Bennett's own *Ballroom* (1978). Anticipating another *A Chorus Line*, both critics and audiences were disappointed. The show quickly closed, but did earn Bennett yet another Tony award for choreography. In an interview he admitted: "I always thought I was prepared for success. No one is. And to be built up as I was

A Chorus Line, and then to do *Ballroom*. Well, it is very interesting when you fall off the pedestal."

Bennett was not off that pedestal for long. His next workshop product, the musical *Dreamgirls* (1981), proved to be almost as well received as *A Chorus Line*. Based on the story of the 1960s singing trio the Supremes, *Dreamgirls* offered theatergoers Bennett's most sophisticated choreography yet and inspired a whole new era of high-tech stagecraft. Critic Frank Rich wrote: "When Broadway history is being made, you feel it. What you feel is a seismic jolt that sends the audience, as one, right out of its wits. While such moments are uncommonly rare these days, I'm here to report that one popped up at the Imperial last night. Broadway history was made at the end of Michael Bennett's beautiful and heartbreaking new musical *Dreamgirls*." The blockbuster brought Bennett his eighth Tony (for choreography).

Back on top, Bennett was poised to take himself and American theater to dizzy new heights. In 1984 he began work on *Scandal*, a daringly frank musical discussion of sexual mores. At the same time he doctored Tune's musical *My One and Only* and Sondheim's musical *Sunday in the Park with George*. He seemed to have the energy of a chorus of people. But suddenly the chorus stumbled. After a year and four workshops, he scrapped *Scandal*. "What's a workshop for?" he asked his dumbstruck collaborators. "To see whether a show should go into production. I have very good instincts and I decided *Scandal* would not work." He added that a musical dealing with sexual experimentation looked like a risky venture in an era threatened with a deadly new disease, AIDS.

As soon as Bennett had abandoned *Scandal*, he drastically cut back his work schedule. His friends were mystified and could only assume that he was pausing after a career setback to rethink his strategy. In 1985 he began casting for the British production of the musical *Chess*, but he was forced to bow out in early 1986, claiming that he was suffering from exercise-induced angina. A year later, after months of seclusion, he announced that he was selling 890 Broadway. His sale of his cherished work space saddened theater lovers, but an even greater cause for alarm was his increasing withdrawal from professional activity. "The real tragedy," Bernard Jacobs said, "is that Michael is sick and does not perceive that he will be working in the foreseeable future." Bennett himself tried to put a better front on the news: "The experience with *Scandal* helped me grow up, and so did selling the building. My life is becoming simpler, and that's always good. I think I'll be able to make my comeback at 44 without a problem."

Bennett was fooling the world and, perhaps, himself. While acknowledging that his illness was life-threatening, he refused to admit it was AIDS-related. In doing this he was following the precedent set by other famous gay men who had already died of AIDS-related causes, such as the fashion designer Perry Ellis (who had claimed to be a victim of sleeping sickness) and the pianist Liberace (who had blamed his suffering on the aftereffects of a watermelon diet). A rare exception to this pattern had been the actor Rock Hudson, whose candor weeks before his 1985 death had helped awaken mainstream America to the full horror of AIDS.

As Bennett's body became scarred with ugly cancer lesions, he withdrew from society altogether. On July 2, 1987, he died at his retreat in Tucson, Arizona. His will stipulated that 15 percent of his $25 million estate should go to organizations involved in AIDS research and the treatment of AIDS patients. To date it is the largest single donation—private or corporate—ever made for these causes, but it represents only part of the huge legacy he left to the ages. "For those of us in the theater world who remain behind," Papp said, "Michael's death has presented us with an enormous task, one he passionately advocated—the creation of new structures to give new and upcoming talent places to work and develop. Michael has set the standards by which we can, from now on, measure our growth as a vital American cultural institution."

Other books of interest from
ALYSON PUBLICATIONS